HEALTH PSYCHOLOGY RESEARCH FOCUS

PSYCHOLOGICAL HEALTH AND NEEDS RESEARCH DEVELOPMENTS

HEALTH PSYCHOLOGY RESEARCH FOCUS

Additional books in this series can be found on Nova's website under the Series tab.

Additional e-books in this series can be found on Nova's website under the e-book tab.

HEALTH PSYCHOLOGY RESEARCH FOCUS

PSYCHOLOGICAL HEALTH AND NEEDS RESEARCH DEVELOPMENTS

RAUL WOLFE
EDITOR

nova publishers
New York

Additional color graphics may be available in the e-book version of this book.

Library of Congress Cataloging-in-Publication Data

ISBN: 978-1-63483-332-5

Published by Nova Science Publishers, Inc. † New York

CONTENTS

PREFACE

The first chapter of this book is a discussion of the three basic psychological needs according to the Self-Determination Theory: autonomy, competence and relatedness, which have been laid out as fundamental nutriments of human experience. The second chapter reviews the research published in the last 10 years on coping skills in adolescence and their association with well-being. The next chapter of the book offers a comprehensive overview of the effectiveness of expressive art based interventions on adolescent mental health. The remaining chapters in this book on psychological health and needs explore the psychological benefits in physical activity and sport; the importance of testing measurement invariance for psychological health research; an examination of the relationships between college student's spiritual well-being, parental rearing attitude and coping strategies with their anxiety and depression; the importance of Health Related Quality of Life (HRQOL) during aging; and lastly, a theoretical framework is proposed by the authors to investigate the mechanisms by which faith-based addition treatment delivers the desirable treatment outcomes.

Chapter 1 - This chapter is a discussion of the three basic psychological needs according to Self-Determination Theory: autonomy, competence, and relatedness, which have been laid out as fundamental nutriments of human experience. The present discussion of these needs is separated into four major components. The first portion of the chapter is devoted to theoretical explanation of the needs including: their independent importance, the benefits of their balance, the conceptual and empirical distinctions between thwarting needs and satisfying them, and how they relate to ideas of ego-involvement, authenticity, and mindfulness. Next the authors turn to the relation between needs and a number of outcomes including relational well-being, physical health, and general well-being. The authors then explore the implications of autonomy, competence, and relatedness for several aspects of psychological health including stress and anxiety, emotional ambivalence, pain, depression, shame, loneliness, and impact on health behavior. Finally, there is a discussion of the utility of these needs for studying populations from a variety of peoples including those from vastly different ideologies and cultures.

Chapter 2 - Attention toward coping in healthy adolescents is the result of the important role of protective and risk factors that could influence well-being. If adolescents improve their coping skills, they can perceive and react to stressors in ways that yield positive health outcomes.

Adolescents experience many stressor situations, ranging from pubertal changes to family and peer relationship conflicts. This chapter will review the research published in the last 10 years on coping skills in adolescence and their association with well-being.

Articles were found using the most relevant electronic databases, PubMed, Psychology and Behavioural Science, PsycINFO, Sciencedirect and Scopus, employing various search strategies: the search terms used included MeSH, headings, text words or keywords relevant to the following terms: "Coping," "adolescent," "well-being," "psychosocial." Text word and thesaurus searches were used to minimize chances of missing relevant articles. Identified articles were examined for additional references. The search was limited to English-language literature published in the last 10 years (2005-2015). The authors considered the full text of the selected papers to examine all the specific characteristics of each study. One of the eligibility criteria was that the papers dealt with adolescents, but the authors also considered studies where parents were the participants, only when they constituted a source of information about their adolescents' coping strategies and health. The authors excluded all the articles related to specific health diseases, such as chronic illnesses (cancer, diabetes, etc.) or other specific pathologies, physical, psychiatric or contextual (i.e., eating disorders, sleep deficits, terrorism/emergency events, mental disorders).

Some important topics associated with adolescents' psycho-social well-being that emerged from the review of the literature were: Health related quality of life and health beliefs area; Mental well-being area (psychopathology symptoms); Perceived stress and coping strategies to front the daily problems area: SES and coping, stable internal resources, positive coping, coping related to academic performance; Relationship and perceived social support area and Family influences on adolescents' well-being.

These information will be discussed and directions for future research and psychological interventions will be proposed.

Chapter 3 - This chapter offers a comprehensive overview of the effectiveness of expressive art based interventions on adolescent mental health, the discussion of which is expanded more concretely through the concept of health humanities. The World Health Organisation has reported that the severity of childhood mental disorders produces a heavy burden on family caregivers, education experts, and national medical expenditures. In particular, the dearth of health professionals and medications in underdeveloped countries worsens their capabilities in coping with this predicament. Such threats pose a dire need for effective and efficient resolutions from scholars, practitioners, and social policy makers. From among a variety of therapies, expressive art based activities become a potential method for children, because they have been used in more creative ways that can cater to various segments of young people who are affected by mental illness. In light of recent research (involving Asian, European, North American, and Middle Eastern participants), findings illustrate a wide spectrum of art forms, including integrative art, painting, music, dance/movement, and drama; which are employed effectively to deal with emotional, behavioural, and social problems, resulting in lowering symptoms of neuro-behavioural difficulties, oppositional defiant disorder, and sensory integration barriers, and in improving academic achievement as well across pre-school, elementary school, secondary school and college students, children with brain injuries, abused or traumatised adolescents, at-risk youth, and teenagers in immigrant and refugee families. These analyses also illuminate improvements in parent-child and teacher-student relationships, because of which social cohesion is enhanced due to better emotional management, communication skills, and self-efficacy. This literature review reveals that intervention programmes are devised in order to accommodate individual characteristics and cultural preferences. It also suggests that expressive art integrates with different therapeutic practices and incorporates into school and professional training curricula for preventive, rehabilitative, remedial, and curative purposes, attaining cross-disciplinary success.

Chapter 4 - The practice of regular and moderate Physical Activity and Sports (PAS) produces positive effects in the health, the well-being and the quality of life of the persons.

An active life benefits children, young women, adults, and disabled persons, from a well-being, preventive and rehabilitation perspective.

More, the practice of PAS helps to reduce anxiety, stress levels and depression, stimulates and supports the cognitive capacities, produces sensations of well-being and favours the establishment of other healthy associate behaviours.

Findings have demonstrated that PAS help to reduce obesity, cardiovascular problems and reduce the addictive behaviours.

The research in this field show a list of motives of the PAS practise such as the amusement, to relate to the others, the health and the competition, to keep fit. On the other hand, some factors which keep people enrolled in these activities have been found (Availability of time and facilities, social support towards the exercise, previous history of exercise, self - efficacy and positive attitude towards the exercise) and others which make people to give up the sport activities like (lack of time, smoking, no habits, no sport history), persistence give up factors (conflict between different activities, lack of time).

In summary, it is suggested to start the sport and physical activity practise since the childhood to acquire the habit to avoid sedentary behaviours and to keep good physical and psychological health levels.

Chapter 5 - Psychological health researchers often explore population heterogeneity regarding unobservable latent variables. The presence of substantial non-equivalence of measurement instruments across different populations creates problems. Often, measurement invariance is just ignored rather than tested. This chapter aims to highlight the importance of testing measurement invariance for Psychological health research, and to clarify biases generated from traditional comparative procedures. The authors designed a sample study to test mean differences of Psychological health constructs between two groups using traditional statistical procedures and multi-group confirmatory factor analysis (CFA) model with structural equation modeling (SEM). The results of the statistical analysis suggested that ignoring measurement invariance across groups may produce invalid findings. It further confirmed that measurement invariance should be tested before any mean difference comparisons of latent constructs across groups. The authors discuss an available remedy option if full measurement invariance does not hold, and propose a new approach. Implications for Psychological health research are suggested.

Chapter 6 - Purpose: The purpose of this study was to exam the relationships between college student's spiritual well-being, parental rearing attitude, and coping strategies with their anxiety and depression.

Methods: This was a cross-sectional descriptive research design. There were 330 college students recruited from a state university in the central USA including 79 male (23.9%) and 251 female (76.1%). The mean age was 25.20 (SD = 6.83). The data were collected by structured questionnaires. The SPSS 20 was used to do the data analysis.

Results: The statistical significant factors related to Anxiety included Spiritual well-being ($r = -0.262$, $p \leq 0.001$), Positive Parental Rearing Attitude including *Inductive Reasoning* ($r = -0.16$, $p \leq 0.01$), *Communication* ($r = -0.154$, $p \leq 0.01$), and *Involvement* ($r = -0.132$, $p \leq 0.05$) as well as Negative Parental Rearing Attitude ($r = 0.22$, $p \leq 0.001$), *Inconsistent Discipline* ($r = 0.18$, $p \leq 0.001$) and *Harsh Discipline* ($r = 0.163$, $p \leq 0.01$). Coping strategies including *Problem Focused Disengagement* ($r = -0.316$, $p \leq 0.001$), *Emotion Focused Engagement* ($r = 0.29$, $p \leq 0.001$), and *Emotion Focused Disengagement* ($r = 0.304$, $p \leq 0.001$) had significant relationships with college students' anxiety. Same as Anxiety, Depression had significant relationships with those variables. Depression also had a significant relationship with Positive Parental Rearing Attitude ($r = -0.164$, $p \leq 0.01$).

Conclusion: Increasing the scores of Spiritual well-being, Positive Parental Rearing Attitude, and using Problem Focused Disengagement coping strategies decreased college students' Anxiety and Depression. Decreasing scores of Negative Parental Rearing Attitude and emotional coping strategies also decreased college students' Anxiety and Depression.

Chapter 7 - Ageing process involves the entire western world and in particular Europe. The analysis of demographic and health changes of the aged population is increasingly urgent in order to answer to the new individual and societal requests. An important concept in this regard is Health Related Quality of Life (HRQOL) during ageing, on which this paper will focus. Firstly, a general framework on demographics and health changes is provided. Secondly, the concept of HRQOL is analyzed, highlighting its strengths as well as its potential limitations. Thirdly, an analysis of HRQOL developmental trends, processes and mechanisms related to these processes is given. Finally, a conceptual dynamic systems model of HRQOL is delineated, in order to summarize the path taken in the paper and to propose new insights in the study of HRQOL in the aged population.

Chapter 8 - Substance addiction is described as a 'chronic relapsing disease', to which the Hong Kong government takes an 'enlightened prohibition' approach to stress on the provision of rehabilitative support to addicts instead of imposing stringent legal sanctions.The treatment and rehabilitation of substance addicts is thus of utmost importance, in which use of faith-based approach to help addict patients keep abstinent is one of the main treatment interventions in Hong Kong. Faith-based addiction treatment is usually conducted and provided by local Christian therapeutic organisations in guidance of a Christian theory of substance addiction that recognises not only the psychological, social and physical determinants of addiction, but also the importance of the religious/spiritual dimension of abusing substance. Despite the desirable treatment outcomes of faith-based treatment found in the West, little research has been performed with regard to its effectiveness and delivery mechanisms, especially in Hong Kong. This chapter will propose a theoretical framework to investigate the mechanisms by which faith-based addiction treatment delivers the desirable treatment outcomes and, in particular, the respective contributing factors in different levels of the treatment mechanisms. Pertinent research designs, measurement and statistical procedures are also addressed. The chapter will finally conclude with implications and contributions stemmed from the proposed study.

In: Psychological Health and Needs Research Developments ISBN: 978-1-63483-332-5
Editor: Raul Wolfe

Chapter 1

THE ROAD TO GOOD PSYCHOLOGICAL HEALTH: BASIC PSYCHOLOGICAL NEED SATISFACTION

Zachary G. Baker*[*,1] and Jennifer L. Bryan[2]
[1]University of Houston, US
[2] Houston Center for Innovations in Quality, Effectiveness and Safety, VA Health Services Research and Development Center, US

ABSTRACT

This chapter is a discussion of the three basic psychological needs according to Self-Determination Theory (Deci & Ryan, 2000): autonomy, competence, and relatedness, which have been laid out as fundamental nutriments of human experience. The present discussion of these needs is separated into four major components. The first portion of the chapter is devoted to theoretical explanation of the needs including: their independent importance, the benefits of their balance, the conceptual and empirical distinctions between thwarting needs and satisfying them, and how they relate to ideas of ego-involvement, authenticity, and mindfulness. Next we turn to the relation between needs and a number of outcomes including relational well-being, physical health, and general well-being. We then explore the implications of autonomy, competence, and relatedness for several aspects of psychological health including stress and anxiety, emotional ambivalence, pain, depression, shame, loneliness, and impact on health behavior. Finally, there is a discussion of the utility of these needs for studying populations from a variety of peoples including those from vastly different ideologies and cultures.

Keywords: Autonomy, competence, relatedness, need fulfillment, well-being

Deci and Ryan (2000) laid out a framework of basic psychological needs according to Self-Determination Theory (SDT) stating that three irreducible needs exist. These needs are

* In preparation for *Psychological Health and Needs Research Developments.* Correspondence concerning this article should be addressed to Zachary G. Baker, Department of Psychology, University of Houston, 126 Heyne Building, Houston, Tx 77204-5022. Email: zbaker@uh.edu. Phone: (713) 743-8500

relatedness, autonomy, and competence and are considered to be bases that cannot be broken down further into more fundamental components. The need for relatedness may be seen as a desire to belong (Baumeister & Leary, 1995). When our relationships lead us to feel that we are making deep connections with others, they tend to satisfy relatedness. Relatedness can be enhanced in a variety a ways ranging from 2 friends having a lengthy conversation on a topic they both enjoy to a smile shared from 2 sports fans wearing their team's jerseys passing each other on the street. The need for autonomy involves ownership and authenticity of one's behaviors – and refers to the need to feel that one's behaviors reflect one's true interests rather than pressures from others or oneself (Deci & Ryan, 1985). It should be noted that this definition of autonomy differs somewhat from a lay conceptualization in which autonomy means acting with the utmost independence. SDT's definition of autonomy is merely concerned with feeling that one is able to choose for oneself. Therefore if in concert with one's thoughts, feelings, and beliefs he or she chooses to go along with the will of others, this action would still satisfy one's need for autonomy. It is this nuance in definition that allows autonomy and relatedness to act in concert, rather than in opposition (Hodgins, Koestner, and Duncan, 1996). An individual may find autonomy in many facets of life. An example would be choosing one's own dinner from a menu at his or her favorite restaurant, however, a sense of autonomy can be derived from diverse circumstances. For instance, if a doctor suggests that an individual should exercise for better health, that individual may choose to start swimming, which they derive pleasure from as opposed to running, which they may loath. Another example would be taking out the trash if an individual values a clean house. Finally, the inclination to master challenges that are optimally difficult describes competence. It is important that these challenges be not too easy but also not too tough as either extreme would not lead to fulfillment of one's competence need (Elliot & Dweck, 2005). Competence can be fostered in a number of ways, from shaving a few seconds off of one's 5k time to obtaining an advanced degree in one's chosen field of study. Self-Determination Theory posits that perceived competence will not lead to greater well-being unless the behavior performed is also autonomous (Ryan, Mims, & Koestner, 1983). For example, imagine that Bob is an excellent tuba player and has been in his high school marching band for 4 years. However, he no longer derives pleasure from playing his Tuba. Bob's parents force him into playing for his college's marching band because he is wonderful at playing the tuba and they enjoy watching him perform at football games. Bob agrees to play tuba to make his parents happy, although his tuba playing competence would not increase his well-being because Bob's behavior is not fulfilling his need for autonomy. Investigation across studies, cultures, methods, and measures have consistently demonstrated that fulfillment of one's needs for relatedness, autonomy, and competence are positively related to one another (e.g., Chen et al., 2014).

Recently, researchers have begun exploring the distinction between need support (i.e., feeling satisfaction of one's needs) and need thwarting (i.e., a deficit in fulfillment of needs). The first experimental investigation of need support and thwarting demonstrated that need thwarting is particularly motivational (Sheldon & Filak, 2008). Subsequent research by Sheldon, Abad, and Hinsch (2011) revealed that need thwarting is not simply the inverse of need satisfaction, but that the two constructs can act in distinct manors. Needs can be thwarted in a variety of ways. Autonomy can be thwarted if one is engaging in behavior that does not align with their values, such as eating meat to fit in with peers' even though they would rather be vegetarian. Competence can be thwarted by an individual consistently choosing to engage in activities that are very easy to them and never engaging in an activity that is challenging. In a similar vein, if an individual chooses activities that are much more advanced than their skill level they may feel overwhelmed, thus thwarting their competence needs. Relatedness may be thwarted if an individual chooses to interact with others in an inauthentic way to gain positive judgement from the others. In a series of studies, Sheldon et al. (2011) found that high levels of relatedness thwarting as well as high levels of relatedness satisfaction were, puzzlingly, both related to more Facebook usage. The authors explained their findings as a 2-process model wherein thwarting of relatedness motivated increased use of Facebook as a coping mechanism and increased Facebook use lead to more feelings of connection. Using experimental and longitudinal studies, the authors found support for this 2-process model. Satisfaction of one's needs has been shown to be beneficial to people in many ways (see below). One pathway through which needs may be helping people to reap benefits is through removal of a focus on the ego (Hadden, Overup, & Knee, 2013). By this we mean that as one's needs are more fulfilled, they view this as providing feedback that those behaviors that would naturally be enacted when acting in accord with one's automatic cognitions and emotions are effective and good, driving one to continue to act in more authentic ways that are truer to the self than those that focus on maintaining a positive self-view (Hodgins and Knee, 2002). Those actions that focus on maintaining a positive self-view should arise from feeling that one's needs are not being fulfilled when acting in accord with one's natural internal states because this would provide feedback that simply being oneself is not enough to be an effective person. Evidence for this mediational pathway has come from unique, but related, perspectives including theory on mindfulness, motivation, and authenticity. Ryan and Brown (2003) suggested that mindfulness, or a willingness to experience what is, arises from need fulfillment and in turn leads to less self-contingencies and more authenticity. Milyavskaya, Nadolny, and Koestner (2015) presented preliminary evidence that overall need satisfaction temporally precedes feelings of authenticity in certain contexts. Similarly, Baker (2015) demonstrated that within-person variations in need fulfillment in the context of one's interactions with others predict greater feelings of authenticity at the end of the day. While this research still suffers from a scarcity of causal demonstrations, the existence of temporal relationships is well-established. Finally, several studies in several domains (see Vallerand, 2000 for a review) demonstrate that need fulfillment's relationship with positive outcomes is consistently mediated by more internally-driven motivations. Ego-involvement, or the need to feel that one is a good, capable person is what unifies each of these concepts. Greater levels of mindfulness, more authenticity, and motivation that is derived from more internalized sources all reflect less focus on appearing in a positive way and instead on acting as one truly desires to act regardless of how one might be seen.

Need Fulfillment and Well-Being

Several positive things arise from fulfillment of one's basic psychological needs including improved relational functioning and general well-being. In a series of studies, Patrick Knee, Canevello, and Lonsbary (2007) demonstrated that need satisfaction in the context of one's relationship, as reported by both partners, positively predicts both one's own and one's partner's general and relational well-being. Using a diary procedure, the authors demonstrated that these relationships were mediated by greater intrinsic motivation to be in one's relationship. That is to say, need fulfillment led to more authentic motivations for relationship presence, which led to greater well-being. The authors also demonstrated that those reporting greater need fulfillment had less defensive responses to conflict with their partners. Together, these more authentic motivations and less defensive responses to conflict lend support to the perspective that need fulfillment leads to benefits through less behavior that focuses on maintaining one's self-esteem (i.e., removal of a focus on one's ego).

A number of studies have presented further evidence that need fulfillment leads to general well-being (e.g., Sheldon & Bettencourt, 2002; Uysal, Lin, & Knee, 2010; Uysal, Lin, Knee, & Bush, 2012). When any of these needs are neglected or unable to be met, suboptimal psychological outcomes are likely to follow (Deci & Ryan, 2000). In two early investigations of this phenomenon, Sheldon and Elliot (1999) followed by Reis, Sheldon, Gable, Roscoe, and Ryan (2000) demonstrated that within-person fluctuations in need fulfillment positively predict analogue fluctuations in several indicators of well-being including positive affect, negative affect, vitality, and physical symptoms. Reis et al., (2000) also found that trait autonomy was correlated with positive mood and vitality, trait competence was negatively correlated with negative mood and physical illness symptoms, and trait relatedness was correlated with positive mood. Similar findings were observed in daily assessments of need satisfaction over time. Autonomy was correlated with positive mood and vitality. Relatedness correlated significantly with positive mood and vitality. Competence was positively correlated with positive mood and vitality while negatively correlated with illness symptoms and negative mood. Moreover, daily fluctuations in well-being were predicted by the satisfaction of needs for autonomy and competence (Sheldon, Ryan, & Reis, 1996).

Deci et al. (2001) revealed that overall basic psychological need satisfaction was positively associated with a greater levels of self-esteem and negatively associated with anxiety symptoms within a cross-cultural sample. Furthermore, autonomy, competence, and relatedness were each found to be positively related to life satisfaction, happiness, satisfaction with the day, positive affect, and negatively associated with negative affect.

Beyond satisfaction and thwarting, questions have been posed as to the importance of individual needs. For instance, if one has high levels of competence, might this compensate for lower levels of autonomy? Sheldon and Niemiec (2006) investigated this question by comparing people who had higher sum reports of need satisfaction to those who had lower sum, but more balanced, reports of need satisfaction. Through four studies, they found that a greater balance in one's need satisfaction is more predictive of greater well-being than higher overall reports of need satisfaction. These results provided evidence that one's needs may not compensate for each other and that instead it is important to have equal fulfillment of all three needs. In other words, it is ideal to have one's needs be balanced rather than have high levels of just 1 or 2 of the needs (recall the example of Bob, whose tuba skills led to a satisfaction of competence but whose autonomy was thwarted because his parents made him play). Advancing upon these findings, Milyavskaya et al. (2009) demonstrated that internationally and across several measures, balanced satisfaction of one's needs within different contexts (i.e., school, home, with friends, and in jobs) is positively predictive of both well-being and adjustment. These findings provide additional support that each of the needs outlined by SDT are irreducible despite their positive relations to each other.

Need Satisfaction Across Cultures

Self-Determination Theory posits that general needs satisfaction (GNS; i.e., the needs for autonomy, competence, and relatedness) is universal among humans just as we universally need shelter, food, and water (Deci & Ryan, 1991). Some cultural psychologists investigated whether GNS was a western phenomenon or truly universal among humans. Early studies demonstrated some cultural variations. Researchers found that satisfaction of one's need for autonomy was a stronger predictor of life satisfaction in countries higher on the individualism spectrum (Oishi, Diener, Lucas, & Suh, 1999). Chen and colleagues (2014) further investigated GNS, as well as the value of the needs cross culturally, in a two part study. Study 1 included adolescents from China and Belgium. Results revealed that participants from both countries saw value in these needs. Autonomy and competence uniquely predicted positive self-esteem and negatively predicted depression and this relationship was not moderated by the individual valuation of these needs. Study 2 looked at a globally diverse population from 4 different continents: China, the US, Belgium, and Peru. Results revealed that all 3 needs uniquely contributed to vitality and autonomy and relatedness satisfaction related uniquely to life satisfaction for each of the 4 cultures. Moreover, need frustration negatively predicted life satisfaction and positively predicted depressive symptoms. These studies taken together help to shape a picture that general needs satisfaction is not simply unique to a western culture and that aspects are needed for a satisfying life for all of mankind.

SDT and Health

When individuals don't act in accordance with their true self (i.e., do not fulfill their need for autonomy), negative outcomes arise. As Uysal et al. (2010) explained, basic needs are not fulfilled when someone chooses to conceal. If a person chooses to hide something from a partner, he or she feels controlled in his or her interactions with that person leading to a decrease in autonomy. Relatedness would be thwarted due to a less genuine interaction with the partner which may lead to feeling distant. Lastly, if a person is choosing to conceal something he or she may begin to believe that what he or she is concealing is worse than he or she had previous thought, leading to a lower self-image and competence.

A related concept is ambivalence over emotional expression (AEE; King and Emmons, 1990) which is when an individual faces an internal struggle in deciding whether to disclose or withhold their emotions. Reis et al. (2000) found that the strongest predictors of relatedness were meaningful talk and feeling understood; most likely, this is something seldom felt by those high in AEE. Similarly, when individuals desire to express their emotions but cannot freely do so, they are unable to communicate their basic needs to other people in order to fulfill them. This, in turn, leads the individual to perceive a lack of social support, whether or not social support is actually present. Researchers have demonstrated that AEE fails to satisfy all three of the basic needs, which has a negative impact on social support (Bryan, Quist, Young, Steers, & Lu, 2015). Research has revealed that AEE is related to depressive symptoms due to lacking fulfillment of the basic needs as well (Lu, Uysal, & Teo 2011). Additionally, a correlation between these needs and the negative emotions of depression, shame, and loneliness were found in a university student population (Wei, Shaffer, Young, &

Zakalik 2005). In other words, AEE failed to fulfill GNS which in turn is related to more shame, depression, and loneliness.

Having the three needs fulfilled can be protective when facing life changes or stressful circumstances both psychologically and physically. In a study with incoming college students in the beginning of the academic year, autonomy predicted emotional and social adjustment as well as GPA several months later, in that those who were more autonomous had a higher emotional adjustment, social adjustment, and GPA. Autonomy accounted for as much variance in GPA as did high school GPA and SAT scores. Those students who reported feeling more autonomous were also more intrinsically motivated and less extrinsically motivated in their college endeavors (Conti, 2000). Autonomy is also beneficial when coping with a chronic disease. Within a population of HIV-positive and AIDS participants, intrinsic motivation behind personal strivings was related positively to well-being and autonomy was related to adjustment to their life threatening disease (Igreja et al., 2000). A review looking at children's adjustment to parental divorce revealed that children were better adjusted if their parents were autonomy supportive and, despite divorce's potential threat to GNS, if basic psychological needs were still met children could thrive (Friendly & Grolnick, 2009). A study investigating elite dancers had them report their autonomy, competence, and relatedness needs 1 month before a major dance solo, researchers then measured their salivary cortisol (a marker of momentary stress) and anxiety before the solo (Quested et al., 2011). Results revealed dancers with higher reported GNS 1 month before the solo had lower cortisol levels and less anxiety directly prior to their solo. These findings bring together the psychological and physical health importance of GNS for both daily life and very stressful situations.

GNS also plays a vital role in health behavior. With regard to weight loss, when an individual autonomously desires, and feels competent to lose weight they tend to be more successful in their endeavors (Silva, et al., 2010a). Moreover, in a randomized clinical trial, participants who received an intervention that facilitated these needs rather than an education control intervention were more likely to lose weight, engage in more physical activity, and more vigorous exercise at the 12 month follow up and also reported more autonomous motivation, a more supportive health care climate, more perceived choice, and more competence (Silya et al., 2010b). SDT can also play a vital role in aiding health care workers to inspire their patients. Many studies have reported that if health care workers are autonomy supportive that the patients report better health behavior outcomes. For example, when physiotherapists' were more autonomy-supportive of patients post-surgery, the patients reported more autonomous treatment motivation which in turn predicted greater rehabilitation adherence (Chan, Lonsdale, Ho, Yung, & Chan, 2009). Similar benefits were found with a sample of individuals who were beginning to exercise such that autonomy support was related to autonomous motivation and intentions to exercise (Rouse, Ntoumanis, Duda, Jolly, & Williams, 2011) as well as with individuals who desired to lose weight (Ng, J. Y. Ntoumanis, & Thogersen-Ntoumani, 2014).

IMPLEMENTING THE BENEFITS OF NEED SATISFACTION

How can a health care worker (or friend) autonomously practice supportive patient interactions? This can be accomplished in multiple ways, such as offering the patient choices that the patient can engage in. An example would be working with a patient to make more healthy eating choices. The provider may suggest to the patient to add more vegetable servings to dinner or to gill meat instead of frying it. The patient would feel more autonomous in their healthy eating journey as they have some choice as to what their first step would be. Another way to increase autonomy support is to demonstrate that the provider understands and validates the patient's perceptions. For instance if the patient has limited exposure to vegetables then incorporating two servings of vegetables into dinner may be overwhelming. The provider could acknowledge that walking into the produce section when not knowing what the majority of the options are, let alone how to prepare them, is indeed scary, but after facing that fear the patient would likely feel accomplished (i.e., competent). The provider could then make a plan with the patient to buy one vegetable that the patient has had a previously pleasant experience with and perhaps to experiment with a new type of vegetable. Another way to engage in autonomy-supportive behavior would be a technique used in motivational interviewing, to reiterate the patients reasons for wanting to do a behavior. An example of this would be the provider saying "So what I am hearing from you is that you want to become more active so that you have the energy and vitality to play with your young children, as being a good parent is important to you." This style of behavior would likely also fulfill relatedness through feelings of connection.

General need satisfaction can also be fostered in the work place. General psychological need satisfaction is related to better work outcomes including job performance, job satisfaction, organizational citizenship behavior, and overall psychological well-being (Gagné & Deci, 2005). Additionally, Guntert (2015) found that autonomy supportive leadership was related to increased job satisfaction, workplace engagement, and decreased turnover intention. Leaders can help their employees flourish by fostering their basic needs. Competence can be increased by allowing employees to take on novel tasks which are optimally challenging. Clearly defining team goals can foster autonomy, as team members' values are likely to align with the goals and serve as a reminder of why the individual is fully present at work each day. Relatedness would be fostered as well because each of the team members would be reminded that they are a team working towards a shared goal. Celebrating benchmarks of major progress or goal completion would also help to foster competence and relatedness. Moreover, leaders could encourage the ownership of work processes. It's possible that the workers may have ideas on how work flow quality could be improved. The ability to make those changes and to have leadership support could foster all three basic needs.

An individual can also choose to foster their own basic needs. For one to increase relatedness they should be true to themselves and interact with others in an autonomous way and not conform to what they think the other's perception of ideal is. Competence can be fostered by getting out of one's comfort zone and trying something optimally challenging. Autonomy can be achieved by acting in accord with one's values and taking ownership in ones actions and choices.

References

Baker, Z. G. (2015). *The Three Basic Psychological Needs as Antecedents to Authenticity.* Unpublished master's thesis, University of Houston, Houston, Texas.

Bryan, J. L., Quist, M. C., Young, C. M., Steers, M.-L. N, & Lu, Q.., (In press). General Needs Satisfaction as a Mediator of the Relationship between Ambivalence over Emotional Expression and Perceived Social Support. *The Journal of Social Psychology*

Baumeister, R. F., & Leary, M. R. (1995). The need to belong: desire for interpersonal attachments as a fundamental human motivation. *Psychological Bulletin*, *117*(3), 497-529.

Chan, D. K., Lonsdale, C., Ho, P. Y., Yung, P. S. H., & Chan, K. M. (2009). Patient motivation and adherence to post-surgery rehabilitation exercise recommendations: The influence of physiotherapists' autonomy supportive behaviors. *Archives of Physical Medicine & Rehabilitation*, 90, 1977-1982.

Chen, B., Vansteenkiste, M., Beyers, W., Boone, L., Deci, E. L., Van der Kaap-Deeder, J., … others. (2014). Basic psychological need satisfaction, need frustration, and need strength across four cultures. *Motivation and Emotion*, 1–21.

Conti, R. (2000). College goals: Do self-determined and carefully considered goals predict intrinsic motivation, academic performance, and adjustment during the first semester? *Social Psychology of Education*, 4(2), 189-211. doi:10.1023/A:1009607907509

Deci, E. L., & Ryan, R. M. (1985). *Intrinsic motivation and self-determination in human behavior*. Springer Science & Business Media.

Deci, E. L., & Ryan, R. M. (1991). A Motivational Approach to Self: Integration in Personality'. In RA Dientsbier (ed.), Perspectives on Motivation: Nebraska Symposium on Motivation. Lincoln, NE: University of Nebraska Press.

Deci, E. L., & Ryan, R. M. (2000). The "What" and "Why" of Goal Pursuits: Human Needs and the Self-Determination of Behavior. *Psychological Inquiry*, *11*(4), 227–268. http://doi.org/10.1207/S15327965PLI1104_01

Deci, E. L., Ryan, R. M., Gagné, M., Leone, D. R., Usunov, J., & Kornazheva, B. P. (2001). Need satisfaction, motivation, and well-being in the work organizations of a former Eastern Bloc country. *Personality and Social Psychology Bulletin*, *27*, 930-942.

Elliot, A. J., & Dweck, C. S. (2005). Competence and motivation. *Handbook of Competence and Motivation*. New York, NY: The Guilford Press

Friendly, R. W., & Grolnick, W. S. (2009). Child adjustment to familial dissolution: An examination of parental factors using a self-determination theory framework. *Journal Of Divorce & Remarriage*, *50*(1), 66-80. doi:10.1080/10502550802365722

Gagné, M., & Deci, E. L. (2005). Self-determination theory and work motivation. *Journal of Organizational Behavior*, *26*(4), 331–362.

Guntert, S. (2015). The impact of work design, autonomy support, and strategy on employee outcomes: A differentiated perspective on self-determination at work. *Motivation and Emotion*, 39, 99-103. doi: 10.1007/s11031-014-9412-7

Hadden, B. W., Øverup, C. S., & Knee, C. R. (2013). Removing the ego: Need fulfillment, self-image goals, and self-presentation. *Self and Identity*, (ahead-of-print), 1–20.

Hodgins, H. S., & Knee, C. R. (2002). The integrating self and conscious experience. In E. L. Deci, & R. M. Ryan (Eds.), *Handbook of self-determination research* (pp. 87-100). Rochester, NY: University of Rochester Press.

Hodgins, H. S., Koestner, R., & Duncan, N. (1996). On the compatibility of autonomy and relatedness. *Personality and Social Psychology Bulletin*, *22*, 227–237.

Igreja, I., Zuroff, D. C., Koestner, R., Saltaris, C., Brouillette, M., & LaLonde, R. (2000). Applying self-determination theory to the prediction and well-being in gay men with HIV and AIDS. Journal Of Applied Social Psychology, 30(4), 686-706. doi:10.1111/j.1559-1816.2000.tb02819.x

King, L. A., & Emmons, R. A. (1990). Conflict over emotional expression: Psychological and physical correlates. *Journal of Personality and Social Psychology*, *58*(5), 864.

Lu, Q., Uysal, A., & Teo, I. (2011). Need satisfaction and catastrophizing: Explaining the relationship among emotional ambivalence, pain, and depressive symptoms. *Journal of Health Psychology*, *16*, 819-827. doi: 10.1177/1359105310392092

Milyavskaya, M., Gingras, I., Mageau, G. A., Koestner, R., Gagnon, H., Fang, J., & Boiché, J. (2009). Balance across contexts: Importance of balanced need satisfaction across various life domains. *Personality and Social Psychology Bulletin*, *35*(8), 1031–1045.

Milyavskaya, M., Nadolny, D., & Koestner, R. (2015). Why do people set more self-concordant goals in need satisfying domains? Testing authenticity as a mediator. *Personality and Individual Differences*, *77*, 131–136.

Ng, J. Y. Y., Ntoumanis, N., & Thogersen-Ntoumani, C. (2014). Autonomy support and control in weight management: What important others do and say matter. British Journal of Health Psychology, 19, 540-552. doi: DOI: 10.1111/bjhp.12054

Oishi, S., Diener, E. F., Lucas, R. E., & Suh, E. M. (1999). Cross-cultural variations in predictors of life satisfaction: Perspectives from needs and values. *Personality And Social Psychology Bulletin*, *25*(8), 980-990. doi:10.1177/01461672992511006

Patrick, H., Knee, C. R., Canevello, A., & Lonsbary, C. (2007). The role of need fulfillment in relationship functioning and well-being: A self-determination theory perspective. *Journal of Personality and Social Psychology*, *92*(3), 434–457. http://doi.org/10.1037/0022-3514.92.3.434

Quested, E., Bosch, J. A., Burns, V. E., Cumming, J., Ntoumanis, N., & Duda, J. L. (2011). Basic psychological need satisfaction, stress-related appraisals, and dancers' cortisol and anxiety responses. *Journal Of Sport & Exercise Psychology*, 33(6), 828-846.

Reis, H. T., Sheldon, K. M., Gable, S. L., Roscoe, J., & Ryan, R. M. (2000). Daily well-being: The role of autonomy, competence, and relatedness. *Personality and Social Psychology Bulletin*, *26*(4), 419–435.

Rouse, P. C., Ntoumanis, N., Duda, J. L., Jolly, K., & Williams, G. C. (2011). In the beginning: Role of autonomy support on the motivation, mental health and intentions of participants entering an exercise referral scheme. *Psychology and Health*, *26*, 729–749.

Ryan, R. M., & Brown, K. W. (2003). Why we don't need self-esteem: On fundamental needs, contingent love, and mindfulness. *Psychological Inquiry*, 71–76.\

Ryan, R. M., Mims, V., & Koestner, R. (1983). Relation of reward contingency and interpersonal context to intrinsic motivation: A review and test using cognitive evaluation theory. *Journal of Personality and Social Psychology*, 45(4), 736-750. doi:10.1037/0022-3514.45.4.736

Sheldon, K. M., Abad, N., & Hinsch, C. (2011). A two-process view of Facebook use and relatedness need-satisfaction: disconnection drives use, and connection rewards it. Retrieved from http://psycnet.apa.org/journals/ppm/1/S/2/

Sheldon, K. M., & Bettencourt, B. (2002). Psychological need-satisfaction and subjective well-being within social groups. *British Journal of Social Psychology*, *41*(1), 25–38.

Sheldon, K. M., & Elliot, A. J. (1999). Goal striving, need satisfaction, and longitudinal well-being: The self-concordance model. *Journal of Personality and Social Psychology*, *76*(3), 482–497. http://doi.org/10.1037/0022-3514.76.3.482

Sheldon, K. M., & Filak, V. (2008). Manipulating autonomy, competence, and relatedness support in a game-learning context: New evidence that all three needs matter. *British Journal of Social Psychology*, *47*(2), 267–283.

Sheldon, K. M., & Niemiec, C. P. (2006). It's not just the amount that counts: balanced need satisfaction also affects well-being. *Journal of Personality and Social Psychology*, *91*(2), 331.

Sheldon, K. M., Ryan, R. M., & Reis, H. T. (1996). What makes for a good day? Competence and autonomy in the day and in the person. *Personality and Social Psychology Bulletin*, (22), 1270–1279.

Silva, M. N., Teixeira, P. J., Markland, D. A., Vieira, P. N., Coutinho, S. R., Carraça, E. V., Palmeira, A. L., Minderico, C. S., Matos, M. G., & Sardinha, L. B. (2010a). Helping overweight women become more active: Need support and motivational regulations for different forms of physical activity. *Psychology of Sport and Exercise*, 11, 591-601.

Silva, M. N., Vieira, P. N., Coutinho, S. R., Minderico, C. S., Matos, M. G., Sardinha, L. B., & Teixeira, P. J. (2010b). Using self-determination theory to promote physical activity and weight control: A randomized controlled trial in women. *Journal of Behavioral Medicine*, 33, 110-122.

Uysal, A., Lin, H. L., & Knee, C. R. (2010). The Role of Need Satisfaction in Self-Concealment and Well-Being. *Personality and Social Psychology Bulletin*, *36*(2), 187–199. http://doi.org/10.1177/0146167209354518

Uysal, A., Lin, H. L., Knee, C. R., & Bush, A. L. (2012). The Association Between Self-Concealment From One's Partner and Relationship Well-Being. *Personality and Social Psychology Bulletin*, *38*(1), 39–51. http://doi.org/10.1177/0146167211429331

Vallerand, R. J. (2000). Deci and Ryan's self-determination theory: A view from the hierarchical model of intrinsic and extrinsic motivation. *Psychological Inquiry*, 312–318.

Wei, M., Shaffer, P. A., Young, S. K., & Zakalik, R. A. (2005). Adult Attachment, Shame, Depression, and Loneliness: The Mediation Role of Basic Psychological Needs Satisfaction. *Journal Of Counseling Psychology*, *52*(4), 591-601. doi:10.1037/0022-0167.52.4.591

In: Psychological Health and Needs Research Developments
Editor: Raul Wolfe
ISBN: 978-1-63483-332-5

Chapter 2

COPING AND WELL-BEING IN ADOLESCENCE

Marta Tremolada*, PhD and Sabrina Bonichini*, PhD
Department of Developmental and Social Psychology,
University of Padua, Italy

ABSTRACT

Attention toward coping in healthy adolescents is the result of the important role of protective and risk factors that could influence well-being. If adolescents improve their coping skills, they can perceive and react to stressors in ways that yield positive health outcomes.

Adolescents experience many stressor situations, ranging from pubertal changes to family and peer relationship conflicts. This chapter will review the research published in the last 10 years on coping skills in adolescence and their association with well-being.

Articles were found using the most relevant electronic databases, PubMed, Psychology and Behavioural Science, PsycINFO, Sciencedirect and Scopus, employing various search strategies: the search terms used included MeSH, headings, text words or keywords relevant to the following terms: "Coping," "adolescent," "well-being," "psychosocial." Text word and thesaurus searches were used to minimize chances of missing relevant articles. Identified articles were examined for additional references. The search was limited to English-language literature published in the last 10 years (2005-2015). We considered the full text of the selected papers to examine all the specific characteristics of each study. One of the eligibility criteria was that the papers dealt with adolescents, but we also considered studies where parents were the participants, only when they constituted a source of information about their adolescents' coping strategies and health. We excluded all the articles related to specific health diseases, such as chronic illnesses (cancer, diabetes, etc.) or other specific pathologies, physical, psychiatric or contextual (i.e., eating disorders, sleep deficits, terrorism/emergency events, mental disorders).

Some important topics associated with adolescents' psycho-social well-being that emerged from the review of the literature were: Health related quality of life and health beliefs area; Mental well-being area (psychopathology symptoms); Perceived stress and

* Corresponding author: Marta Tremolada, PhD, Department of Developmental and Social Psychology, University of Padua, Italy, Via Venezia 15 – 35131 Padova, Italy. tel.+39 3474868835. e-mail: marta.tremolada@unipd.it

coping strategies to front the daily problems area: SES and coping, stable internal resources, positive coping, coping related to academic performance; Relationship and perceived social support area and Family influences on adolescents' well-being.

These information will be discussed and directions for future research and psychological interventions will be proposed.

1. Introduction

1.1. Adolescence: A Complex Developmental Period of the Life Cycle

Adolescence is a developmental complex period, in which girls and boys live moments very intense and crucial of their lives. According to the American Psychological Association (APA), adolescence is the period of life between 10 and 18 years of age. The World Health Organization (WHO) suggests extending the period up to and including 20 years. In fact it is very difficult to define adolescence in a limited time because the risk is to be reductive in wanting to treat it an unified manner. In fact, the features and development tasks that define adolescence tend to be influenced by individual differences, different social contexts and historical period. In more general terms it is preferred to treat, then, adolescence as the period of the life cycle that lasts from late childhood to the first young adulthood (Albiero, 2012).

The modern trend is to match this evolutionary period with the period of the conflict. Literature, film and media in fact depict mainly the problematic aspects by creating a distorted idea. Despite the many problems that characterize adolescence, the latest research will instead highlight a positive image (Bonino et al., 2003). On the one hand, it is true that adolescence is a complex period, but, on the other hand, there is an important increasing number of teenagers who have passed the difficulties encountered along the growth path and who have achieved their development objectives, gradually closer to those in adulthood, showing a source of well-being and a good adaptation.

In light of the fact that every teenager lives in a unique and original way this stage, so that it would be simplistic to enter adolescence within stakes rigid, however we could synthesize, as proposed by Palmonari (1997), two key aspects of this phase of the life cycle.

1. In all adolescences the protagonist faces a considerable amount of problems. Sometimes, they are distributed evenly along the path of growth, so as not to be impossible to deal with; other times, these problems are more complex and require more energy to be successfully overcome. This success depends not only on the individual characteristics of the subject, the so-called coping, but also on the availability of resources from outside and from the characteristics of the cultural context in which the adolescent is inserted.
2. In all adolescences the protagonist is never completely alone. The adolescent forms meaningful relationships with family and significant others, with new friends and special people with which to build a relationship sentimentally rewarding. Sometimes these relationships are a source of satisfaction, sometimes a reason for conflict, but it is true that the perceived social support is a source of psychosocial well-being for the adolescent.

1.2. The Well-Being in Adolescence: An Overview

For the World Health Organization, health, both physical and mental, is a resource for life, a capital that enables individuals to achieve the goals they have set and their own welfare. Studying how individuals perceive their health status becomes critical, because this is not only one of the components of quality of life, but it comes almost to coincide with the concept of well-being. Adolescence is the period of transition in which the boys and girls are facing many new challenges that impact on their health and well-being perceptions. Following the bio-psycho-social model, the health professionals are interested in the health promotion related to the personal well-being. In this perspective, the focus on adolescent health is crucial: It is at this age that teenagers define their own lifestyle that is then strongly predictive of disease/disability levels of adulthood; it is the meeting/clash with the cultural context in which we live every day that young people construct their own way of being in the world and their idea of health and well-being.

Before analyzing the research studies that are interested in the health of adolescents, it is necessary to deepen an important aspect of the life of the young, or the challenges that he/she has to deal with in this period of life that determine consistently his/her quality of life and the physical and mental well-being. The continuous adaptation between individual and environment characterizes human development, leading to the search for a dynamic balance between the demands of both sides. It is just in periods of transition, like in adolescence, that the search for balance is essential. The young, who, as previously stated, is an active protagonist of his growth, searches equilibrium with its life context by addressing the "development tasks." Robert Havighurst (1952) has identified critical developmental tasks that occur throughout the life span, defining a "development task" as one that arises at a certain period in our lives, the successful achievement of which leads to happiness and success with later tasks; while leads to unhappiness, social disapproval, and difficulty with later tasks. Havighurst uses lightly different age groupings, but the basic divisions are quite similar to those used in this chapter. He identifies three sources of developmental tasks:

- Tasks that arise from physical maturation. For example, learning to walk, talk, and behave acceptably with the opposite sex during adolescence; adjusting to menopause during middle age
- Tasks that from personal sources. For example, those that emerge from the maturing personality and take the form of personal values and aspirations, such as learning the necessary skills for job success.
- Tasks that have their source in the pressures of society. For example, learning to read or learning the role of a responsible citizen.

According to our biopsychosocial model, the first source corresponds to the "bio" part of the model, the second to the "psycho," and the third to the "social" aspect.

Specifically, the developmental tasks of adolescence are the following:

1. Achieving new and more mature relations with age-mates of both sexes
2. Achieving a masculine or feminine social role
3. Accepting one's physique and using the body effectively

4. Achieving emotional independence of parents and other adults
5. Preparing for marriage and family life
6. Preparing for an economic career
7. Acquiring a set of values and an ethical system as a guide to behavior; developing an ideology
8. Desiring and achieving socially responsible behavior.

The way the adolescent faces the tasks of development characterizes his/her psychological well-being: If the adolescent successfully overcomes the problems, he/she will experience a sense of satisfaction, joy and a self-confidence increase; in the unsuccessful case, he/she would feel sadness, distrust and a self-esteem decrease (Vianello, 2003). For this reason we are interested in studying the psychosocial well-being of the adolescent and young adult and the perception of the quality of life in the light of the tasks of development, as are the characteristics tied to the overcoming of the latter.

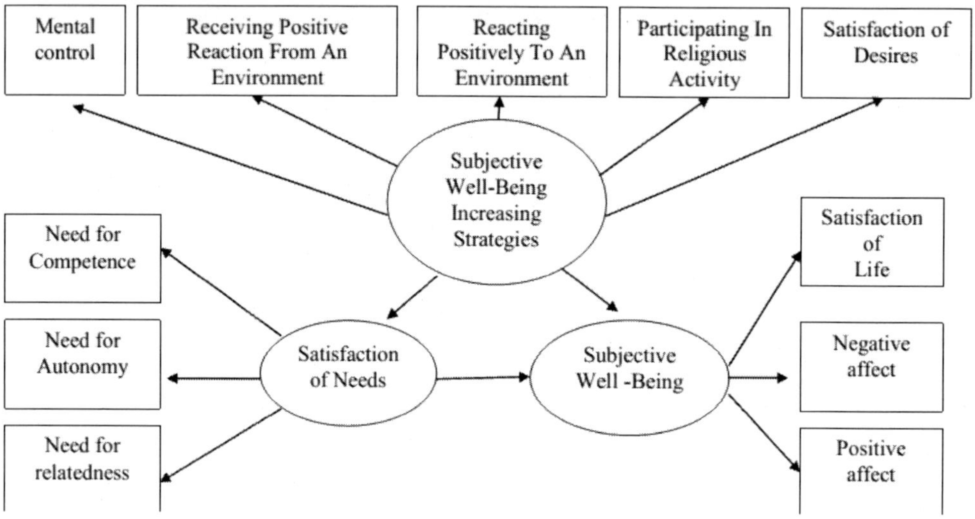

Figure 1. A model related to subjective well-being of adolescents in high school—satisfaction of needs and employment of strategies for improving subjective well-being (Eryılmaz, 2012, p. 283).

A model of subjective well-being in adolescence is developed based on subjective well-being increasing strategies and satisfaction of needs (Eryılmaz, 2012). Eryılmaz (2012) stressed that the satisfaction of adolescents' needs goes in parallel with the increase in their subjective wellbeing, showing similar relationships between satisfaction of needs and subjective well-being even in different developmental stages.

1.3. Coping Strategies of Adolescents and Young Adults: Models

As underlined by Olbrich (1990), adolescence can be considered as a period of coping, adapting production: In fact, the teenager has to invest a lot of themselves to build their own identity and tackle the tasks of development, which show to adapt constructively, without falling into crisis situations.

Although there are many definitions and theoretical approaches used to understand coping, it can be generally defined as a cognitive and/or behavioral attempt to manage (reduce or tolerate) situations that are appraised as a stressful to an individual. Moreover, no single coping strategy or dimension can be considered (mal)adaptive. The quality of the coping strategy and process should be evaluated according to its impact on the outcome of importance (Aldridge & Roesch, 2007). From the previous conceptual definition, Lazarus and Folkman (1984) have distinguished two primary categories of coping: Emotion-focused and problem-focused. These coping categories describe efforts to either alter the source of stress in the environment or to alleviate the personal emotional stress induced by the stressors. The emotion-coping dimension includes strategies that involve self-preoccupation, fantasy, or other conscious activities related to affect regulation, including for example social support for emotional reasons and positive reappraisal. The problem-focused coping dimension, on the other hand, involves strategies that attempt to solve, reconceptualize, or minimize the effects of a stressful situation, including for example instrumental social support and planful problem-solving (Lazarus and Folkman, 1984).

Initial research studies on coping in adolescence had used the classification proposed by Lazarus for adults, but only later it was decided to use a classification specific for this development stage. Among the models that explain the main strategies to address the problems in adolescence we find the model of Seiffge-Krenke (1995), the phenomenological approach of Frydenberg (1997) and the strategic approach proposed by the research group of the Laboratory of Toulouse coordinated by Pierre Tap (Tap, et al.,1997).

The first model of Seiffge-Krenke (1995) considers the coping as a mediator between the stressful event and the result of action, and it is influenced by internal variables (self-concept, personality) and social resources (relationships with family and friends). The author hypothesized twenty different coping strategies that can be summarized in three distinct styles: Active coping (search for information, talking about the problem with an expert), Internal coping (use the compromise, expect the worst), Avoidance coping (trying to forget the problem by making use of alcohol and drugs).

The approach of Frydenberg (1997) emphasizes the role of personality: the coping is both a function of the person and of the situation, but, above all, the personal perception of a difficult event. The author highlights eighteen coping strategies grouped into three styles: solution of the problem (work hard, focus on the problem), refer to the other (invest on close friends, search for spiritual support), not productive coping (not to act, withdraw into themselves).

Tap and his research team propose a model multidimensional and dynamic of coping (Tap et al.,1997), in which you need to consider the specific contexts. Coping covers three different areas: The action, or the behavioral context, regarding management strategies to overcome the problems; the information, the cognitive domain, concerning the knowledge gathered to face difficult event; the emotion, or the affective domain, stackable in emotional reactions and feelings that arise when you face stress.

These three different areas originate four distinct coping strategies: Control (cognitive, emotional and adjustment activities), withdrawal (avoidance of the problem, social withdrawal and behavioral), social support (informational support, emotional support, cooperation), rejection (denial, distraction, alexithymia).

2. METHOD

Our goal is to contribute to a broad and up-to-date picture of the literature on adolescents' coping and well-being. Studies on these topics have been increasing considerably in recent times, but there is still a gap in the literature in terms of discussion and organization of this information that would allow a clearer idea of the methodologies adopted and the formulation of general conclusions from these existing data. The focus of the present chapter will be a systematic and updated review of the main bodies of knowledge on coping skills in adolescence and their association with well-being, summarizing the principal results and indicating the possible future directions of research. Fifty-nine research articles were found using the most relevant electronic databases, PubMed, Psychology and Behavioural Science, PsycINFO, Sciencedirect and Scopus, employing various search strategies: the search terms used included MeSH, headings, text words or keywords relevant to the following terms: "Coping," "adolescent," "well-being," "psychosocial." Text word and thesaurus searches were used to minimize chances of missing relevant articles. Identified articles were examined for additional references. The search was limited to English-language literature published in the last 10 years (2005-2015). We considered the full text of the 59 selected papers to examine all the specific characteristics of each study. One of the eligibility criteria was that the papers dealt with adolescents, but we also considered studies where parents were the participants, only when they constituted a source of information about their adolescents' coping strategies and health. We excluded all the articles related to specific health diseases, such as chronic illnesses (cancer, diabetes, etc.) or other specific pathologies, physical, psychiatric or contextual (i.e., eating disorders, terrorism/emergency events, mental disorders) or the articles on therapeutic interventions. We treated separately the reviews, putting the findings of these un the discussion of each area.

3. RESULTS

In trying to give an overall picture of how boys and girls perceive their mental well-being and the coping strategies adopted, we decided to analyze this important component of life, dividing it in the main areas that define this construct.

1. Health related quality of life and health beliefs area (addictive behaviors, sleep disturbances);
2. Mental well-being area (psychopathology symptoms);
3. Perceived stress and coping strategies to front the daily problems area: SES and coping, stable internal resources, positive coping, coping related to academic performance;
4. Relationship and perceived social support area and their relationship with depressive symptoms;
5. Family influences on adolescents' well-being.

We will analyze each area discussing the main results of the studies and the methodology adopted.

3.1. Health Related Quality of Life (HRQoL) and Health Beliefs Area

Twelve studies belong to this area, 4 related to health beliefs and 8 related to HRQoL. (Table 1). Five studies had a longitudinal design, three were only descriptive, the other four had a cross-sectional design. The health related quality of life is a multidimensional key issue and several subdomains are associated to it: Physical subdomain, Healthy/Non healthy lifestyle behaviors and Well-being, Health beliefs. Physical dimension belongs to: Physical self-concept, Physical activity, Sleep functioning, Diet, Alterations in the stress-sensitive hypothalamic–pituitary–adrenal axis. Health behaviors and Well-being refer to: Loneliness, Concerns and hopes, Stress, Emotional and psycho-social well-being, Problem behavior, Social connection, Lifestyle behaviors, Addictive behaviors (Polydrug use, alcohol use, smoking), Conduct problems, Defiant attitude, High school non-completion, Academic performance, Life satisfaction, Leisure-time, Life change events. Health beliefs deal with: Cognitive and structural social capital, Social constructionism, Social support, Social representations, Cultural beliefs about adversity, Cognitive social maturity. From these studies we could stress that several factors contribute substantially to a holistic construction and meaning of health and wellbeing, such as: Effective communication, mutual respect, support from significant others, relationships, daily actions, identity, stressful life events. For example, having a low level of physical self-concept could be associated with an increasing risk of being inactive, a worse life satisfaction perceptions and adherence to the diet (Grao-Cruces et al., 2014). Or unhealthy sleep practices could be related with conduct problems, poor academic performance, low levels of emotional well-being and defiant attitudes (Lin et al., 2015). Adolescents' substance abuse (drug/alcohol) behaviors versus healthy life-style behaviors, could be associated with social thought processes towards their recent life events (levers-Landis et al., 2006), but also with their social capital, broadly defined as the resources that individuals access through their social networks (i.e., structural family social capital, cognitive school social capital – Cc Clercq et al., 2014 -, social connection – Sladek et al., 2015 -socio-economic disparities beliefs - Shek et al., 2005 -, family composition – Lee et al., 2014). These unhealthy behaviors were also predictive of a school non-completion (Kelly et al., 2014).

3.2. Mental Well-Being Area (Psychopathology Symptoms)

Polanczyk et al., 2015 presented a meta-analysis of the worldwide prevalence of mental disorders in children and adolescents The worldwide pooled prevalence of mental disorders was 13.4% (range: 11.3–15.9). The worldwide prevalence of any anxiety disorder was 6.5% (range: 4.7–9.1), any depressive disorder was 2.6% (range: 1.7–3.9), attention-deficit hyperactivity disorder was 3.4% (range: 2.6–4.5), and any disruptive disorder was 5.7% (range 4.0–8.1). Significant heterogeneity was detected for all pooled estimates. Beside this review, we found 6 studies specifically related to mental well-being and psychopathology symptoms in adolescence (Table 2). Four studies had a longitudinal design, taking into account the developmental difference of mental well-being across age, 1 was a one-time point study and the last was a cross-cultural study throughout different cultures.

Table 1. Health related quality of life (HRQoL) and health beliefs area

First Author/ Publication yr	Sample	Age range	Study design	Timing	Variables and functional area assessed	Measures	Main results
Antilla et al., 2015	N=70 Finnish admitted to psychiatric hospital wards or involved in a brief intervention	Aged 15-17	Descriptive	Interventional group	Concerns and hopes	Short essays analyzed by the Depis.Net Internet program and thematic analysis	Four main themes were formed to represent areas of life where concerns and hopes emerged: relationships, daily actions, identity, and well-being
Ce Clercq et al., 2014	N=8453 from Belgium	Mean=15.2 (SD=1.90); Range 12-18	Cross-sectional	One-time point	Adolescent smoking Cognitive and structural social capital	Individual, Parental, Peer Smoking frequency; The Family Affluence Scale (FAS); participation in clubs or organizations; Flemish Health Behavior in School-Aged Children (HBSC) survey	Only structural family social capital and cognitive school social capital variables negatively related to regular smoking. No interactions between socio-economic status and social capital variables were found
Glozah, 2015	N=11 Ghanaian adolescents	Average age of 16.86 years	Descriptive	One-time point	Social support Stress Health and wellbeing Social constructionism	semi-structured interviews	Effective communication, mutual respect, and support from significant others, in the midst of stressful life events, contribute substantially to a holistic construction and meaning of health and wellbeing by Ghanaian adolescents.
Grao-Cruces et al., 2014	N=1.808 Spanish adolescents	14.35±1.31 years, 12-16 years; body mass index: 22.26±4.32 kg/m2	Cross-sectional	During the 2011/2012 academic year.	Physical self-concept, physical activity, life satisfaction, Mediterranean diet	Physical Self Questionnaire, Moderate-to-Vigorous Physical Activity Screening Measure, Intention to be Physically Active Scale, Satisfaction with Life Scale, and Mediterranean Diet Quality Index	Having a low level of physical self-concept increases the risk of being inactive and of having a low level of intention to be physically active, life satisfaction and adherence to the Mediterranean diet

First Author/ Publication yr	Sample	Age range	Study design	Timing	Variables and functional area assessed	Measures	Main results
Kelly et al., 2014	The youngest cohort (n=804) The middle cohort (n=955) The oldest cohort (n=973) from Australia	The youngest cohort: mean age=15.15 The middle cohort: mean age= 14.99 The oldest cohort: mean age= 14.89	Longitudinal	The youngest Cohort: seven-wave study from grade 5 (10 ys) to post-high school, except 8 The middle cohort: four waves (grades 7–9 and post-high school). The oldest cohort: three waves (grades 9/10/post-high school).	Polydrug use, alcohol use and high school non-completion Depressive symtoms	Communities That Care Youth Survey Non-completion of grade 12 (assessed in the final wave). Drug use by questions on past-month use Academic failure School commitment Peer drug use Short Mood and Feelings Questionnaire	Mid-adolescent polydrug use in Australia predicts subsequent school non-completion after accounting for a range of potential confounding factors. Adolescents who mainly consume alcohol are also at elevated risk of school non-completion
Lee et al., 2011	N=2014 Chinese adolescents	aged 10–19	Cross-sectional	One-time point	Lifestyle behaviours and psychosocial well-being	Chinese version of the modified Adolescents' Lifestyle Questionnaire (C-ALQ)	Socio-economic disparities, family composition and age group are the key factors associated with adolescents' healthy lifestyle behaviors
levers-Landis et al.., 2006	N= 1322 High schools students in Midwest	Mean = 15.15 ys; (SD=0.80 ys); range: 12-18 ys	Longitudinal	Mean time between pre- and post-tests: 18.84 days (SD=7.87)	Cognitive social maturity Life change events Substance use	Children's Social Desirability (CSD) Adolescent Life Change Event Scale Substance abuse	Adolescents' social thought processes are related to their recent life events, which in turn are related to their substance use behaviors
Lin et al. 2015	N=2683 from Taiwan at wave 2 two cohorts: J1 (first year of junior-high school) J3 (third year of junior-high school)	Youth were aged 14–18 (M = 14.3, SD = 0.48) at wave 2	Longitudinal	Subjects followed annually for 8 years.	Sleep functioning Emotional well-being Conduct problems Academic performance Defiant attitude	short sleep, social jetlag, and sleep problems; Symptom Checklist-90-Revised; keeping up-to-date with their school work; students' rank in their class based on GPA; factor with major subjects the student had failed; Students' lack of impulse control and attitude; Skipping class; fighting and substance abuse	All the measures of unhealthy sleep practices were related to conduct problems and they were differently related to poor academic performance, low levels of emotional well-being, and defiant attitudes.

Table 1. (Continued)

First Author/ Publication yr	Sample	Age range	Study design	Timing	Variables and functional area assessed	Measures	Main results
Moreira et al., 2013	N=316 from State of Bahia	aged between 13 and 19 years old	Descriptive	One-time point	Quality of Life: social representations	Evocation of Words program, from the inductive term "quality of life"	Associated elements with QoL: sports/healthy lifestyle habits, being influenced by the desires, curiosities and pleasures (sex, football, the use of marijuana), work as a way to provide the resources needed to live well and in peace with his family means.
Sabiston et al., 2008	N=857 from Vancouver, British Columbia, Canada	Aged 15-18	Cross-sectional	One-time point	Adolescent leisure-time and physical activity	Perceived Competence Scale for Exercising, Regularly Personal efficacy expectations, Self- and Task-Perception Questionnaire, Leisure-Time Exercise Questionnaire, Perceptions of Significant Others' Influences	Expectancy-value (EV) model is demonstrated as a useful key to study leisure-time and physical activity
Shek, 2005	N=199 Chinese adolescents with financial difficulties	Mean age=14.2 ys	Longitudinal	Time 1: first assessment Time 2: 1 year post	Cultural beliefs about adversity Psychological well-being Problem behavior	Chinese Beliefs about Adversity Scale, Existential Well-Being Scale, Life Satisfaction Scale, Mastery Scale, Chinese Self-Esteem Scale, Chinese version GHQ-30 Substance abuse Delinquency	Identification with Chinese cultural beliefs about adversity is an important factor that influences the psychosocial adjustment of Chinese adolescents experiencing economic disadvantage
Sladek et al., 2015	N=71 Adolescents at their first year of college in Arizona	Mean age = 18.85	Longitudinal	In high school at the first assessment (T1). Identical procedures during the fall (T2) and spring (T3) semester	Sleep Alterations in the stress-sensitive hypothalamic–pituitary–adrenal axis Loneliness Social connection	Daily diary reports of social connections, objective measures of sleep (actigraphy), and naturalistic salivary assessment, The UCLA Loneliness Scale	More daily social connection with others than usual may predict improved sleep quantity for lonely adolescents and a physiological index of anticipating upcoming daily demands in general.

Table 2. Mental well-being area (psychopathology symptoms)

First Author/ Publication yr	Sample	Age range	Study design	Timing	Variables and functional area assessed	Measures	Main results
Garcia, 2014	N=69 Swedish adolescents	38 boys age mean 17.15 ± 0.98 31 girls age mean 16.83 ± 0.78	Longitudinal	T1: baseline: high SWB/PWB vs low SWB/PWB T2: 1week after for the interpretation and memory Tasks T3: 2 days after the recall	Subjective (SWB) and Psychological Well-Being (PWB), Life events, Autobiographical memory	Background and Health Questionnaire, Satisfaction With Life Scale, Positive Affect and Negative Affect Schedule, Ryff's Measure of Psychological Well-being, Recollection and Interpretation of Life Events, The Interpretation and Recognition for Words in a Short Story	The high well-being groups remembered more positive than negative life events. Conversely to the other groups, the high PWB group interpreted positive and negative life events equally and had no preference for recognition of positive words. The number of words rated as positive predicted false recognition of positive words among the high well-being groups.
Navarro et al., 2015	N=93 students from Girona (north-east of Spain)	-in the fifth year of primary (9–10 years old) -up to the third year of secondary (13–14 years old)	Longitudinal	Students from the fifth year of primary to the third year of secondary education for two consecutive academic years	Subjective well-being	Personal Well-Being Index (PWI-7), Satisfaction With Life Scale (SWLS), Brief Multidimensional Students' Life Satisfaction Scale (BMSLSS)	Well-being is related to both affects and attitudes, relations with family and friends being key factors in it. Children scoring lower in SWB tend to refer more to relationships with friends and basic needs covered, whereas those scoring higher tend to refer more to family relationships and not having problems
Sijtsema et al., 2014	N=2230 Dutch adolscents	T1 mean age=11.09 years (SD = 0.55) T2 mean age: 13.56 years (SD = 0.53)	Longitudinal	T1: primary school: T2: two-and-a-half years after, secondary school	Psychopathology and Academic Performance, Social Well-Being, and Social Preference at School	YSR/CBC; TRAILS for academic performance; Social Production Functions questionnaire; Social preference was derived from the peer nominations.	Teacher reports of psychopathology, especially regarding attention problems and withdrawn/depressed problems, followed by parent reports regarding hyperactivity, were most strongly associated with academic performance. The same held for social preference. Social well-being was best predicted by child reports (at primary school) of affective problems. In girls, the association between ADHD problems and poor academic performance was stronger than in boys and conduct problems were more often associated with poor school functioning in general

Table 2. (Continued)

First Author/ Publication yr	Sample	Age range	Study design	Timing	Variables and functional area assessed	Measures	Main results
Singh et al., 2015	N=539 Indian students	age 13-18	One-time point	Assessment at school in once a time	Mental health and distress, psychosocial functioning	Mental Health Continuum Short Form, Depression Anxiety and Stress Scales-21, Strengths and Difficulties Questionnaire	Findings showed that 46.4% participants were flourishing, 51.2% were moderately mentally healthy, and only 2.4% were languishing. A higher number of girls and younger adolescents were flourishing compared to boys and older adolescents. Moreover, flourishing youths reported lower prevalence of depression and adjustment difficulties, and more prosocial behavior
Sujoldzic et al., 2007	N=2000 adolescents from Croatia	15-18 years of age	Cross-cultural	Different cultures: Croatia, Bosnia and Herzegovina, Albania, Kosovo, Italia and Austria	BMI, Body Image and Psychological Well-Being	body mass index (BMI), Hopkins Symptom Checklist and Reynolds Adolescent Depression Scale	Strong relationship between BMI and body dissatisfaction, between body image and dietary habits, and strong effects of body image on all indicators of psychosocial health. Gender and significant intracultural variations related to socioeconomic status or to other specific social and cultural contexts.
Wight et al., 2006	N=18.417 adolescents from USA in grades 7 through 12	11-18 ys old	Longitudinal	Students in 7th through 12th grade	Internalizing problems (depressive symptoms) and Externalizing problems (minor delinquency and violent behavior) Socioeconomic disadvantage	Center for Epidemiologic Studies—Depression Scale frequency of various delinquent and physical aggressive activities Social support-7-item scale Socioeconomic disadvantage	Socioeconomic disadvantage is positively associated with depressive symptoms, negatively associated with minor delinquency. High perceived support offsets poor mental health, but is most protective in areas of low socioeconomic disadvantage.

The methodology adopted to analyze mental functioning was limited to self-report or proxy-report questionnaires or psychological tests (i.e., Recollection and interpretation of life events, Recognition for words in a short story) that identified the possible predictive factors of a worse psychological well-being: Negative life events (Garcia, 2014), lower satisfaction with their relationships with friends and with their needs covered (Navarro et al., 2015), lower social well-being, attention problems, conduct problems and poor academic performance reported by teachers (Sijtsema et al., 2014), body dissatisfaction (Sujoldzic et al., 2007), socioeconomic disadvantage (Wight et al., 2006).

Gender differences could be found: girls' ADHD problems were related with poor academic performance, while boys reported more conduct problems related to poor academic performance (Sijtsema et al., 2014). Girls and younger adolescents were more in health and reported more prosocial behavior than boys and older adolescents (Singh et al., 2015).

3.3. Perceived Stress and Coping Strategies to Front the Daily Problems Area: SES and Coping, Stable Internal Resources, Positive Coping, Coping Related to Academic Performance

This is a pregnant area for the purpose of this review, because this area itself globally was constituted by 24 studies. The results were organized by using this classification: SES stable factors (gender, age, socio-economic status, residential context) (Table 3a, including 7 studies), Internal stable resources (i.e., intellectual and temperance strengths, interpersonal strengths, self-esteem, Extraversion, Neuroticism, Conscientiousness, Persistence, Self-directedness, curiosity, trait emotional intelligence) (Table 3b, including 7 studies), positive coping strategies (Table 3c), especially related to a good academic performance (including 10 studies).

All the studies related to possible differences of coping by SES had a cross-sectional design at one-time point; the studies about stable internal resources were divided into 2 longitudinal, 4 cross-sectional and 1 one-time point. Finally, the studies on positive coping strategies were principally cross-sectional or cross-informant (N=6), longitudinal (N=3) and one-time point (N=2). The methodology adopted consisted principally in self- or proxy-report questionnaires, only one used a narrative approach.

There are numerous studies that were interested to investigate the existence of gender and age differences in the use of coping strategies. The literature on differences by gender in adults agreed that women use coping strategies focused on emotions more than men, in particular the seek for social support. Men preferred more active coping strategies, focused on problem solving.

Dealing with adolescents' research results were not yet so clear.

A summary of the most recent studies that investigate the coping strategies implemented by teenagers, shows that the most used are: problem solving, spending time with his girlfriend or boyfriend, seek solace in the network of social support, family or outside the family, listen to the music, sports, think of the positive aspects of situations, daydreaming open, pray and seek solace in religion, cry and cut themselves, behave disturbing food as food refusal or binge, to take aggressive behaviors (Seiffge-Krenke, 2011).

Many studies have shown that girls tend to seek more frequently the support of family and friends in solving problems, while boys use more active strategies, such as engaging in physical activities or recreational leisure (Frydenberg, Lewis 1991). The girls make more use than boys to strategies like wishful thinking (or daydreams, fantasies, hope in miracles) and withdrawal. Most of the girls, more than boys, uses strategies such as: discuss problems with parents, ask for help to friends and get help from people in general, think about the problem and the solution to solve it, to accept that there will always be problems, vent their aggression, anger and despair, and the withdrawal from the situations that are perceived as not changeable (Cicognani et al., 2011). Girls made more use of social support, in particular the call for help and advice as well as the share with others own experiences or to enjoy some moments of distraction. The boys preferred the use of control strategies. These results are consistent with another study (Casas et al., 2007), where boys scored significantly higher on the materialistic values dimension and the capacities and knowledge related values dimension, while girls scored higher on the interpersonal relationship related values dimension. Female adolescents seemed to use more maladaptive coping styles than males and (Hampel et al., 2005; Al-Bahrani et al., 2013) and they presented lower average than boys for the Satisfaction with life scale and for the happiness measure (Bedin et al., 2015). Boys with higher academic achievement were happier but not more satisfied, the opposite holds true for girls (Chui et al., 2015).

One explanation for these differences is due to the nature of the stressful events that happen every day in the lives of boys and girls. Girls are probably affected more by stressful events of relational and affective nature. An alternative explanation, offered by Seiffge-Krenke, points out that females are not subjected to the most stressful events in terms of quantity than males, but perceive the same events as more stressful because of gender stereotypes culturally transmitted, underestimating their ability to cope with the difficulties.

Also residential context, the social class and the type of school adolescents belong, seemed to influence their well-being: the adolescents from lower middle class, less satisfied with their living context and attending government schools, were more at risk for a decrease in their well-being levels (Cicognani et al., 2008; Bedin et al., 2015; Sweeting et al., 2014; Singh et al., 2015). Higher happiness was related to a good self-esteem and life satisfaction as stable internal coping and with having more close friends as external coping (Chui et al., 2015).

As for the age variable, as explained above, the coping is a feature that changes and matures during the life cycle because of changes in cognitive, social, behavioral skills and the emergence of stressful events of a different nature (Frydenberg 1997). Studies related to this variable does unfortunately not lead to results sufficiently firm.

Some studies on the development of coping strategies in children and adolescents between 8 and 14 years have shown an increase in the use of maladaptive strategies, such as resignation, rumination, self-criticism and aggression, with increasing age (Hampel, Petermann 2005) or in general a decrease in the mean of personal well-being, Satisfaction with life perceptions and happiness when increasing age (Bedin et al., 2015). Another study declared that the use of adaptive or maladaptive coping styles increased with age (Al-Bahrani et al., 2013).

It is sure, however, that with increasing age, complex stressful events with which to cope increase and become more and more, thus also the coping strategies improve. In particular, the use of strategies to reduce tension increases, such as the use of alcohol and drugs, and the use of strategies of self consequently to the development of formal thought - abstract and cognitive skills more elaborate.

However, there were no changes in the use of problem solving, research, social support and the ability to give instructions on how to solve the problem, according to some research, they are acquired in childhood and remain stable over time. Adolescents anticipated future-related problems but did not portray their futures negatively. In addition, they dealt with future-related stress actively and showed high levels of coping competence. Adolescents used active coping strategies most frequently, followed by thinking about possible solutions. Dysfunctional coping strategies were used much less often (Seiffge-Krenke et al., 2010). The tendency not to worry about dealing with a problem decreased with age, while the ability to reflect and find solutions and strategy of compromise increased, especially after the age of 15 (Cicognani 2011). The youngest adolescents scored higher on materialistic values, while the oldest scored higher on interpersonal relationships related values (Casas et al., 2007).

After the SES factors related to coping, it is necessary to take into consideration also the stable internal resources (Table 3b) and the positive coping strategies (Table 3c) in adolescence. Seven studies dealt with this theme and stressed the following stable internal resources that were associated with a better subjective/psychological well-being and school performance/well-being and minor frequency of risk behaviors: intellectual and temperance strengths (Shoshani et al., 2013), neuroticism, extraversion, conscientiousness, persistence and self-directedness (Garcia et al., 2014), self-esteem (Biro et al., 2006; Tian et al., 2013), the emotional self-efficacy (Valois et al., 2015), curiosity (Jovanovic et al., 2012), trait emotional intelligence (Gugliandolo et al., 2014).

Positive coping skills identified by the several studies were: active coping strategies (Seiifge-Krenke et al., 2010, see above), perfectionism, perceived competence self-determined motivation related to adolescent athletes (Mouratidis et al., 2011), active and internally focused strategies (Cicognani et al., 2011, see above), the passive coping style that mediated the association between lower self-esteem and same-sex attraction (Bos et al., 2014), meaning-making strategy (Tavernier et al., 2012), attitudes towards Christianity (Goeke-Morey et al., 2014), resilience resources such as personality, mother-child communication, social support, school coherence and teacher support (Noor et al., 2013). Coping strategies related specifically to best academic performance were recognized as: self-determined motivation, task-oriented coping (Thompson et al., 2006), sense of coherence and problem-focused strategy (Cohen et al., 2008), generalized self-efficacy and scholastic self-efficacy (De Caroli et al., 2014).

4. Relationship and Perceived Social Support Area

Major part of the studies belonging to this area (N=13) had a cross-sectional design (N=6), followed respectively by a one-time point (N=4) and by longitudinal ones (N=3). Self and proxy-report surveys were the most used, followed by structured interviews utilized in only one study (Table 4). Social support is the set of activities, resources and social networks, that the individual can use when they need advice, help, assistance, approval or protection from someone significant. The support means that the people involved are part of a network of communication and mutual duties and contains within it the concept of caring for each other, mutual respect and the value given to the relationship (Cobb, 1976).

Table 3a. Perceived stress and coping strategies to front the daily problems area: SES and coping

First Author/ Publication yr	Sample	Age range	Study design	Timing	Variables and functional area assessed	Measures	Main results
Al-Bahrani et al., 2013	N=1.843 Omani adolescents	Mean age=15.75, SD=2.08	Cross-sectional	One-time point study	Coping styles	Problems Scale, Coping Style Scale	Adolescents' high levels of perceived problems were associated with higher levels of maladaptive coping styles Female adolescents seem to use maladaptive coping styles more than males. The use of adaptive and maladaptive coping styles increase with age.
Bedin et al., 2015	N=543 adolescents and their respective parents	Adolescents aged between 12 and 16 years (68.3% girls)	Parent–child Comparative study	One-time point study	Subjective well-being	Personal Wellbeing Index (PWI), Satisfaction With Life Scale (SWLS), Brief Multidimensional Students' Life Satisfaction Scale (BMSLSS), Happiness measure (HM) and happiness overall life (HOL), Overall life satisfaction (OLS)	Girls as mothers present lower average than boys and parents for the Satisfaction with Life Scale and for the happiness measure. Considering age, in general there were no significant differences found for adolescents and parents, despite a decrease in the mean for several measures for adolescents when increasing age. There were differences in social class, and the means of well-being are lower for participants from lower middle class.
Chui et al., 2015	N=1.428 Hong Kong adolescents	Range= 10-19 years old	Cross-sectional	One-time point study	Happiness and Life Satisfaction; Relationships and Self-Concept	Oxford Happiness Questionnaire; satisfaction with life; Number of Close Friends, Parents' Marital Status, and Siblings; Academic Satisfaction, Purpose in Life questionnaire, Rosenberg Self-Esteem Scale	While self-esteem and purpose in life are associated with higher happiness and life satisfaction, having more close friends is related to higher happiness, but not necessarily life satisfaction. On the other hand, boys with higher academic achievement are happier, but not more satisfied; the opposite holds true for girls.

First Author/ Publication yr	Sample	Age range	Study design	Timing	Variables and functional area assessed	Measures	Main results
Cicognani et al., 2008	N=297Italian adolescents	203 adolescents (14–19 years old) and 94 young adults (20–27 years old)	Cross-sectional	One-time point study	Residential context; Stressful life events; Subjective Well being; Emotional Well being; Psychological Well being; Sense of Community; Social Support;	Perceived Residential Environment Quality Scale; The Sense of Community Scale for Adolescents; The Multidimensional Scale of Perceived Social Support; Generalized Perceived Self-Efficacy; Keyes's Subjective Well being	Results confirm the significant impact of the residential context on youngsters' perceived residential quality, Stress and Subjective Well-being outcomes Adolescents are less satisfied of their living context and enjoy lower well-being than young adults. Social resources (Friend and Family Support) significantly buffer the effect of a deprived residential context of youngsters' Well-being, whereas personal resources (Self-Efficacy) directly increase Well-being levels.
Hampel et al., 2005	N=1.123 German adolescents	8-13 years Mean age = 10.76, SD = 1.58, 526 males, 597 females	Cross-sectional	One-time point study	Coping	German Coping Questionnaire	Female early adolescents coped maladaptively with common stressors
Hampel et al., 2005	N=1.123 German adolescents	8-13 years Mean age = 10.76, SD = 1.58, 526 males, 597 females	Cross-sectional	One-time point study	Coping	German Coping Questionnaire	Female early adolescents coped maladaptively with common stressors
Singh et al., 2014	N=1.327 Indian students	aged 11–21 years; mean age = 15.36 years (SD = 1.42 years)	Cross-sectional	One-time point study	Perceived quality of life	WHOQOL-BREF	Adolescents who attended private school possessed significantly better quality of life (overall), physical health, psychological well-being and environmental conditions as compared to adolescents who attended government school. Rural adolescents had significantly higher perceived quality of life (overall), physical health, psychological well-being, social relationships and environmental conditions as compared to urban adolescents.

Table 3a. (Continued)

First Author/ Publication yr	Sample	Age range	Study design	Timing	Variables and functional area assessed	Measures	Main results
Sweeting et al., 2014	N=2.503 Scottish adolescents	13-15 year-olds	Cross-sectional	One-time point study	Socio-economic and school-based social status, health and well-being	Scottish Index of Multiple Deprivation, Family affluence scale, Subjective SES, SSS-school dimensions, physical symptoms, 12-item General Health Questionnaire (GHQ-12)	Associations between objective SES and health/well-being were weak and inconsistent. Objective and subjective SES had weaker associations with health/well-being than did school-based SSS dimensions

Table 3b. Perceived stress and coping strategies to front the daily problems area: stable internal resources

First Author/ Publication yr	Sample	Age range	Study design	Timing	Variables and functional area assessed	Measures	Main results
Biro et al., 2006	N= 2379 girls, 1213 black and 1166 white	Girls were recruited at ages 9 and 10 years, and followed to age 22 years	Longit-udinal	ages 9–12 (I), 13–15 (II), and 17–22 (III)	Self-esteem, BMI, Socio-demographic variables	The Harter Self-Perception Profile, Global Self-Worth Scale, SES and BMI	Race and BMI are important predictors of self-esteem. Self-esteem is consistent across the phases of adolescence, andcomparable with other personality traits. Lower levels of self-esteem may increase the vulnerability of adolescents to risky behaviors
Garcia, 2011	N=289 high school pupils from Sweden	Big Five group: 91 (age mean = 16.73, SD = 0.93) TCI group: 98 (age mean = 16.70, SD = 0.91) Mixed group: 100 (age mean = 16.69, SD = 0.91)	The adoles-cents were randomly assigned to three different groups	1.Big Five model 2.TCI (Psychobiological Model) 3.Mixed group (both models)	Temperament and Character Well-being, Psychological Well-Being and Subjective Well-Being	Temperament and Character Inventory (TCI), NEO Personality Inventory – Revised (NEO-PI-R), Psychological Well-Being (PWB) and Subjective Well-Being (SWB)	Neuroticism, Extraversion, Conscientiousness, Persistence, and Self-Directedness were strongly related to well-being. In the Mixed group, Self-Directedness was strongly related to PWB, Life Satisfaction, and to the absence of Negative Affect.
Gugliandolo et al., 2014	N=263 Italian adoles-cents 8133 males and 130 females) and their parents	Age varied between 13 and 17 years (Male: M = 14.99, SD = 1.43; Female: M = 15.02, SD = 1.41)	Cross-informant	Self- and other-ratings in personality and adolescent behavior	Trait emotional intelligence and behavioral problems	Two forms of the Trait Emotional Intelligence Questionnaire (TEIQue-AF and TEIQue-360) and the Child Behavior CheckList (CBCL-YSR and CBCL-parents' report).	Both fathers and mothers attributed higher Well-being and Self-control to their children than the children attributed to themselves. The findings showed that while multisource ratings of trait EI generally converge, they are differentially predictive of external criteria.

Table 3b. (Continued)

First Author/ Publication yr	Sample	Age range	Study design	Timing	Variables and functional area assessed	Measures	Main results
Jovanovic et al., 2012	N=408 Serbian high school students,	Average age of 16.6 years (SD = 0.88) with a range of 15–19.	One-time point	Assessment during the last week of the first term	Trait curiosity and the well-being	Curiosity and Exploration Inventory-II (CEI-II), Multidimensional Students' Life Satisfaction Scale, Children's Hope Scale, Life Engagement Test, The Serbian Inventory of Affect based on the Positive and Negative Affect Schedule-X, De Jong Gierveld Loneliness Scale, The Serbian version of the Depression Anxiety and Stress Scale	Curiosity is a specific predictor of positive well-being and gave support to the two continua model of mental health, which view positive and negative well-being as relatively independent constructs.
Shoshani et al., 2013	N=417 Israel students and 13 teachers	Aged 12.1–13.8 (212 girls, 205 boys, Mean age = 12.55 years)	Longitudinal	T1: during the middle of seventh grade T2: again during the middle of eighth grade	Character Strengths, Subjective Well-Being, and School Adjustment	The VIA Inventory of Strengths for Youth (VIA-Y), The 45-item School Engagement Survey, The Friends subscale of The School Adjustment Report, Positive and Negative Affectivity Scale-Child Version; Satisfaction with Life Scale	Intellectual and temperance strengths were central in the prediction of students' school performance and achievements. Interpersonal strengths were significantly related to social functioning at school. Temperance and transcendence strengths were robust positive predictors of students' SWB
Tian et al., 2013	N(1)=221 early Chinese adolescents N(2)=140 middle Adolescents	Mean age(1) = 13.6 Mean age (2) = 16.4	Cross-sectional	Early adolescents (junior high school) versus middle adolescents (senior high school)	Perceived Social Support and School Well-Being, Self-esteem	Network of Relationships Inventory, Adolescent's School Well-Being Scale (ASW-BS), Rosenberg's Self-Esteem Scale	Among early adolescents, parent and teacher support related significantly to positive school well-being. Among middle adolescents, friend and teacher support significantly related to school wellbeing. For both early and middle adolescents, global self-esteem mediated relations between teacher support and school well-being. For early adolescents, global self-esteem mediated relations between parent support and school well-being; whereas for middle adolescents, global self-esteem mediated relations between friend support and school well-being.

First Author/ Publication yr	**Sample**	**Age range**	**Study design**	**Timing**	**Variables and functional area assessed**	**Measures**	**Main results**
Valois et al., 2015	N=3.836 students in South Carolina	Student participants were in grades 9–12 with ages ranging from 12 to 18 year	Cross-sectional	Four race/sex groups	Suicide Ideation, Suicide Attempts and Emotional Self-Efficacy	The Emotional Self-Efficacy (ESE) Scale, Four standard YRBS suicide ideation and attempts questions	Nearly all suicide variables were significantly related to emotional self-efficacy in the unadjusted models for the four race/sex groups. In adjusted models, suicide ideation, planning a suicide attempt, attempting suicide and a suicide attempt resulting in injury were associated with reduced emotional self-efficacy for black females. For white males, suicide ideation, attempting suicide and a suicide attempt resulting in injury were associated with reduced emotional self-efficacy. Suicide ideation for black males was associated with reduced emotional self-efficacy. No significant associations were established for white females.

Table 3c. Perceived stress and coping strategies to front the daily problems area: positive coping skills

First Author/ Publication yr	Sample	Age range	Study design	Timing	Variables and functional area assessed	Measures	Main results
Bos et al., 2014	N=1.546 high school Dutch students (802 boys and 744 girls)	Mean age= 13.57 years (SD=1.03), range=11–17 years			Same-sex attraction, Sexual orientation, Coping, Psychological adjustment	Same-sex attraction question, Rosenberg Self-Esteem Scale, Brief Symptom Inventory,Utrecht Coping List for Adolescent	Same-sex attraction was found to predict lower levels of self-esteem and higher levels of psychological distress. Further analyses showed that passive coping style partly mediated these associations
Casas et al., 2007	N=1.618 Spanish adolescents	Age from 12 to 16 years	One-time point		Values aspirations, well-being	Satisfaction with 19 specific life domains, Personal Well-Being Index, overall satisfaction with life	Boys scored significantly higher on the materialistic values dimension and the capacities and knowledge related values dimension, while girls scored higher on the interpersonal relationship related values. The youngest adolescents scored higher on materialistic values, while the oldest scored higher on interpersonal relationships related values. Values aspired to can be considered a well-being related construct. An important change appears in the Spanish sample: Family values no longer fit with the interpersonal relationships related values dimension
Cicognani, 2011	N=342 adolescents Italian origin living in a large city in North Italy	14–19 years	Cross-sectional		Coping strategies, Social Support, Self-Efficacy, and Psychological Well-Being	Coping Across Situations Questionnaire, Multidimensional Scale of Perceived Social Support, General Self-Efficacy Scale, Berne Questionnaire on Adolescents' Subjective Well-Being	The most frequently used strategies were active and internally focused. Females used a wider range of coping strategies than did males. Significant correlations were found among coping strategies and coping resources. Moreover, the adoption of some strategies significantly affected adolescents' psychological well-being.

First Author/ Publication yr	Sample	Age range	Study design	Timing	Variables and functional area assessed	Measures	Main results
Cohen et al., 2008	N=216 1st-year undergraduates at a major university in the north of Israel	The sample was 86.6% women, and the mean age was 23.11 years (SD 4.20, range 18–49)	Short term prospective	T1: last session of the second semester of academic year before the final exam T2: exams took place 2 to 4 weeks later	Sense of Coherence (SOC), Coping Strategies, Test Anxiety, Test Performance	Short SOC Scale, Short COPE Scale, Test Anxiety, Test Performance	SOC to be negatively related to test anxiety, whereas emotion-focused coping and avoidance were positively related to it. Problem-focused coping contributed positively to performance on the test, and avoidance coping adversely affected test grades. The data suggest that test anxiety is minimally associated with performance grades, and the 2 measures are related somewhat differentially to coping strategies and SOC
De Caroli et al., 2014	N=136 Italian adolescents (64 boys and 72 girls)	between 14 and 18 years of age	Cross-sectional		Generalized Self-Efficacy, Well-Being, Scholastic Self-Efficacy	Generalized Self-Efficacy Scale (GSES), Psychological Well-Being Scale (PWBS), Scholastic Self-Efficacy	Positive relationships between GSES and PWB (with mastery, personal growth, and self-acceptance). Except for the autonomy, the highest scores in PWB were obtained by 16yrs. adolescents, while the lowest scores were reached by 14yrs. and 18yrs. ones. Boys expressed greater GSES and PWB than girls Additionally, highly efficient adolescents expressed higher scores in PWB
Goeke-Morey et al., 2014	N=667 mother/adolescent dyads in Belfast, Northern Ireland	Mean age=15.75 years old 50% male	Longitudinal	fifth and sixth annual waves	Religious coping and relationship, Well-being	Francis Attitudes toward Christianity scale, Brief Symptom Inventory-18, General Health Questionnaire (GHQ-12), 4-item subscale from a multidimensional coping inventory (COPE)	Greater internalizing problems predict a weaker relationship with God 1 year later. Significant moderation analyses suggest that a stronger relationship with God predicted fewer depression and anxiety symptoms for youth whose mothers used more religious coping.

Table 3c. (Continued)

First Author/ Publication yr	Sample	Age range	Study design	Timing	Variables and functional area assessed	Measures	Main results
Mouratidis et al., 2011	Study 1: N=333 Greek adolescent athletes Study 2: N=63 adolescent athletes	Study 1: Mean age = 15.59 years; SD=2.37 Study 2: Mean age= 14.40 years, SD=1.58)	Cross-sectional (Study 1), short-term longitudinal (Study 2).	Study 2: three-week summer basketball camp	perfectionism, perceived competence, self-determined motivation, and sport-related coping skills	Multidimensional Perfectionism Scale, Psychological Need Satisfaction in Exercise Scale, Behavioral Regulation in Sport Questionnaire, Athletic Coping Skills Inventory	Athletes with high personal standards are more likely to report effective coping or to put more effort if they become (or remain) autonomously motivated. In contrast, athletes with concerns over mistakes are more likely to exhibit controlled motivation and, in turn, to report poorer coping skills or to put less effort compared to autonomous motivated athletes.
Noor et al., 2013	N=197 adolescents in Malaysia	Aged 12–16 years Mean age = 13.77, SD= 1.49)	Cross-informant	Parent, teacher and self-report	Stressors and well-being, resilience resources	Life Events Checklist, The Problem Questionnaire, International Personality	Resilient adolescents were found to have significantly higher scores on all the identified resilience resources (personality, mother–child communication, social support, school coherence, and teacher support) compared to the non-resilient maladjusted group.
						Item Pool, Mother–child Communication Scale, Multidimensional Scale of Perceived Social Support, Sense of School Coherence Scale. Teacher Support Scale, Brief Multidimensional Students' Life Satisfaction Scale, General Health Questionnaire	Results showed that these resilience resources acted both as mediator and moderator in the relationship between stressors and well-being

First Author/ Publication yr	Sample	Age range	Study design	Timing	Variables and functional area assessed	Measures	Main results
Seiffge-Krenke et al., 2010	N=3.154 adolescents from four countries	mean age of 15 years	Cross-cultural	1.071 Italians 1.433 Germans 308 French 341 British	Competence in Coping with Future-Related Stress	Problem Questionnaire, Coping Across Situations Questionnaire	German and British adolescents showed low levels of stress, whereas French and Italian adolescents had high levels. All adolescents anticipated future-related problems but did not portray their futures negatively. In addition, they dealt with future-related stress actively and showed high levels of coping competence. Adolescents used active coping strategies most frequently,f ollowed by thinking about possible solutions. Dysfunctional coping strategies were used much less often.
Tavernier et al., 2012	N= 418 Grade 12 students in southern Ontario, Canada	Mean age)=17 years, 3 months	This Cross-sectional study was part of a larger longitudinal-sequential project		Meaning-Making, Turning points and Psychological Well-Being	The turning point question, 20-item Center for Epidemiological Depression Scale, the 14-item Social Anxiety-related symptoms Scale, the 10-item Rosenberg Self-Esteem Scale, 21-item list of daily hassles with friends, peers, school	Meaning-making was significantly associated with higher psychological well-being, controlling for Grade 9 scores on well-being. Importantly, adolescents who reported meaning-making in Grade 12 did not differ on well-being prior to the experience of their turning point event, when they were in Grade 9, from adolescents who did not report meaning-making.
Thompson et al., 2008	N=299 undergraduate students of Ottawa	undergraduate students		T1: two weeks prior to midterm T2: two weeks after midterm exams	Academic motivation, dispositional optimism and pessimism, coping utilization	Dispositional optimism and pessimism (LOT), Academic Motivation Scale, Brief COPE	Self-determined motivation mediated the relationship between dispositional optimism and task-oriented coping, whereas non-self-determined motivation mediated the relationship between dispositional pessimism and disengagement-oriented coping. Furthermore, task-oriented coping was associated with an increase in self-determined motivation from Time 1 to Time 2

Social support is both a coping strategy and a resource that the individual can use to deal with more security problems that life places before (Cicognani, 2011). The perception of support is a better predictor of psychosocial well-being of the person with respect to the actual support received (Wethington, Kessler, 1986).

Adolescence is a time when social relations undergo a change: young people move away gradually from the protection of the family to look for support and companionship in relationships with peers. This is also the time when the first romantic relationships begin. The literature highlights that creating and perpetuating oneself in stable relationships is one of the fundamental human motivations (Baumeister, Leary, 1995).

Poor interpersonal relationships in adolescence and low perceived social support are associated with a poor perception of psychosocial well-being and low values in the quality of daily life and the risk of developing high levels of anxiety and depression (Nilsen et al., 2013; O'Shea et al., 2014)

The perception of social support from family and peers is associated also to a high use of positive coping strategies based on the search for help and advice from other people. In particular, the support received by the family is positively correlated to the use of strategies such as discussion and sharing of problems to search a solution, the search for information and address the problem with the person concerned. Social support correlates negatively with strategies such as disadvantageous to surrender, catastrophization, behaving as if all was well and the abuse of substances such as alcohol and drugs. The support received from friends correlates positively in particular by asking for help when needed. Being aware of the possibility of receiving support can then help the child to avoid the use of dysfunctional coping strategies (Cicognani, 2011).

Coping and support patterns were found related to friendship closeness and conflict (Man Chow et al., 2011). Peer acceptance had a direct effect on school life satisfaction which in turn was related to euphoria together with family harmony (Jun et al., 2015).

Social capital and resilience could link formal family support interventions to adolescent coping (Pinkerton et al., 2007), revealing negative associations between perceived parental autonomy support and adolescents' depressive symptoms, both in early and middle adolescents (Van der Giessen et al., 2014). The influence of friends' affiliation was strongest when support from friends was high and parental support low (Espinoza et al., 2014).

Resilience played a mediational role in the association between quality of relationship to significant figures and well-being (Mota et al., 2015); loneliness mediated the relation between positive/negative affect and life satisfaction (Inguglia et al., 2014); self- reported empathy and social support were related with grandiose narcissism, in turn associated with self-reported aggression (Barry et al., 2014).

Also online friendship was analyzed by several studies. Desjarlais et al. (2010) stressed that social anxiety of male adolescents moderated the relation using computers with friends and friendship quality, while in girls this direct effect is the main one. In another study (Berntsson et al., 2014) positive relationships by web together with other health activities (reading books, visiting friends, listening to music, activity in organizations) were positively associated with absence of psychosomatic complaints and better life perceptions. Using social networking site for social purpose was associated with user's well-being, whereas the use by entertainment was not. Online self-disclosure was a significant predictor of users' friendship quality (Wang et al., 2014).

Table 4. Relationship and perceived social support area

First Author/ Publication yr	Sample	Age range	Study design	Timing	Variables and functional area assessed	Measures	Main results
Barry et al., 2014	N=185 adolescents 159 male, 26 female, Southern Missisipi	Mean age = 16.95 years, SD =0.73; ages 16 to 18;.	One-time point	In classrooms in a series of three to four 45-minute sessions over the course of approximately three weeks.	Self-Perceptions of Empathy and Social Support; Narcissism and Aggression	Pathological Narcissism Inventory, Narcissistic Personality Inventory for Children, Peer Conflict Scale, Social Support Scale, Toronto Empathy Questionnaire	Grandiose narcissism was positively associated with reports of social support and empathy. Each narcissism dimension was positively correlated with self-reported aggression, but vulnerable narcissism and non-pathological narcissism predicted unique variance in aggression. Furthermore, the association between each form of narcissism and aggression was exacerbated by low self-reported empathy.
Berntsson et al., 2014	N=1.461 Swedish children	children aged 2–17; three age groups 2–6 years, 7–12 years and 13–17 years.	Cross-sectional	Data from 2011 were used and compared with data from 1984 and 1996.	Health, leisure time activities	three questions on Health, the absence of Long Term Illness, 13 diagnoses, the absence of psychosomatic complaints, six symptoms, six	The health of Swedish children declined between 1984 and 2011. Positive relationships were found between some activities and health as well as other activities related to ill health.
						items of well-being) and 12 activities	I.e., 'Reading books', 'visiting friends', 'listening to music' and 'activity in organisations' were related to an absence of PSC, LTI and well-being. 'Surfing/blogging on the Internet' was negatively related to LTI, PSC and well-being

Table 4. (Continued)

First Author/ Publication yr	Sample	Age range	Study design	Timing	Variables and functional area assessed	Measures	Main results
Chow et al., 2011	N=113 pairs of college friends in Texas	78 pairs of women and 35 pairs of men, with mean age=23.7 years	Cross sectional	Comparative study	Actor–Partner Interdependence Model, attachment theory, coping, dyadic coping, friendship quality, support-giving	Prototypic coping patterns, 32-item Caregiving Questionnaire, Network of Relationships Inventory	Using of support coping was associated with friends' responsive support-giving, overwhelmed coping was associated with overinvolved support-giving, and distance coping was associated with disengage support-giving. Coping and support patterns were found related in theoretically expected ways to ratings of friendship closeness and conflict
Dan He et al., 2014	N=300 (169 males and 131 females) in China	The participants' ages ranged in age from 12 to 17, with an average of 14.50 years (SD = 1.06).	Cross-sectional	Comparative study: two mid-sized cities in the middle and southern part of China	Core self-evaluations, Positive and negative affect, Loneliness, Life satisfaction	the Core Self evaluations Scale (CSE), Positive and Negative Affect Scale, UCLA Loneliness and Satisfaction with Life Scale	Positive and negative affect, and loneliness fully mediated the relationship between CSE and life satisfaction. The relationship between CSE and loneliness was partially mediated by positive and negative affect. Loneliness partially mediated the relation between positive and negative affect and life satisfaction. Significant paths from CSE through positive and negative affect and loneliness to life satisfaction
Desjarlais et al., 2010	N=1.050 Adolescents in Ontario	Time 1: average age of 14.27 (SD = 0.53). Time 2: average age of 15.99 (SD = 0.37) Time 3: average age of 17.29 (SD = 0.50)	Longitudinal	Assessment T1: adolescents in grade 9 T2: in grade 11 T3: in grade 12	Computer use with friends and friendship quality; Sport activities; Support	Using computers with friends either in person or over the Internet, Online chat, Organized sport activities, 18-item scale measuring attachment to one's friends, 18-item scale measuring attachment to one's friends	For girls, there was a main effect of using computers with friends on friendship quality; For boys social anxiety moderated this relation. These findings were identical for online communication and were stable throughout adolescence. Furthermore, participating in organized sports did not compensate for social anxiety for either adolescent girls or boys.

First Author/ Publication yr	Sample	Age range	Study design	Timing	Variables and functional area assessed	Measures	Main results
Espinoza et al., 2014	N=412 49% male Mexican or Mexican-American	ages 14–16, Mean =15.46 8SD = 0.65)	One-time point	Ninth and tenth grade classrooms at both schools. Each week throughout the school	Friend affiliations, Friend support, Parental support, School adjustment	Friend affiliations, Deviant Affiliation Scale, Achievement-Oriented Affiliation Scale, Friend's Support Scale, Parent Support Scale, School Adjustment, Future Education Aspirations, Attendance and academic problems	Although results revealed few direct associations between friend affiliations and school adjustment, several moderations emerged. In general, the influence of friends' affiliation was strongest when support from friends was high and parental support was low.
Inguglia et al., 2014	N=325 adolescents and emerging adults living in Sicily (southern Italy)	Age range: 17-26 years Adolescents= 143(mean age= 17.86, SD=0.66) Emerging adults =182 (mean age=22.96, SD=2.21)	Cross sectional	Comparative study	Autonomy, Relatedness, Psychological distress, Parental support	Basic Psychological Needs Scale, Perceptions of Parents Scale, Youth Self-Report (YSR), Adult Self-Report (ASR), UCLA Loneliness Scale, Depression Anxiety Stress Scale-21,	Autonomy and relatedness are fundamental needs for both teens and emerging adults related to parental support and psychological health. Age moderated some of the investigated relationships
Jun et al., 2015	N=343 Korean middle school students	The mean age of the adolescents was 13.9 years (SD = 0.784).	One time point study		Peer acceptance, School life satisfaction, Happiness, Euphoria, Psychological well-being	Korean Peer Nomination Inventory, GPA, friendships,and school representation activities, family harmony, parental communication, SES, SLS and euphoria	Peer acceptance did not have a direct effect on euphoria, but that an indirect influence was applied through school life satisfaction. Of the school and family factors, family harmony showed a direct and an indirect (via school satisfaction) influence on euphoria.
Mota et al., 2015	N=246 Portuguese adolescents under institutional care	aged 12–18. Mean age=14.87; SD=1.79	One-time point		Institutionalization, Resilience process, Well-being, Significant figures	Relationship to Significant Figures Questionnaire, Resilience Scale, Psychological Well-Being Manifestation Measure Scale	Resilience plays a mediational role in the association between quality of relationship to significant figures and well-being. The attachment theory stresses the importance of safe haven and secure base provided by significant figures for the individual's adaptation and development

Table 4. (Continued)

First Author/ Publication yr	Sample	Age range	Study design	Timing	Variables and functional area assessed	Measures	Main results
O'Shea et al., 2013	N=31one clinically diagnosed depressed adolescents matched with 31 non-depressed adolescents adolescents	The 62 participants were aged between 12 and 19 years and comprised 18 male and 44 female	Cross-sectional	Comparative study	Interpersonal Psychotherapy, Depression, Attachment, Interpersonal Skills, Life Events	Structured interview. The fifth revision of the K-SADS-E, Children's Global Assessment Scale, 21-item Beck Depression Inventory II, Life Events Record, Attachment Style Questionnaire, Social Skills Questionnaire (SSQ), Social Competence with Peers Questionnaire, Conflict Behaviour Questionnaire	Depressed adolescents reported a greater number of negative interpersonal life events, a less secure attachment style and scored higher on all insecure attachment styles compared with the non-depressed adolescents. In addition, depressed adolescents demonstrated lower levels of social skill (on both adolescent and parent report), a poorer quality of relationship with parents (on both adolescent and parent report) and lower social competence (adolescent report only
Pinkerton et al., 2007	N=172 West of Ireland	Age range: 11–18 years	Longitudinal	Assessments over the 9 months and annually thereafter for at least 3 years	Family support, social capital, resilience and coping	Social Provisions Scale (SPS), Social Network Questionnaire (SNQ), Adolescent Wellbeing Scale (AWS), Adolescent Perceived Events Scale (APES)	It was suggested a conceptual model that draws on social support theory to harness the ideas of social capital and resilience in a way that can link formal family support interventions to adolescent coping.
Van der Giessen et al., 2014	N=923 early adolescents N=390 middle adolescents	age range from 12 to 20. First wave: mean age=12.42 years (SD= 0.59) - early adolescence Mean age= 16.68 years (SD = 0.80) - middle adolescence	Longitudinal	During five consecutive years, annual assessments	Perceived autonomy support; Depressive symptoms; Parent-adolescent relationships; Friendships	Balanced relatedness scale, Children's Depression Inventory	Results revealed concurrent and longitudinal negative associations between perceived parental autonomy support and adolescents' depressive symptoms. No concurrent and longitudinal associations were found between perceived best friends' autonomy support and adolescents' depressive symptoms. Results were similar for early and middle adolescent boys and girls.

First Author/ Publication yr	Sample	Age range	Study design	Timing	Variables and functional area assessed	Measures	Main results
Wang et al., 2014	N=337 from Southwestern China	College students undergraduate	Cross-sectional	One-time point, spring 2013	Social Networking Site (SNS) use on college students' friendship and well-being	Qzone usage, Amount of Self-disclosure Scale, Social Anxiety Scale for Adolescents, Friendship quality, The Satisfaction with Life Scale	''Social'' type SNS use was positively related to users' well-being, whereas ''entertainment'' type SNS use was not. Online self-disclosure was a significant predictor of users' friendship quality. However, there was an inverse relationship between ''social'' SNS use and online self-disclosure, and no relationship between friendship quality based on SNS use and well-being.

Table 4a. Social support as predictor of depression or suicidal ideation

First Author/ Publication yr	Sample	Age range	Study design	Timing	Variables and functional area assessed	Measures	Main results
Dunn et al., 2015	N= 16.172 US students and N=2.118 Neighbor-hoods	Mean age = 15.6 years; (SD= 1.7)	Cross-sectional	Wave 1 A random sample (N=20.745) complete a more detailed in-home interview. 17.670 caregivers provided information	Schools and Neighborhoods, Depressive Symptoms	19-item adaptation of the Center for Epidemiological Studies Depression Scale, SES	The school-level random effect was significant and more than 3 times the neighborhood-level random effect, even after individual-level characteristics had been taken into account. Individual-level indicators (e.g., race/ethnicity, socioeconomic status) were associated with depressive symptoms, but there was no association with either school- or neighborhood-level fixed effects. The between-level variance in depressive symptoms was driven largely by schools as opposed to neighborhoods.
Farrel et al., 2015	N=7.240 in the Mobile, Alabama metro-politan statistical area	Mean age range throughout the waves=11.6 -13.1	Longi-tudinal	Data from 1998 to 2011. Single wave of data=4.334 Two waves contributions=2.456 Three waves contribution= 1.730 Four waves contribution= 1.267 Five or more waves: 2.600	Social support, Social context, Suicide attempt,	Parental Warmth, Overall Peer Support, Sense of Community, Contextual Safety, Inevitability of Violence, Hopelessness, Victim of Violence, Perpetrator of Violence	Increased peer support reduced the risk of suicide attempt, and increased perceived inevitability of violence led to an increase in risk among 9-year-old children. As children age, the effect of overall peer support remains consistent, while there is a reduction in the effect of inevitability of violence.
Frison et al., 2015	N = 910 from Belgium	Mean age of 15.44 years (SD = 1.71)	One-time point		Daily stress, depressed mood, social support through Facebook	The Adolescent Stress Questionnaire (ASQ), Social support seeking through Facebook or normal, adapted version of the Multidimensional Scale of Perceived Social Support, Perceived social support, Epidemiological Studies Depression Scale for Children	Daily stress positively predicted adolescents' seeking of social support through Facebook. In addition, when social support was sought on Facebook and subsequently perceived, social support seeking through Facebook decreased adolescents' depressed mood. However, when social support was sought on Facebook, but not perceived, social support seeking through, Facebook increased adolescents' depressed mood

First Author/ Publication yr	Sample	Age range	Study design	Timing	Variables and functional area assessed	Measures	Main results
Miller et al., 2015	N= 143 adolescents in the Mid-Atlantic area	Range: 12-18 years; Mean age= 15.38; SD= 1.43	One time point		Social Support, Suicidal Ideation (SI), Suicide Attempts (SA)	Child and Adolescent Social Support Scale, Scale for Suicidal Ideation, Self-Injurious Thoughts and Behaviors Interview, Youth Inventory-4	Perceptions of lower school support independently predicted greater severity of SI, accounting for parent and close friend support. The relationship between lower perceived school support and SI was the strongest among those who perceived lower versus higher parental support. Perceptions of lower parental support independently predicted SA history, accounting for school and close friend support. Those who perceived lower support from school and close friends reported the greatest odds of an SA history
Millings et al., 2012	N=5022 UK adolescents	aged 11–16. Mean age= 13.43 (SD 1.12)	One-time point		School connectedness, Peer attachment, and self-esteem, Depression	Short Mood and Feelings Questionnaire, Rosenberg Self-Esteem Scale, Attachment Questionnaire for Children, Short form of the Psychological Sense of School Membership Scale	The relationship between School Connectedness and low mood was reduced by the inclusion of Self Esteem and peer attachment style. Peer attachment style was the largest predictor of low mood. The relationship between SC and low mood was not moderated by SE or peer attachment style.
Nilsen et al., 2013	N=566 in early Norwegian adolescents N=375 Late adolescents N=456 middle adolescents N tot at T1=929	Mean age early adolescence = 12.5 Mean age late adolescence = 16.5 Mean age middle adolescents = 14.5	Longi-tudinal	Six further waves (t2–t7); with the adolescents responding to questionnaires at ages 12.5 (t5), 14.5 (t6), and 16.5 (t7).	Social skills, Depressive symptoms, Social support	13-item Short Mood and Feelings Questionnaire, 24-item self-reported version of the Social Skills Rating System, Social support (Friend, Teacher, Parent)	Low levels of social skills in early adolescence predicted increases in depressive symptoms for both girls and boys. Low levels of friend support in middle adolescence mediated this relationship for girls, but not boys.

Table 4a. (Continued)

First Author/ Publication yr	Sample	Age range	Study design	Timing	Variables and functional area assessed	Measures	Main results
Rawana, 2013	N = 4587 form Canada	Mean age= 14.95 (SD = 1.55); 49% female.	Longi-tudinal	Wave 1:1994/1995 Wave 2:1996	Body change strategies, Weight perception, Perceived social support, Sself-esteem, Depressive symptoms	Centre of Epidemiologic Studies Depression Scale, Weight perception, Body change strategies, Parent expressive support, Perceived peer support, Perceived school support, Self-esteem	Body change strategies related to losing weight and overweight perceptions predicted depressive symptoms above and beyond established risk factors. Self-esteem moderated the relationship between trying to lose weight and depressive symptoms.
Zhao et al., 2015	N= 504 Chinese adolescents	aged 16-18 (316 girls and 188 boys) Mean age =16.86, SD=0.68)	One-time point	Public upper secondary schools. Six classes (of 12 classes) of Grade 11	Emotion regulation, Depressive symptoms. School connectedness	The Emotion Regulation Questionnaire, Psychological Sense of School Membership Scale, self-reported Center for Epidemiological Studies Depression Scale for Children,	Reappraisal and suppression significantly associated with school connectedness and depressive symptoms, and school connectedness mediated the link between emotion regulation and depressive symptoms, even when the general emotion experiences were controlled. The hypothesized model was invariant across gender except for the link between suppression and depressive symptom

A group of studies (Table 4a) identified the social support as a possible predictor of depressive symptoms. Lower level of social skill, friend support (Nilsen et al., 2013) and social competence, a poorer relationship with parents were related with an increase of depressive symptoms (O'Shea et al., 2013). Seeking of social support through Facebook, if it was sought and perceived, decreased adolescents' depressed mood (Frison et al., 2015). Body change strategies related to losing weight and overweight perceptions predicted depressive symptoms with self-esteem as moderator (Rawana, 2013). Reappraisal and suppression strategies significantly were associated with school connectedness and depressive symptoms, and school connectedness mediated the link between emotion regulation and depressive symptoms (Zhao et al., 2015), even if beside school connectedness also self-esteem and peer attachment style reentry in an explanation model of depressive symptoms (Millings et al., 2012).

There were also individual-level indicators (e.g., race/ethnicity, socioeconomic status) associated with depressive symptoms more than neighborhood level random effect (Dunn et al., 2015).

Suicidal ideation (SI) and suicidal attempt (SA) were also investigated by 8 studies.

In these studies the longitudinal design was used in 3 studies, the one-time point design in 4 studies and the cross-sectional one in only 1 study. Also here the unique method adopted was self and proxy-report surveys.

Perceptions of lower school support independently predicted greater severity of SI, accounting for parent and close friend support. Perceptions of lower parental support independently predicted SA history, accounting for school and close friends' support (Miller et al., 2015). Increased peer support was a protective factor for the risk of suicide attempt, while increased perceived inevitability of violence was a risk factor (Farrel et al., 2015).

5. Family Influences on Adolescents' Well-Being

This area was composed by 12 studies with several designs: 5 longitudinal, 4 one-time point, 3 cross-informant/cross-sectional. The methodology adopted was only derived from self and proxy-reports (Table 5).

Low levels of family warmth and parental support perceived by the adolescent were more easily associated with depressive symptoms and with non-suicidal self-injury (Baetens e tal., 2015), with sleep problems and with alcohol/drug using (Vazsonyi et al., 2015). The intrusiveness and excessive control were, however, experienced as greater difficulty associated with psychosocial adjustment and negative levels of well-being (Barnes et al., 2000). Self-psychological control was a better predictor of internalizing distress compared to low autonomy-support (Costa et al., 2015). Paternal and maternal rejection in their attachment style and paternal control were the strongest predictors of adolescents' self-destructive thoughts and behaviors (Cruz et al., 2014).

Table 5. Family influences on adolescents' well-being area

First Author/ Publication yr	Sample	Age range	Study design	Timing	Functional area assessed	Measures	Main results
Baetens et al., 2015	N=358 Belgian students	Age range: 12-20 years old; Mean age = 16.07 years (SD = 1.12)	One-time point		Non-suicidal self-injury, Self-criticism, Perceived parental expressed emotions, Depression	The brief NSSI (Non-suicidal self-injury) assessment tool, Children's Depression Inventory, Self Rating Scale, the self-report questionnaire of the level of expressed emotion	The relationship between self criticism and NSSI is mediated by depressive symptoms. Perceived lack of parental emotional support had a direct effect on frequency of NSSI, as well as an indirect effect via depressive symptoms. Perceived parental criticism showed only an indirect effect through self-criticism.
Ce Clercq et al., 2014	N=8453 from Belgium	Mean=15.2 (SD=1.90); Range 12-18	Cross-sectional	One-time point	Adolescent smoking Cognitive and structural social capital	Individual, Parental, Peer Smoking frequency; The Family Affluence Scale (FAS); participation in clubs or organizations; Flemish Health Behavior in School-Aged Children (HBSC) survey	Only structural family social capital and cognitive school social capital variables negatively related to regular smoking. No interactions between socio-economic status and social capital variables were found
Costa et al., 2015	N=121 female Italian college students	Age ranged from 18 to 24 years with a mean of 20.30 (SD = 1.34).	One-time point		Parenting, Adjustment, Psychological needs	8-item Psychological Control Scale–Youth Self-Report, Perceptions of Parent Scale, Basic Psychological Needs Satisfaction Scale-general version, Profile of Mood States	Satisfaction of basic psychological needs was a full mediator of the relationship between perceptions of psychological control and internalizing distress. Psychological control was a better predictor of internalizing distress compared to low autonomy-support
Cruz et al., 2014	N= 1.266 Portuguese adolescents	Mean age of 15.9 years ((SD = 2.11). Age range 11-21	One-time point		Self-destruction, Parenting, Attachment, Cohesion	Paternal and Maternal Parenting Styles EMBU-A; the father/mother attachment questionnaire (FMAQ), family adaptability and cohesion evaluation scale—FACES-II, Reports of Self-Destructive Thoughts and Behavior	Paternal and maternal rejection and paternal control were the most accurate predictors of SDTB (Self-Destructive thoughts and behaviors), emphasizing their role as risk factors for maladaptive trajectories with reports of SDTB. Additionally, a mediation effect of cohesion and a moderation of sex were also found

First Author/ Publication yr	Sample	Age range	Study design	Timing	Variables and functional area assessed	Measures	Main results
Goeke-Morey et al., 2014	N=667 mother/adolescent dyads in Belfast, Northern Ireland	Mean age=15.75 years old 50% male	Longitudinal	Fifth and sixth annual waves	Social ecological model of children's exposure to political violence	Francis Attitudes toward Christianity scale, Brief Symptom Inventory-18, General Health Questionnaire (GHQ-12), 4-item subscale from a multidimensional coping inventory (COPE)	Greater internalizing problems predict a weaker relationship with God 1 year later. Significant moderation analyses suggest that a stronger relationship with God predicted fewer depression and anxiety symptoms for youth whose mothers used more religious coping.
Gugliandolo et al., 2014	N=263 Italian adolescents 8133 males and 130 females) and their parents	Age varied between 13 and 17 years (Male: M = 14.99, SD = 1.43; Female: M = 15.02, SD = 1.41)	Cross-informant	Self- and other-ratings in personality and adolescent behavior	Trait emotional intelligence and behavioral problems	Two forms of the Trait Emotional Intelligence Questionnaire (TEIQue-AF and TEIQue-360) and the Child Behavior CheckList (CBCL-YSR and CBCL-parents' report).	Both fathers and mothers attributed higher Well-being and Self-control to their children than the children attributed to themselves. The findings showed that while multisource ratings of trait EI generally converge, they are differentially predictive of external criteria.
Nor et al., 2013	N=197 adolescents in Malaysia	Aged 12–16 years Mean age = 13.77, SD= 1.49)	Cross-informant	Parent, teacher and self-report	Stressors and well-being resilience resources	Life Events Checklist, The Problem Questionnaire, International Personality Item Pool, Mother–child Communication Scale, Multidimensional Scale of Perceived Social Support, Sense of School Coherence Scale. Teacher Support Scale, Brief Multidimensional Students' Life Satisfaction Scale, General Health Questionnaire	Resilient adolescents were found to have significantly higher scores on all the identified resilience resources (personality, mother–child communication, social support, school coherence, and teacher support) compared to the non-resilient maladjusted group. Results showed that these resilience resources acted both as mediator and moderator in the relationship between stressors and well-being

Table 5. (Continued)

First Author/ Publication yr	Sample	Age range	Study design	Timing	Variables and functional area assessed	Measures	Main results
Petts, 2014	N=5.739 USA	between the ages of 10 and 25	Longitudinal	Youth contributed up to eight data points	Family, Parenting, Religious attendance, Psychological well-being	Center for Epidemiological Studies Depression scale, Family structure (form interviews), Family structure transition, Parent–child relationship quality (from interviews), Religious Attendance	parental interaction and attending religious services with parent(s) in late childhood are associated with higher psychological well-being, whereas conflict with parents and residing in a nontraditional family in late childhood are associated with lower well-being among youth.
Shek, 2005	At Time 1 N=3.017; At Time 2 N= 2.758; At T3 N= 2.559. Chinese secondary school students	Mean age at T1= 12.65 years N=280 experiencing economic disadvantage N=2.187 not experiencing	Longitudinal	Wave 1, Wave 2 and Wave 3: three data assessment, one for each year	Perceived family life quality and emotional well-being	Assessment of family quality of life (Parenting quality); Assessment of family quality of life (Parent-child relational quality); Assessment of emotional well-being	Participants experiencing economic disadvantage generally had more negative perceptions of parenting quality and parent-child relational quality. The differences were more pronounced for the father-adolescent dyad Emotional well-being was also different in adolescents with and without economic disadvantage.
Sijtsema et al., 2014	N=2230 Dutch adolscents	T1 mean age=11.09 years (SD = 0.55) T2 mean age: 13.56 years (SD = 0.53)	Longitudinal	T1: primary school: T2: two-and-a-half years after, secondary school	Psychopathology and Academic Performance, Social Well-Being, and Social Preference at School	YSR/CBC; TRAILS for academic performance; Social Production Functions questionnaire; Social preference was derived from the peer nominations.	Teacher reports of psychopathology, especially regarding attention problems and withdrawn/depressed problems, followed by parent reports regarding hyperactivity, were most strongly associated with academic performance. The same held for social preference. Social well-being was best predicted by child reports (at primary school) of affective problems. In girls, the association between ADHD problems and poor academic performance was stronger than in boys and conduct problems were more often associated with poor school functioning in general

First Author/ Publication yr	Sample	Age range	Study design	Timing	Variables and functional area assessed	Measures	Main results
Stuart et al., 2012	N= 972 adolescent–parent dyads in New Zealand	At Year One: 40% (384) were aged 10–11 (Year 6), 30% (284) were aged 12–13 (Year 8), and 30% (277) were aged 14–15 (Year 10)	Longitudinal	Data collected at two time points separated by one year were analyzed.	Family dynamics, well-being, discrepancies	Family Climate Inventory, Family Adaptability and Cohesion Evaluation Scale, Ryff Well-Being Scales	Significant discrepancies between adolescents' and parents' perceptions of family functioning were found for all positive family dynamics, but not for family conflict. Discrepancies increased over time and larger discrepancies were noted for older adolescents. Discrepancies were bidirectionally related to adolescent well-being. In addition, age was found to moderate the predictive model. 14–15 year olds were found to be more stable in their well-being over time than younger adolescents.
Vazsonyi et al., 2015	two nationally representative samples of - Georgian adolescents (N = 6.992) -Swiss adolescents (N = 5.575)	Mean age Georgian= 15.83 (SD = 0.82); Mean age Swiss=17.17 (SD = 0.82)	One-time point		Parenting, Closeness, Sleep hygiene, Delinquency, Deviance	Affective parent–adolescent relationship quality or family attachment, Sleep Quality and Quantity, Alcohol use, Illegal Drug Use	Both sleep quality and sleep quantity independently and cumulatively mediated the effects of parental warmth on each of the three problem behaviors in both samples, with one exception

Mother-child communication (Noor et al., 2013) and mother's using of more religious coping (Goeke-Morey et al., 2014) were identified as resilience resources for adolescents associated with less anxiety and depressive symptoms. Parental interaction and the adolescent's attending religious services with parents in late childhood, were associated with higher psychological well-being, whereas conflict with parents was associated with lower well-being among youth (Petts, 2014). Adolescents experiencing economic disadvantage had generally more negative perceptions of parenting quality and parent-child relational quality, especially for the father-adolescent dyad (Shek, 2005).

Parents attributed higher well-being and self-control to their daughters and sons than the adolescents attributed to themselves, especially in the external behavior problems (Gugliandolo et al., 2014). Significant discrepancies between adolescents' and parents' perceptions of family functioning were found for all positive family dynamics, but not for family conflict. Discrepancies increased over time and larger discrepancies were noted for older adolescents. Discrepancies were bidirectionally related to adolescent well-being (Stuart et al., 2012). Parents' reports regarding hyperactivity were associated with academic performance (Sijtsema et al., 2014) and structural family social capital was negatively related to regular smoking (Ce Clercq et al., 2014).

Conclusion and Future Directions

The perception of health in adolescents presents a trend consistent with the presence / absence of anxious and depressive symptoms, with the success / failure in school, with the quality of communication with their parents and a positive or negative school experience especially in hard transition from middle school to high school and college.

Well-being is also associated with life perceptions closely related to the non-use of substances and to higher levels of physical activity. Somatic and psychological symptoms can be considered common in growth and change period, requiring simultaneously the management of several requests from inside and outside, but if too frequent, it can be a symptom of great distress for the young. In adolescence there is, in fact, intense and sudden mood swings.

In this period of the life cycle negative feelings, sadness, withdraw into themselves, irritation, nervousness will be intensified, strengthened by the idea of not being understood and the disillusionment with the people and places frequented. These experiences, although normal and temporary, often cause suffering, lead to the search for simple but harmful solutions (use of maladaptive coping strategies such as denial and substance abuse) and to perceive themselves ineffective in dealing with the normal developmental tasks for this age.

At this purpose we have to stress that the perception of health and well-being and the coping strategies adopted of adolescents are influenced by the many requests coming from the historical, social and cultural context in which they were inserted, impacting heavily on their ability to deal with the tasks of development. Sometimes if an adolescent lives in a poor stimulating and full of adversity context, he/she will perceive less healthy and perhaps his/her choices do not lead to positive development trajectories, but towards taking risk behaviors.

In particular, factors influencing adolescent's life are:

- the change that characterizes adolescent's relations, because it increases the interest in peers, who, sometimes, are unfortunately,not positive models to follow. This increases the chance to experience and adopt behaviors that may have adverse health consequences, only to be accepted by the group, or to emulate the most influential leaders;
- school climate as the school is the context where the adolescent spends most of his day. Many researches reveal that the well-being at school appears to have positive effects on health and general well-being of adolescents. The adolescents who claim to experience more negative episodes and atmosphere at school, are more likely to adopt negative behaviors such as substance abuse and show more physical and mental disorders and a lower quality of life. Among these behaviors the use of legal substances, such as smoking and alcohol, or illegal onesm such as cannabis or other psychoactive substances, are noteworthy.

The availability of social support and certain personality characteristics (self-confidence, extroversion, ability to deal with the difficulties so active without being overwhelmed by them) are very important for the adolescents, expecially in dealing with the difficulties in which a teenager can stumble. As described in the above sections, a rich social network is a key factor: Friends, especially at this age, are the main figures of reference to confide in and talk freely to.

The studies related to these key elements of well-being and coping in adolescence were very rich, however, the methodology adopted was quite exclusively based on questionnaires and the longitudinal design was not much often used, with the preference for cross-sectional/cross-informant design or one-time point, with the subsequent limitations to results' intepretations.

Future directions in the assessment of coping in adolescents could focus more to the use of longitudinal design and the adoption of a multi-method approach, taking into consideration both surveys and narratives of parents and adolescents. Another future direction could be to build and test models on stable and modifiable predictors on adolescents' well-being taking into consideration contemporaneity all the possible predictors so to have a clinical screening for a worse well-being. To know the best and effective coping strategies could be useful to teach them to adolescents and to their parents and trainee them for a good short- and long-term psycho-social well-being.

REFERENCES

Al-Bahrani, M., Aldhafri, S., Alkharusi, H., Kazem, A., Alzubiadi, A. (2013). Age and gender differences in coping style across various problems: Omani adolescents' perspective. *J. Adolesc*, 36, 303-9.

Albiero, P. (2012). Il benessere psicosociale in adolescenza. Prospettive multidisciplinari. Carocci editore, Roma.

Aldridge, A.A., Roesch, S.C. (2007). Coping and adjustment in children with cancer: a meta-analytic study. *J. Behav. Med.*, 30, 115-29.

Anttila, K., Anttila, M., Kurki, M., Hätönen, H., Marttunen, M., Välimäki, M. (2015). Concerns and hopes among adolescents attending adolescent psychiatric outpatient clinics. *Child and Adolescent Mental Health* 20, 81–88.

Baetens, I., Claes, L., Hasking, P., Smits, D., Grietens, H., Onghena, P., Martin, G. (2015). The relationship between parental expressed emotions and non-suicidal self-injury: The mediating roles of self-criticism and depression. *J. Child Fam. Stud.,* 24, 491–498.

Barry, C., Kauten R.L., & Lui J.H.L. (2014). Self-perceptions of empathy and social support as potential moderators in the relation between adolescent narcissism and aggression. *Individual Differences Research*, 12, 170-179

Baumeister, R.F., & Leary, M.R. (1995). The need to belong: Desire for interpersonal attachments as a fundamental human motivation, *Psychological Bulletin*, 117, 497-529.

Bedin, L.M., & Sarriera, J.C. (2015). A comparative study of the subjective well-being of parents and adolescents considering gender, age and social class. *Soc Indic Res*, 120, 79–95.

Berntsson, L.T., & Ringsberg, K.C (2014). Health and relationships with leisure time activities in Swedish children aged 2–17 years. *Scand J Caring Sci*, 28, 552–563.

Biro, F.M., Striegel-Moore, R., Franko, D.L., Padgett, J. & Bean, J.A. (2006). Self-esteem in adolescent females. *Journal of Adolescent Health*, 39, 501–507.

Bonino, S., Cattelino E., Ciairano, S. (2003). Adolescenti e Rischio, comportamenti, funzioni e fattori di protezione. Giunti, Firenze.

Bos, H, van Beusekom, G., & Sandfort, T. (2014). Sexual attraction and psychological adjustment in Dutch adolescents: Coping style as a mediator. *Arch. Sex Behav.*, 43, 1579–1588

Casas, F., Sarriera, J.C., Alfaro, J., Gonzalez, M., Bedin, L., Abs, D., Figuer, C., & Valdenegro, B. (2015). Reconsidering life domains that contribute to subjective well-being among adolescents with data from three countries. *J. Happiness Stud.*, 16, 491–513.

Chow, C.M., & Buhrmester, D. (2011). Interdependent patterns of coping and support among close friends. *Journal of Social and Personal Relationships*, 28, 684–70.

Chui, W.H., & Wong, M. Y. H. (2015). Gender differences in happiness and life satisfaction among adolescents in Hong Kong: Relationships and self-concept. *Soc. Indic. Res.*, DOI 10.1007/s11205-015-0867-z

Cicognani, E., Albanesi, C., & Zani, B. (2008). The impact of residential context on adolescents' subjective well-being. *J. Community Appl. Soc. Psychol.*, 18, 558–575

Cicognani, E. (2011). Coping strategies with minor stressors in adolescence: Relationships with social support, self-efficacy, and psychological well-being, *Journal of Applied Social Psychology*, 41, 559–578.

Cobb S. (1976). Social support as a moderator of life stress. *Psychosom. Med*, 38, 300-314.

Cohen, M., Ben-Zur, H., & Rosenfeld, M.J. (2008). Sense of coherence, coping strategies, and test anxiety as predictors of test performance among college students. *International Journal of Stress Management*, 15, 289–303.

Costa, S., Soenens, B., Gugliandolo, M.C., Cuzzocrea, F., Larcan, R. (2015). The mediating role of experiences of need satisfaction in associations between parental psychological control and internalizing problems: A study among Italian college students. *J. Child Fam. Stud.*, 24, 1106–1116.

Cruz, D., Narciso, I., Pereira, C.R., Sampaio, D. (2014). Risk trajectories of self-destructiveness in adolescence: Family core influences. *J. Child Fam. Stud.*, 23, 1172–1181.

De Caroli, M.E., & Sagone, E. (2014). Generalized self-efficacy and well-being in adolescents with high vs. low scholastic self-efficacy. *Procedia - Social and Behavioral Sciences*, 141, 867 – 874.

De Clercq, B., Pfoertner, T.K., Elgar, F.J., Hublet A., Meas L. (2014). Social capital and adolescent smoking in schools and communities: A cross-classified multilevel analysis. *Social Science & Medicine,* 119, 81-87.

Desjarlais, M., & Willoughby, T. (2010). A longitudinal study of the relation between adolescent boys and girls' computer use with friends and friendship quality: Support for the social compensation or the rich-get-richer hypothesis? *Computers in Human Behavior*, 26, 896–905.

Dunn, E.C., Milliren, C.E., Evans, C.R., Subramanian, S.V., Richmond, T.K. (2015). Disentangling the relative influence of schools and neighborhoods on adolescents' risk for depressive symptoms. *American Journal of Public Health*, 105, 732-740.

Eryılmaz, A. (2012). A model of subjective well-being for adolescents in high school, *J. Happiness Stud.*, 13, 275–289.

Espinoza, G., O'Neel, C.G., Gonzales, N.A., Fuligni A.J. (2014). Friend affiliations and school adjustment among mexican-american adolescents: The moderating role of peer and parent support. *J. Youth Adolescence*, 43, 1969–1981.

Farrel, C.T., Bolland, J.M., Cockerham, W.C. (2015). The role of social support and social context on the incidence of attempted suicide among adolescents living in extremely impoverished communities, *Journal of Adolescent Health,* 56, 59-65.

Frison, E., & Eggermont, S. (2015). The impact of daily stress on adolescents' depressed mood: The role of social support seeking through Facebook. *Computers in Human Behavior*, 44, 315–325.

Frydenberg, E. (1997). Adolescent coping: Research and theoretical perspectives. London: Routledge.

Frydenberg, E. & Lewis, R. (1991). Adolescent coping styles and strategies: Is there functional and dysfunctional coping? *Australian Journal of Guidance and Counselling*, 1, 1-8.

Garcia, D. (2014). La Vie en Rose: High levels of well-being and events inside and outside autobiographical memory, *J. Happiness Stud.*, 15, 657–672.

Glozah, F.N. (2015). Exploring Ghanaian adolescents' meaning of health and wellbeing: A psychosocial perspective. *Int. J. Qualitative Stud Health Well-being*, 10, http://dx.doi.org/10.3402/qhw.v10.26370

Goeke-Morey, M.C., Taylor, L.K., Merrilees, C.E., Shirlow, P., Cummings E. M. (2014). Adolescents' relationship with God and internalizing adjustment over time: The moderating role of maternal religious coping. *Journal of Family Psychology*, 28, 749–758.

Grao-Cruces, A., Nuviala, A., Fernández-Martínez, A., Pérez-Turpin, J.A. (2014). Association of physical activity, life satisfaction and Mediterranean diet in adolescents, *Kinesiology* 46, 3-11.

Gugliandolo M. C., Costa, S., Cuzzocrea, F., Larcan, R., Petrides, K.V. (2015). Trait emotional intelligence and behavioral problems among adolescents: A cross-informant design. *Personality and Individual Differences*, 74, 16–21.

Hampel, P., & Petermann, F. (2005). Age and gender effects on coping in children and adolescents. *Journal of Youth and Adolescence*, 34, 73–83.

Havinghurst, Robert James, (1952). Human Development and Education, p. 7.

Inguglia, C., Ingoglia, S., Liga, F., Lo Coco, A., Lo Cricchio, M.G. (2015). Autonomy and relatedness in adolescence and emerging adulthood: Relationships with parental support and psychological distress. *J. Adult Dev.,* 22, 1–13.

Jovanovic, V., & Brdaric, D. (2012). Did curiosity kill the cat? Evidence from subjective well-being in adolescents. *Personality and Individual Differences*, 52, 380–384.

Jun, Y.., & Shin, J. (2015). The effect of peer acceptance on euphoria among Korean adolescents. *Social behavior and personality*, 43, 63-74.

Kelly, A.B., Evans-Whipp, T.J., Smith, R., Chan, G.C.K., Toumbourou, J.W., et al. (2014). A longitudinal study of the association of adolescent polydrug use, alcohol use and high school non-completion. *Addiction*, 110, 627–635.

Lazarus, R. S., & Folkman, S. (1984). Stress, appraisal, and coping. New York: Springer.

Lee, R.L.T., & Loke, A.Y. (2011). Lifestyle behaviours and psychosocial well-being of Chinese adolescentsin Hong Kong and Guangzhou, China: a cross-sectional comparative survey. *Journal of Clinical Nursing*, 20, 2733–2743.

Ievers-Landis, C.E., Greenley, R.N., Burant, C., Borawski, E. (2006). Cognitive social maturity, life change events, and health risk behaviors among adolescents: Development of a structural equation model, *Journal of Clinical Psychology in Medical Settings*, 13, 111-120.

Lin, W.H., & Yi C.C. (2015). Unhealthy sleep practices, conduct problems, and daytime functioning during adolescence. *J. Youth Adolescence*, 44, 431–446.

Miller, A.B., Esposito-Smythers, C., & Leichtweis, R.N. (2015). Role of social support in adolescent suicidal ideation and suicide attempts. *Journal of Adolescent Health*, xxx, 1-7

Millings, A., Buck, R., Montgomery, A., Spears M., Stallard, P. (2012). School connectedness, peer attachment, and self-esteem as predictors of adolescent depression. *Journal of Adolescence*, 35, 1061–1067.

Mota, C.P., & Matos, P.M. (2015). Adolescents in institutional care: Significant adults, resilience and well-being. *Child Youth Care Forum*, 44, 209–224.

Mouratidis, A., & Michou, A. (2011). Perfectionism, self-determined motivation, and coping among adolescent athletes. *Psychology of Sport and Exercise*, 12, 355-367.

Navarro, D., Montserrat, C., Malo, S., González, M., Casas, F., Crous, G. (2015). Subjective well-being: what do adolescents say?, *Child and Family Social Work*, 1-10, doi:10.1111/cfs.12215

Nilsen, W., Karevold, E., Røysamb, E., Gustavson, K., Mathiesen, K.S. (2013). Social skills and depressive symptoms across adolescence: Social support as a mediator in girls versus boys. *Journal of Adolescence*, 36, 11–20.

Noor, N.M., & Alwi, A. (2013). Stressors and well-being in low socio-economic status Malaysian adolescents: The role of resilience resources. *Asian Journal of Social Psychology*, 16, 292–306.

O'Shea, G., Spence, S.H., & Donovan, C.L. (2014). Interpersonal factors associated with depression in adolescents: Are these consistent with theories underpinning interpersonal psychotherapy? *Clin. Psychol. Psychother.*, 21, 548–558.

Olbrich, E. (1990). Coping and development. In H. Bosma & S. Jackson (Eds.), Coping and self-concept in adolescence (pp. 35–47). Berlin, Germany: Springer-Verlag.

Palmonari, A. (Ed.). Psicologia dell'adolescenza; Bologna; Il Mulino, 1997.

Petts, R.J. (2014). Family, religious attendance, and trajectories of psychological well-being among youth, *Journal of Family Psychology*, 28, 759–768.

Pinkerton, J., & Dolan, P. (2007). Family support, social capital, resilience and adolescent coping. *Child and Family Social Work*, 12, 219–228.

Polanczyk, G.V., Salum, G.A., Sugaya, L.S., Caye, A., Rohde, L.A. (2015). Annual Research Review: A meta-analysis of the worldwide prevalence of mental disorders in children and adolescents. *Journal of Child Psychology and Psychiatry*, 1-21, doi:10.1111/jcpp.12381.

Rawana, J.S. (2013). The relative importance of body change strategies, weight perception, Perceived social support, and self-esteem on adolescent depressive symptoms: Longitudinal findings from a national sample. *Journal of Psychosomatic Research*, 75, 49–54.

Sabiston, C.M., Crocker, P.R.E. (2008). Exploring self-perceptions and social influences as correlates of adolescent leisure-time physical activity. *Journal of Sport & Exercise Psychology*, 30, 3-22.

Seiffge-Krenke, I. (1995). Stress, coping, and relationships in adolescence. Mahwah, NJ: Lawrence Erlbaum.

Seiffge-Krenke, I. (2011). Coping with relationship stressors: A decade review. Journal of Research on Adolescence, 21, 196 – 210.

Seiffge-Krenke, I., Molinar, R., Ciariano, S., Menna, P., Michel, G., Hoareau, E., Kloep, M., Hendry, L.B. (2010). Competence in coping with future-related stress in adolescents from France, Italy, Great Britain, and Germany. *J. Happiness Stud.*, 11, 703–720.

Shek, D.T.L. (2005). A longitudinal study of Chinese cultural beliefs about adversity, psychological well-being, delinquency and substance abuse in Chinese adolescents with economic disadvantage. *Social Indicators Research*, 71, 385–409.

Shoshani, A., & Slone, M. (2013). Middle school transition from the strengths perspective: Young adolescents' character strengths, subjective well-being, and school adjustment. *J. Happiness Stud.*, 14, 1163–1181.

Sijtsema, J.J., Verboom, C.E., Penninx, B.W.J.H., Verhulst, F.C., Orme J. (2014). Psychopathology and academic performance, social well-being, and social preference at school: The TRAILS Study. *Child Psychiatry Hum Dev.*, 45, 273–284.

Singh, K., Bassi, M., Junnarkar, M., Negri, L. (2015). Mental health and psychosocial functioning in adolescence: An investigation among Indian students from Delhi. *Journal of Adolescence*, 39, 59-69.

Singh, K., & Junnarkar, M. (2014). Validation and effect of demographic variables on perceived quality of life by adolescents. *Asian Journal of Psychiatry*, 12, 88–94.

Sladek, M.R., & Doane, L.D. (2015). Daily diary reports of social connection, objective sleep, and the cortisol awakening response during adolescents' first year of college. *J. Youth Adolescence*, 44:298–316.

Stuart, J., & Jose, P.E. (2012) The influence of discrepancies between adolescent and parent ratings of family dynamics on the well-Being of adolescents. *Journal of Family Psychology*, 26, 858–868.

Sujoldzic, A., & De Lucia, A. (2007). A cross-cultural study of adolescents – BMI, body image and psychological well-being. *Coll. Antropol.*, 31, 123–130.

Sweeting, H., Hunt, K. (2014). Adolescent socio-economic and school-based social status, health and well-being. *Social Science & Medicine*, 121, 39-47.

Tap, P., Esparbés-Pistre, S., & Sordes-Ader, F. (1997). Identité et strategies de personnalisation. *Bulletin de Psychologie*, 50, 185-196.

Tavernier, R., & Willoughbyù, T. (2012). Adolescent turning points: The association between meaning-making and psychological well-being. *Developmental Psychology*, 48, 1058–1068.

Thompson, A., & Gaudreau, P. (2006). From optimism and pessimism to coping: The mediating role of academic motivation. International. *Journal of Stress Management,* 15, 269–288.

Tian, L., Liu, B., Huang, S, Scott Huebner, E. (2013). Perceived social support and school well-being among Chinese early and middle adolescents: The mediational role of self-esteem. *Soc. Indic Res.*, 113, 991–1008.

Valois, R.F., Zullig, K.J., Hunter, A.A. (2015). Association between adolescent suicide ideation, suicide attempts and emotional self-efficacy. *J. Child Fam. Stud.*, 24, 237–248.

Van der Giessen, D., Branje, S., Meeus, W. (2014). Perceived autonomy support from parents and best friends: Longitudinal associations with adolescents' depressive symptoms. *Social Development,* 23, 537–555.

Vazsonyi, A.T., Harris, C., Terveer, A.M., Pagava, K., Phagava, H., Michaud, P.A. (2015). Parallel mediation effects by sleep on the parental warmth-problem behavior links: Evidence from National probability samples of Georgian and Swiss adolescents. *J. Youth Adolescence*, 44, 331–345.

Vianello, R. (2003). Psicologia dello sviluppo: adolescenza, età adulta, età senile. Bergamo: Edizioni Junior.

Wang, J.L., Jackson, L.A., Gaskin, J., Wang, H.Z. (2014). The effects of Social Networking Site (SNS) use on college students' friendship and well-being. *Computers in Human Behavior*, 37, 229–236.

Wethington, E., & Kessler, R.C. (1986). Perceived support, received support and adjustment to stressful life events. *Journal of Health and Social Behavior*, 27, 78-79.

Wight, R.G., Botticello, A.L., Aneshensel, C.S. (2006). Socioeconomic context, social support, and adolescent mental health: A multilevel investigation. *Journal of Youth and Adolescence*, 35, 115–126.

Zhao, Y., & Zhao, G. (2015). Emotion regulation and depressive symptoms: Examining the mediation effects of school connectedness in Chinese late adolescents. *Journal of Adolescence*, 40, 14-23.

In: Psychological Health and Needs Research Developments ISBN: 978-1-63483-332-5
Editor: Raul Wolfe

Chapter 3

EFFECTS OF EXPRESSIVE ART BASED INTERVENTIONS ON ADOLESCENT MENTAL HEALTH

***Fung Kei Cheng*, PhD**[*]
Hong Kong, The People's Republic of China

ABSTRACT

This chapter offers a comprehensive overview of the effectiveness of expressive art based interventions on adolescent mental health, the discussion of which is expanded more concretely through the concept of health humanities. The World Health Organisation has reported that the severity of childhood mental disorders produces a heavy burden on family caregivers, education experts, and national medical expenditures. In particular, the dearth of health professionals and medications in underdeveloped countries worsens their capabilities in coping with this predicament. Such threats pose a dire need for effective and efficient resolutions from scholars, practitioners, and social policy makers. From among a variety of therapies, expressive art based activities become a potential method for children, because they have been used in more creative ways that can cater to various segments of young people who are affected by mental illness. In light of recent research (involving Asian, European, North American, and Middle Eastern participants), findings illustrate a wide spectrum of art forms, including integrative art, painting, music, dance/movement, and drama; which are employed effectively to deal with emotional, behavioural, and social problems, resulting in lowering symptoms of neuro-behavioural difficulties, oppositional defiant disorder, and sensory integration barriers, and in improving academic achievement as well across pre-school, elementary school, secondary school and college students, children with brain injuries, abused or traumatised adolescents, at-risk youth, and teenagers in immigrant and refugee families. These analyses also illuminate improvements in parent-child and teacher-student relationships, because of which social cohesion is enhanced due to better emotional management, communication skills, and self-efficacy. This literature review reveals that intervention programmes are devised in order to accommodate individual characteristics and cultural preferences. It also suggests that expressive art integrates with different therapeutic practices and incorporates into school and professional training curricula for

---

[*] oasischeng@yahoo.com

preventive, rehabilitative, remedial, and curative purposes, attaining cross-disciplinary success.

Keywords: Dance/movement therapy, drama therapy, emotional disorder, health humanities, literature review, music therapy, visual art

INTRODUCTION

Neuropsychiatric problems produce disabilities among the young, and 10-20% of adolescents worldwide experience different levels of mental disorders (World Health Organisation, 2015) such as developmental disorders (World Health Organisation, 2013) that adversely affect their health, emotion and behaviour, self-esteem, educational accomplishment, and social life (World Health Organisation, 2012). These childhood defects then extend into adulthood to reduce productivity at work (World Health Organisation, 2003) and increase mortality (Perou et al., 2013) due to suicidal risks (Social Exclusion Unit, 2004), resulting in the devastation of their overall function over their lifespan (Schwartz et al., 2009). Such damages to youthful well-being incur an enormous burden on both family resources (Padilla-Frausto, Grant, Aydin, & Aguilar-Gaxiola, 2014) and public finance (Buchanan, 2015), which marks the considerable social costs involved (Knapp et al., 2014). Thus, programmes for mental health promotion have become a serious need (McKay et al., 2004) by the way of prevention and cure (National Research Council and Institute of Medicine, 2009).

A wealth of research has addressed a feasible link between mental illness and creativity (Sussman, 2007) owing to the activation of brain functions (Kruk, Aravich, Deaver, & deBeus, 2014). Although this postulate is controversial (Kyaga et al., 2011), it hints at the plausible adaptation of art-related therapies in dealing with mental disorders. The use of expressive art in healing began with the ancient Egyptians and Greeks (Farrington, 2015), and emerged in the Western psychiatric field starting in the late 19th century (Malchiodi, 2005), following which it has been developed by psychotherapists as a non-verbal stream of interventions in physical health, mental care, and rehabilitation (Stuckey & Nobel, 2010; Wexler, 2014). Since this approach involves visual, auditory, tactile, and bodily senses, it contributes to the advancement of multiple intelligences (Groff, 2013), concerning verbal-linguistic, logical-mathematical, visual-spatial, bodily-kinesthetic, musical-rhythmic, intrapersonal, interpersonal, and natural domains; providing space for self-expression, self-exploration, innovation, engagement, and body-mind interplay. These characteristics have been presented through effective outcomes in interventions for children (Phelps, undated), such as in the area of autism (Parteli, 1995).

Expressive art therapy consists of various forms, and consists mainly of four modalities: art making, music, dance/movement, and drama (Odell-Miller, Hughes, & Westacott, 2006), which indicates positive effects in cognitive, emotional, and social enhancements among adolescents (Henley, 1998). This non-conventional variety enriches their creativity, imagination, self-awareness (Potash, Chen, Lam, & Chau, 2014; Sundaram, 1995), and self-care (Ko, 2014) through novel, playful, and experiential involvement.

Art therapy, largely pertaining to art making, has developed symbolic and representational communications to reduce defence mechanisms, clarify confusion, and make latent agendas visible (Miller, Rubin, & Irwin, 2011). This non-threatening and personal medium can accommodate a wide range of populations, including prisoners (Djurichkovic, 2011), and also children (Henley, 2001; Henley, 2000; Meijer-Degen, 2014; Riley, 2001) through a "meditative, tactile, and internal process" (Milia, 2013, p. 137).

Clinical evidence reports the effectiveness of art therapy on psychological health (Lamont, Sutton, & Brunero, 2009), which invites a growing trend in using it in mental care (Coqueiro, Vieira, & Freitas, 2010). In particular, art therapy has become a prevalent means to cope with mental illnesses (Lloyd, Wong, & Petchkovsky, 2007; Morrison, 2004); for example, attention deficit hyperactivity disorder (Henley, 1998), anxiety (Boehm, Cramer, Staroszynski, & Ostermann, 2014), depression (Gussak, 2007), bipolar disorder (Fish, 1989), schizophrenia (Bitonte & De Santo, 2014; Morrow, 1985; Richardson, Jones, Evans, Stevens, & Rowe, 2007), panic disorder, stress (Bolwerk, Mack-Andrick, Lang, Dorfler, & Maihofner, 2014), and posttraumatic stress disorder (Lobban, 2014).

Music offers a path towards aesthetic feeling and emotional expression (Brauer, 2012; Gao, 2007), relaxation, social connection (Gold et al., 2013), and creativity (Baines & Danko, 2010). These functions are conducive to the neutralisation of negative emotions, an increase in stress endurance, and inner harmonisation (Sze & Yu, 2004). A body of research reports the usefulness of music training in physical impairments (Jung et al., 2012) and improvements in general intelligence and visual-spatial skills (Flohr, 2010).

In employing musical instruments and techniques, music therapy indicates enhancements in brain development to prevent the occurrence of mental illnesses (Frank, 2014), and therefore to tackle mental problems (Odell-Miller, 2005; Solli & Rolvsjord, 2015; Solli, Rolvsjord, & Marit, 2013), including anxiety (Fagen, 1982; Guetin, Soua, Voiriot, Picot, & Herisson, 2009; Simavli et al., 2014), depression (Erkkila et al., 2011; Gardstrom, Bartkowski, Willenbrink, & Diestelkamp, 2013; Maratos, Crawford, & Procter, 2011), schizophrenia (Mössler, Chen, Heldal, & Gold, 2013; Talwar et al., 2006), and dementia (Brotons & Koger, 2000). These results reveal the helpfulness of utilising music for teenagers with emotional and behavioural disorders, especially during their childhood developmental stages (Gao, 2008).

Physical exercises and activities exhibit effects on mental health (Taylor, Sallis, & Needle, 1985), among which dance is one of the popular methods. Dance represents a natural form of emotional expression that cultivates emotional recognition (Van Dyck, Vansteenkiste, Lenoir, Lesaffre, & Leman, 2014) and a feeling of self control over body movement. Stimulating the right brain, it increases body awareness and bodily feelings, resulting in mind-body therapeutic functionality (de Valenzuela, 2014).

Dance therapy, through free movement, presents a holistic mode of intervention, implicitly covering physical, cognitive, perceptual, emotional, psychological, and social capabilities (Homann, 2010; Lorenzo-Lasa, Ideishi, & Ideishi, 2007; Pallaro & Fischlein-Rupp, 2002; Scharoun, Reinders, Bryden, & Fletcher, 2014). It has been extensively used not only in mental illness, such as depression (Koch, Morlinghaus, & Fuchs, 2007; Pinniger, Brown, Thorsteinsson, & McKinley, 2012), schizophrenia (Ren & Xia, 2013), and eating disorders (Levy, 1988), but also in the enhancement of quality of life (Bräuninger, 2014; Kaltsatou, Kouidi, Anifanti, Douka, & Deligiannis, 2014; Koch, Kunz, Lykou, & Cruz, 2014). Its coverage extends to various target participants; for instance, breast cancer survivors (Dibbell-Hope, 2000; Ho, 2000), and maltreated children (Betty, 2013) in many countries, including the USA, Canada, Spain, Norway, Finland, Japan, India, and Haiti (Capello, 2008).

Drama is a "particular medium of expression" (Johnson, 1982, p. 184) that includes a sophisticated set of performances, involving visual, verbal, sound, light, symbols, and bodily presentation. By incorporating these components into treatment, drama therapy, as a "therapeutic theatre" (Snow, D'Amico, & Tanguay, 2003, p. 73), adopts dramatic methods or training in a group setting for therapeutic purposes (Kedem-Tahar & Kellermann, 1996). It has been employed to deal with a variety of mental problems (Cassidy, Turnbull, & Gumley, 2014); for example, posttraumatic stress disorder (Morris, 2014), eating disorders (Radmall, 1997), and speech impairment (Couroucli-Robertson, 2001), particularly for youngsters (Cattanach, 1995) and disturbed adolescents (Willis, 1988).

The present literature review offers a comprehensive overview of how recent practitioners manage mental health promotion and tackle mental disorders, along with behavioural and social problems by means of expressive art based interventions (in which integrative art, dance/movement, drama, music, painting, and a combination of these therapies are applied). Therefore, it plays a role in the rapid development of health humanities in mental care, and in art-based research (Finley, 2014).

RESEARCH METHOD

The search strategy of this review utilises 52 major electronic databases in ProQuest, covering British Nursing Index, ERIC, MEDLINE, PILOTS, PsycArticles, and PsycINFO. Boolean operators (such as "and") and truncation methods (for instance, "neuro*") were used. Inputs include three categories: in the first place, "art" or "dance" or "drama" or "movement" or "music"; in the second place, "brain" or "emotion*" or "neuro*" or "psycho*"; and in the third place, "adolescen*" or "child*" or "teen*" or "young*" or "youth." In addition to sourcing digitalised channels, more potential works have also been obtained from the reference lists of the reviewed manuscripts. A retrieval of 188 outputs has been searched for initial selection. Subsequently, abstracts of the retrieved works were gone through, from which 33 projects that complied with the inclusion criteria were finally chosen for detailed review.

The eligibility criteria are threefold: first, they must be peer-reviewed articles published between 2000 and 2014, including Online First publications; second, they must be empirical projects regarding quantitative, qualitative, and mixed methods; and third, only full texts are selected. The excluded papers include editorials, commentaries, literature reviews, book reviews, case reports, letters to editors, and dissertations.

FINDINGS AND DISCUSSION

The reviewed 33 research projects (refer to Table 1) cover an extensive age spectrum from 3-24 years old (unspecified ages in eight studies), involving more than 4,454 participants (the number of persons in three research projects were unspecified) across Asia (n=1 in China; n=1 in Korea), Europe (n=1 in Northern Ireland; n=1 in Italy; n=1 in Finland), North America (n=5 in Canada; n=21 in USA), and the Middle East (n=1 in Turkey; n=1 in Israel). Their publication years centre around 2010-2014 (61%): 2014 (n=2), 2013 (n=5),

2012 (n=4), 2011 (n=4), 2010 (n=5), 2009 (n=1), 2008 (n=1), 2007 (n=2), 2006 (n=1), 2005 (n=4), 2004 (n=1), 2002 (n=2), and 2001 (n=1). In terms of research methods, there are 13 quantitative inquiries (in which two projects were randomised controlled trials), 13 qualitative studies, and seven mixed-method programmes.

Among the reviewed research, comprising integrative art (n=9), painting (n=1), music (n=5), dance/movement (n=7), and drama (n=11), seven projects dealt with immigrants and refugee children who had adaptive problems that adversely affected their psychological well-being, four pertained to adolescents with brain injuries that traumatised their mental health, and six regarded those who suffered from developmental disorders such as autism, and attention deficit hyperactivity disorder. In addition to these subjects, the remainder studied a wide scope of participants: children with mental illnesses (for example, eating disorders, bipolar disorder, and depression), with oppositional and disruptive behaviours, vulnerable populations (including abused children, those with chronic pain, and paediatric inpatients), and various age groups (from pre-school, primary school, and nursing college, to transition age youth).

Childhood Mental Illnesses

Adolescence is a risky period in which mood disorders can arise because of immature brain development (Murphey, Barry, & Vaughn, 2013). Thus, sensory integration difficulties are not rare among children, and cause a diverse group of mental problems (Ghanizadeh, 2011), such as learning disabilities, autism, Asperger's syndrome, and attention deficit hyperactivity disorder (Pollock, 2009); all of which strongly associate with stress, anxiety, and inharmonious interpersonal relationships (Ben-Avi1, Almagor, & Engel-Yeger, 2012).

General Mental Health

A multi-centred single-blinded randomised controlled trial in Northern Ireland aimed to evaluate the effectiveness of music therapy on childhood psychological health (Porter et al., 2012). One hundred and ninety-eight children in six centres, ranging 8-16 years old, were randomly assigned to the intervention (n=99) and the control (n=99) groups. Participants in the intervention group received normal clinical care and 30-minutes of weekly music training for 12 weeks. Pre- and post-assessments were performed with both the participants and their parent(s). Positive indicators were apparent in communication and interaction skills, self-esteem, and social functioning. Supported by financial cost-effectiveness analysis, this study proposed a greater use of music therapy in promoting mental wellness.

Having recruited 60 kindergarten students aged 3-6 years old, another quantitative study examined how dance could benefit their motor skills and emotional expression (Walter & Sat, 2013). The participants were assigned to either an experimental group (n=30) or the control group (n=30). Those in the experimental group attended folk dance lessons, guided by four instructors, throughout the entire school year, in which they got involved in 30-minute weekly training sessions. Measurements in November and May reported not only better adaptability, assertiveness, and emotion identification, but also significant improvements in emotional intelligence abilities and cultivation of empathy. Such positive indicators were also exhibited in a clinical observation of two pre-adolescent boys with attention deficit and hyperactivity disorder (Novy, 2005). The informants showed better communication skills and more willingness to cooperate with other people, after receiving 25 45-minute drama therapy sessions.

Sensory Integration Problems

One single case study with a 5-year old boy who had sensory integration difficulties investigated the effects of art therapy on his problems (Kearns, 2004). The programme was devised along an A-B-A-B mode, in which "A" represents the non-treatment condition and "B" refers to the intervention. It took 10 weeks, in which the informant received 20-minute daily training sessions for a variety of art training, including easel painting, oil-based clay work, and finger painting, together with another ten control sessions. Measurements were carried out before and after the intervention, indicating an enhancement in positive behaviour and postponement of negative behaviour. This pilot study also displayed the usefulness of art activities in training for kinesthetic experience, personal expression, and visual stimulation.

Music was applied to helping children in an integrative class develop compassion. Four children, aged 9-10 years, took part in a music therapy programme, which comprised two normal girls and two boys with pervasive developmental disorders (Gilboa & Ben-Shetrit, 2009). A total of 14 30-minute weekly sessions were offered, and assessments were carried out via quantitative and qualitative measures. Despite the small sample size of this mixed research, the results illuminated the fact that the participants could develop compassion gradually during their interactions.

Autism

Xu and her team members (2010) attempted to identify pictures, types of music, and combinations of pictures and music for emotional stimulation in children with autism. Twelve different pictures and four types of music, covering silent, nursery rhymes, Samba percussion, and soothing piano music, were presented to 14 Chinese participants, 8-12 years old. They showed the longest attention durations when seeing pictures of food and hearing disparate types of music, rather than during silent portions. One encouraging outcome pertained to feedback received from the autistic children, such as speech, smiles, and positive emotional responses.

Comparable results were also achieved by 38 children with autism who completed group movement therapy (Hartshorn et al., 2001). After four 30-minute biweekly sessions, the participants reduced stress, wandering time, resistance to teachers, and negative responses to touching, while increasing on-task behaviour and attentive behaviour.

Another combined programme which encompassed music and dance/movement therapy was assessed regarding how it could treat psychopathological disorders (Mateos-Moreno & Atencia-Dona, 2013). Sixteen children with severe autism were assigned to either the intervention group (n=8) or the control group (n=8). The former completed 36 one-hour sessions within 17 weeks, presenting more significant improvements in physical and psychological wellness than those in the control group, including attention capability, emotional control, and self-regulation of impulsive behaviours.

Bipolar Disorder

"Naming the Enemy" (an art therapy programme) was employed for children with bipolar disorder and difficulties with emotion control, in which one girl and three boys who were 9-

15 years old completed the programme (Henley, 2007). This clinical observation reported an increase in the self-awareness of how their behaviour affected their social life and overall quality of life. The informants also achieved better responsible self-regulation and stabilisation of impulsive behaviour.

Eating Disorders

Pellicciari and colleagues (2013) devised the "Metamorphosis Project," a theatre workshop, to cope with eating behaviours and patterns. They recruited 15 children from 15 to 18 years old in Bologna, Italy, who attended six to fifteen weekly sessions. Quantitative assessments were taken and qualitative data were collected after the intervention. Findings reported an increase in knowledge of obesity symptoms and improvements in obsessive mood and thoughts. However, in addition to a small sample size that is not able to convincingly conclude the results, the inconsistent number of sessions that the participants joined reduced the reliability of the data analysis.

Oppositional Defiant Disorder

Thirty elementary school boys with oppositional defiant disorder, aged 7-12 years, took part in painting therapy sessions (Khadar, Babapour, & Sabourimoghaddam, 2013). They were assigned to either an experimental group (n=15) or a control group (n=15). The former learned mainly painting and sculpting, but also dancing, drama performing, storytelling, and poem writing. The class involved 40 minutes per session and assessments were taken prior to and after the therapy. Outcomes exhibited a significant reduction in symptoms: increasing adaptive emotion and behaviour, and improving communication skills.

A group of children from military families, aged 11-13 years and with opposition and disruptive behaviours, participated in expressive art therapy to develop psychosocial ability (Kim, Kirchhoff, & Whitsett, 2011). This eight-session programme involved visual art making, painting, sculpture, drama, musical instrument playing, and movement. Each session lasted 75 minutes. In qualitative interviews, they gave feedback on what they felt, indicating enhancements in interpersonal and social skills.

Summary

Research such as that denoted above elucidates the effects of expressive based art therapy (including integrative art, dance, drama, music, and painting) on a large sphere of childhood mental problems, covering general psychological health, sensory integration disorder, autism, oppositional defiant disorder, bipolar disorder and eating disorders. Findings evince a reduction in psychiatric symptoms, and improvements in adaptability, self-expression, and attention. Since participants increased self-awareness and were able to control emotion more easily, their positive behaviours increased and negative behaviours decreased. Furthermore, when their interpersonal and communication skills were enhanced, they gained more self-esteem and self-efficacy benefiting from non-judgemental empowerment. These results supported the predictions that teenagers would attain better mental well-being and social life.

Adolescents with Brain Injuries and Chronic Pain

Clinical data reveals a close relationship between mental illnesses and brain injury (Barrett, 1999; Schwartzbold et al., 2008) and chronic pain (Mangerud, Bjerkeset, Lydersen, & Indredavik, 2013).

One boy who was 10 years old suffered from post-traumatic stress disorder due to brain injury. He underwent 15 art therapy sessions, half of which arranged weekly and the other half biweekly in order to develop his physical, verbal, sensory, cognitive, emotional, psychological, and social abilities (Mallay, 2002). His withdrawal behaviours and psychophysiological symptomology were evidently reduced, and his feelings of control and self-esteem increased.

Two other children, who were 12 and 15 years old and suffered from neuro-behavioural disorders incurred by traumatic brain injury, improved their communication skills and social interaction after 30-minute weekly music therapy sessions over eight weeks (Magee et al., 2011). These qualitative case studies reveal the effects of this treatment on psychosocial premises.

Similar outcomes were achieved by a mixed method project which looked into the effects of drama on social skill training (Agnihotri et al., 2012). Two female adolescents aged 16 and 17 years old who had childhood brain injuries participated in a four-hour daily programme for three weeks focusing on collaboration, awareness of self, others and their environment, relaxation, listening, and curiosity and imagination, along with eight months post-treatment. The workshop was guided by three theatre artists and three occupational therapy students. In addition to pre- and post-tests, three focus group interviews collected feedback from the participants, their parents, and the trainers at the end of the intervention. The findings reported enhancements in social skills, self awareness, self-esteem, self-efficacy, abstract thinking, and adaptability to social environment. However, the small sample size that resulted from difficulties in recruiting participants yielded inconclusive results.

In spite of this limitation, Agnihotri and colleagues (2014) kicked off a longitudinal multiple descriptive project with five adolescents who were 13-16 years old and who had suffered brain injuries in order to examine how theatre training could improve social skills and community participation. Four were placed in the treatment group and one in the control group. They received four-hour daily sessions for four weeks under the guidance of two theatre artists and one occupational therapy student. Apart from the pre- and post-tests, follow-up assessments were conducted between six and eight months after the intervention. The findings of this pilot study included positive changes in social and communication skills, and increases in self confidence.

The interplay between physiological and psychological impacts becomes an explicit concern for paediatricians. Two girls who suffered from chronic pain that also affected their emotional health received six dance and drama therapies sessions (Christie, Hood, & Griffin, 2006). However, while one adolescent reported a reintegration of body and mind, resulting in better emotional expression, the other adolescent showed insignificant effects caused by her lack of active engagement with the intervention. The inconsistent outcomes of these case studies address the importance of the intensity of therapeutic involvement.

Paediatric Inpatients

A pilot study assessed a paediatric orientation programme (Basso, 2010), to which 38 children in paediatric inpatient wards, aged 4-12 years, were invited. It lasted for three months of expressive art activities, and their parents and nine nursing staff were involved in participatory observations. Pre- and post-measurements were undertaken. The outcomes of this mixed research revealed not only decreases in stress, anger, withdrawal and fear, but also improvements in emotional regulation.

Students

Expressive based art therapy has been applied to a full range of students from pre-school, primary school, high school, college, and nursing school.

Through observation, Thom (2010) explored how pre-school students can develop socio-emotional capacities through dance/movement therapy. Her results evidenced better emotional stability in 15 children aged three years old after a seven-month intervention period. In addition, the participants gained a stronger sense of self from a holistic perspective in terms of emotion, cognition, and socialisation. However, the overly heavy reliance on observation did not suffice to approve this project convincingly.

"All's Well That Eats Well" (a drama programme) was assessed for its effects on children's eating behaviours (Perry, Zauner, Oakes, Taylor, & Bishop, 2002). A large scale quantitative study recruited 2,893 1st-6th grade students in 20 elementary schools, aged 5-12 years old. The programme consisted of 40-minute sessions, and follow-up activities in class and at home. Pre- and post-tests were conducted. Participants learned healthier food-related knowledge and food choices, and their food recall pertained more to fruits and vegetables.

A team of 90 fourth and fifth grade students in Finland, aged 10-12 years, took part in a school-based drama programme for social and emotional learning (Joronen, Hakamies, & Astedt-Kurki, 2011), made up of 50 and 40 girls and boys respectively. The programme consisted of 90-minute monthly sessions spanning eight months, home assignments, and three evening gathering sessions with parents. Children completed from four to eight sessions, and between 13 and 50 parents participated in the gatherings. Outputs generated from the quantitative data and four focus group interviews revealed that this programme enhanced social and emotional learning and pro-social behaviour in more friendly positive interactions because the children understood diversity and the consequences of bullying. However, the absence of a control group and the use of retrospective data reduced the reliability of this mixed research study.

Forty Korean middle school seniors with mild depression were recruited in order to look into the effects of dance therapy on neuro-hormone related emotions (Jeong & Hong, 2005). They were randomly assigned to either the intervention (n=20) or the control (n=20) groups. The first group underwent a programme that contained 45 minutes per week, thrice weekly sessions for 12 weeks. This preliminary research indicated positive signs, noting the moderation of serotonin and dopamine and the reduction of psychological distress.

A quasi-experimental study investigated how expressive art can help youngsters foster communication skills and empathy (Ozcan, Bilgin, & Eracar, 2011). Five groups of nursing students (n=48) in Istanbul took part in a group learning programme, which comprised music, painting, sculpture, literature, storytelling, movement, and drama. Each weekly session lasted

105-135 minutes, and the sessions continued for 12 weeks. Pre- and post-tests were measured and which reported the development of empathic and interpersonal skills.

Immigrants and Refugee Adolescents

Adverse experiences in childhood heavily trigger greater risks of mental problems (Read & Bentall, 2012), including psychosis symptoms. Immigrant and refugee children experience organised violence, poverty, dangerous physical and social environments, and persecution (Birman et al., 2005; Rousseau & Guzder, 2008), all of which damage their psychological health.

Choi (2010) identified psychological problems among refugee youth from North Korea through the use of a music therapy programme. She designed a multiple case analysis with nine children aged 8 to 24 years old; albeit some of these refugee youngsters entered school later than do normal students. The programme focused on five themes: feelings about self, feelings about family, feelings about community, problem solving, and loss healing. The findings reported that the participants were hobbled by avoidance, distrust, loneliness, feelings of loss, and fear.

School-based drama therapy was offered to 40 immigrant adolescents with behavioural disorders to facilitate them in the expression and regulation of emotion (Moneta & Rousseau, 2008). The participants, aged 13-16 years, were divided equally and assigned to two special classes, attending 16 75-minute sessions over eight weeks. A focus group interview with teachers was arranged after the fifth session. The qualitative data imply that the children began to express their emotions more easily, especially with regard to anger, indicating the effectiveness of drama on emotional and social learning. Furthermore, this training helped teachers address children's emotions. Although not every participant shared the experience, this attempt revealed the significance of emotional ventilation.

A Laotian woman, who was 22 years old and suffered from stress, took part in a community-based mental health programme (project FOCUS) (Shik, 2013), in which she joined four creative art activities that pertained to creating a self-box, drawing personal dreams and goals, drawing a self-portrait on a blank canvas, and writing a letter to herself. She reduced her stress levels and improved her relationship with her mother as well as her own daughter following the six-month intervention period. This case study illustrates how an Asian American transition-age young person dealt with her emotional disorder through making art. It also portrays the use of expressive art in developing mother-child relationships (Lai, 2011).

Having assessed how a creative programme can prevent emotional and behavioural disorders for immigrants and refugee children (Rousseau, Drapeau, Lacroix, Bagilishya, & Heusch, 2005), one research project in Montreal recruited 138 adolescents (7-13 years old) from this specific group who were studying in two integrated classes from two schools. The intervention group consisted of 73 students, whereas there were 65 in the control group. The programme was conducted with two-hour weekly sessions for 12 weeks. The pre- and post-test results of the intervention group reported a reduction in internalising and externalising symptoms and an increase in feelings of popularity and satisfaction. Supported by another qualitative project, these populations showed positive changes in behaviour and self-esteem after joining ten 70-minute weekly drama training sessions (Rousseau, Gauthier, et al., 2005).

Further research, also led by Rousseau (2007), analysed a school-based drama therapy programme in order to prevent emotional and behavioural problems among immigrant and refugee children. It recruited 123 newly arrived immigrant and refugee adolescents in five integrated classes who were 12-18 years old and had learned French (the official language in Quebec), among whom 66 were placed into the experimental group (n=26 girls, n=40 boys) and 57 in the control group (n=27 girls, n=30 boys). Moreover, it invited two teachers to join this study. The pre- and post-tests involved both students and teachers. Data reported lower impairment levels (particularly in girls), better mathematics performance (particularly among boys), and better social adjustment.

Rousseau and team (2012) continued their studies to assess the combined effects of drama and language workshops. They recruited 55 immigrant and refugee adolescents in four classes from two high schools. Twenty-seven of them were placed into the experimental group (n=14 girls, n=13 boys), and another 28 in the control group (n=16 girls, n=12 boys). The former group experienced 90-minute plurilingual weekly drama sessions for 12 weeks. The findings, collected through quantitative analyses, observation, and interviews with the students and teachers, were three-fold: stronger feelings of empowerment and social bonds, improved expression of experience and feelings, and reductions in impairment.

The first randomised controlled trial by Rousseau's research team (2014) evaluated how a school-based drama programme improved the emotional and behavioural health and academic results of immigrant and refugee youth. The team invited 477 secondary school students in a highly multi-ethnic school. The participants were randomly assigned to either the drama (n=157), the tutoring (n=180), or the control (n=140) groups. Members in the drama group received 90-minute weekly training sessions for 12 weeks. Stronger evidence of improvements in impairment and academic performance were found in the second generation of immigrants than in the first generation.

Abused Children and At-risk Youth

Associations with mood disorders and child abuse (Afifi, Mota, Dasiewicz, MacMillan, & Sareen, 2012) have a substantial impact on medical expenses (Wada & Igarashi, 2014) and social costs, particularly in higher rates of suicide attempts in female victims (Afifi et al., 2014). This urges immediate attention towards adequate treatments, among which making art is apparently a feasible instrument for use with traumatised children (Brumleve, 2010).

One abused child with autism spectrum disorder participated in dance/movement therapy for nine months, which consisted of 90-minute weekly sessions (Baudino, 2010). This clinical case demonstrates how such therapy can enhance self confidence and freedom of choice.

Through a quasi-experimental design, 108 at-risk young people (n=53 girls, n=55 boys) were recruited to evaluate the effects of a prodigy programme on their mental health and academic achievements (Rapp-Paglicci, Stewart, & Rowe, 2011). They were between 15 and 18 years old, and received a variety of training, including visual, performing, musical, media, and theatre arts over a period of eight weeks, in which a three-hour weekly session was offered. Pre- and post measurements were carried out for both the participants and their parents. The research outputs covered significant improvements: a reduction in mental health symptoms and aggressive and externalising behaviours, an increase in self-efficacy and self-regulatory capability, and enhancements in academic performance. However, a lack of programme details restricts further examination of this intervention, and eliminates the repeatability of this study.

Source	Objective(s)	Target participants	Research method	Intervention / Data collection	Results	Research location
Integrative art (n=9)						
Shik, 2013	To illustrate how creative art can improve mental health.	Asian American transition-age youth with mental disorder.	A case study.	One Laotian American woman (n=1) aged 22 years, who suffered from stress. Project FOCUS, a community-based mental health programme. 4 creative art activities (producing a self-box, drawing personal goals and dreams, drawing a self-portrait, and writing a letter to herself), 6 months.	Reduced anxiety. Improved relationships with her mother and daughter.	USA.
Kim et al., 2011	To investigate the effects of expressive art therapy on psychosocial development.	Middle school youth with oppositional and disruptive behaviour in military families.	A qualitative study.	Children (unspecified number of participants) aged 11-13 years in a public school (unspecified number). 8 75-minute sessions (unspecified intervention duration) (including visual art making, painting, sculpture, musical instrument, movement and drama).	Enhanced interpersonal and social skills.	USA.
Ozcan et al., 2011	To look into the effects of expressive art on communication and empathic skills.	Nursing students.	A quasi-experimental research design.	Assigned nursing students (n=48) (unspecified age range) to 5 groups. 105-135 minute weekly session, 12 weeks. Group learning (including music, painting, sculpture, literature, storytelling, movement, and drama). Pre- and post-tests.	Developed empathic and interpersonal skills.	Turkey.
Rapp-Paglicci et al., 2011	To evaluate a prodigy programme for mental health and academic achievements.	At risk youth.	A quasi-experimental design.	n=108 participants aged 15-18 years (n=53 girls, n=55 boys). 3 hours per week for 8 weeks. Included visual, performing, musical, media, and theatre arts. Pre- and post-tests. Participants and parents took part in the measures.	Reduced mental health symptoms, improved aggressive and externalising behaviour, academic performance, enhanced self-regulatory skills, and increased self-efficacy.	USA.
Basso, 2010	To test a paediatric orientation group.	Paediatric inpatient children.	A mixed study. A pilot study.	n=38 participants aged 4-12 years, plus 9 nursing staff and parents. 3 months. Pre- and post-group tests.	Decreased stress, withdrawal, anger, and fear. Improved emotional	USA.

Source	Objective(s)	Target participants	Research method	Intervention / Data collection	Results	Research location
					regulation.	
Henley, 2007	To evaluate the effects of an art therapy programme (Naming the Enemy) on emotional control.	Children with bipolar.	Clinical observations.	n=4 participants aged 9-15 years (n=1 girl, n=3 boys). A total number of 32 sessions. Note: The project involved 16 children in a total of 184 sessions in 2.5 years. This article reported four cases only.	Increased self-awareness, and emotional regulation.	USA.
Rousseau, Drapeau, et al., 2005	To assess the effect of a creative expression programme on preventing emotional and behavioural disorders.	Immigrant and refugee children.	A quantitative study.	n=138 participants aged 7-13 years, immigrants and refugee children in integrated classes in 2 schools (n=57 girls, n=81 boys) (n=73 in the experimental group, n=65 in the control group) (n=51 in integration classes, n=87 in regular classes). 2-hour weekly session, 12 weeks. Pre- and post-tests.	Lowered internalising and externalising symptoms. Increased feelings of popularity and satisfaction.	Canada.
Kearns, 2004	To examine the effects of art therapy on sensory integration difficulties (for example, attention deficit hyperactivity disorder and Asperger's syndrome).	A boy who have sensory integration difficulties.	A single case study. A pilot study.	n=1 boy, 5 years old. A-B-A-B mode where A represented the no-treatment condition and B represented the intervention. 10-week training. Oil-based clay work (9 sessions), finger painting (8 sessions), and easel painting (10 sessions), and 12 control sessions. 20-minute daily session. Pre- and post-tests. Measured classroom performance.	Daily reports indicated an increase in positive behaviour and postponement of negative behaviour.	USA.
Mallay, 2002	To test the effects of art therapy on posttraumatic stress disorder.	Traumatised youth with brain injury.	A case study.	n=1 boy aged 10 years. 15 sessions; half weekly and half biweekly. Trained with sensory, cognitive, social, emotional, psychological, physical, and verbal abilities.	Reduced withdrawal behaviour and psychophysiological symptomology. Increased feelings of control and self-esteem.	USA.

Figure 1. (Continued).

Source	Objective(s)	Target participants	Research method	Intervention / Data collection	Results	Research location
Painting (n=1)						
Khadar et al., 2013	To examine the effects of painting therapy on reducing symptoms.	Elementary school boy with oppositional defiant order.	A mixed method.	n=30 participants aged 7-12 years (n=15 in the intervention group, n=15 in the control group). 40-minute per session, twice per week, 6 weeks. Art lessons involved painting, sculpting, writing a poem, telling a story, dance, and drama.	Significantly reduced symptoms. Increased adaptive behaviour and emotion. Improved communication skills.	USA.
Music (n=5)						
Porter et al., 2012	To test the effects of music therapy on mental health.	Adolescents with emotional, behavioural, and social problems.	A multi-centred single-blind randomised controlled trial.	n=198 participants aged 8-16 years from 6 centres. Randomly assigned to the intervention group (n=99), and to the control group (n=99). 30-minute per week for 12 weeks intervention (normal clinical care and music therapy). Pre- and post-tests with participants and their parents.	Improved communication and interaction skills, self-esteem, and social functioning.	Northern Ireland.
Magee et al., 2011	To assess the effects of music therapy on communication skills and social interaction.	Youth with neurobehavioural disorders due to traumatic brain injury.	Case studies.	n=2 participants aged 12-15 years. 30-minute weekly session, 8 weeks.	Improved communication skills and social interaction.	USA.
Choi, 2010	To identify psychological problems through a music therapy programme.	Refugee youth from North Korea.	A multiple case analysis.	n=9 participants aged 8-24 years (n=4 girls, n=5 boys). 25 45-minute sessions within 5 focuses (feelings about ourselves, problem solving, feelings about our family, feelings about our community, and loss healing goodbye).	Reported avoidance, distrust, loneliness, feelings of loss, and fear.	USA.
Xu et al., 2010	To test the effects of different combinations of pictures and music on	Autistic children.	A cross-sectional design.	n=14 participants aged 8-12 years. 12 pictures and 4 types of music (soundless, nursery rhyme, Samba	Showed longest attention duration to pictures of food.	China.

Source	Objective(s)	Target participants	Research method	Intervention / Data collection	Results	Research location
	emotional stimulation.			percussion, and soothing piano music).	Received longer attention period to music than to silence. 9 out of 14 children showed speech and emotional responses, for example, smiles.	
Gilboa & Ben-Shetrit, 2009	To examine how children develop compassion in a music therapy integration group.	Integrating children.	A mixed study.	n=4 participants aged 9-10 years (n=2 normal girls, n=2 boys with pervasive developmental disorder). 14 30-minute weekly sessions.	Developed compassion gradually.	USA.
Dance/movement (n=7)						
Mateos-Moreno & Atencia-Dona, 2013	To assess the effects of a combined dance and music therapy on psychopathological disorder.	Children with severe autism.	A quantitative study.	n=16 participants (unspecified age range and gender ratio) assigned to the intervention group and the control group in an equal number. 36 60-minute sessions in 17 weeks.	Enhanced attention ability, self-control and impulses.	USA.
Walter & Sat, 2013	To examine the effects of folk dance or circle dance on motor skills and emotion expression.	Kindergarten children.	A quantitative study.	Assigned participants (aged 3-6 years) to the experimental group (n=30) (n=11 girls, n=19 boys) for folk dance lessons, plus 4 staff; and to the control group (n=30) (n=13 girls, n=17 boys), plus 5 staff. 30-minute per week throughout the entire school year. Measurements in November and May.	Better adaptability, assertiveness, and identifying emotions. Significantly improved emotional intelligence abilities, and cultivation of empathy.	Israel.
Baudino, 2010	To assess the effects of dance/movement therapy on autism spectrum disorder.	Abused children.	A clinical case.	Unspecified age range and number of participant. 90-minute weekly session, 9 months.	Increased self confidence, and freedom of choice.	USA.

Figure 1. (Continued).

Source	Objective(s)	Target participants	Research method	Intervention / Data collection	Results	Research location
Thom, 2010	To explore the effects of dance/movement therapy on socio-emotional development.	Pre-school children.	Observations.	n=15 participants aged 3 years. 7 months.	Improved emotional stability. Achieved a stronger sense of self regarding an emotional, social, and cognitive being.	USA.
Christie et al., 2006	To examine the physical-psycho effects of dance and drama therapies.	Adolescents with chronic pain that affects their psychological health.	Case studies.	n=2 participants (unspecified ages). 6 sessions.	One girl reported her reintegration of body and mind and better emotional expression. Another girl showed insignificant effects while she was inactive engaged.	USA.
Jeong & Hong, 2005	To investigate the effects of dance therapy on neurohormones related to emotions.	Middle school seniors with mild depression.	A quantitative study. A preliminary study.	Randomly assigned participants (unspecified age range) to the intervention (n=20 girls) group, and to the control group (n=20 girls). 45-minute per session, 3 times per week, 12 weeks.	Moderated serotonin and dopamine. Improved psychological distress.	Korea.
Hartshorn et al., 2001	To examine the effects of movement therapy on developmental disorders.	Children with autism.	A quantitative study.	n=38 participants aged 3-7 years. 30-minute biweekly sessions, totally four sessions.	Reduced wandering time, resistance to teachers, stress, and negative responses to touching. Increased attentive behaviour and on-task behaviour.	USA.
Drama (n=11)						
Agnihotri et al., 2014	To look into the effects of theatre training on social skills and community participation.	Children with acquired brain injury.	A longitudinal multiple descriptive case study design. A pilot study.	Assigned participants (aged 13-16 years) to the intervention group (n=4), and to the control group (n=1). 4 hours per day, 4 weeks. 2 theatre artists and 1 occupational therapy students at Master level. Measured at baseline, the 4th week, and 6-8 months post interventions.	Improved social and communication skills. Increased self confidence.	USA.

Source	Objective(s)	Target participants	Research method	Intervention / Data collection	Results	Research location
Rousseau et al., 2014	To evaluate a school-based drama intervention for immigrant and refugee youth to improve mental health (emotional and behavioural) and academic results.	Secondary school students in a high multiethnic density school.	A randomised controlled trial.	Randomly assigned participants to the drama group (n=157), to the tutoring group (n=180), and to the control group (n=140); a total of n=477 students (unspecified age range). 90-minute per week, 12 weeks.	Slightly improved impairment in the first generation immigrant youth but achieved a greater improvement in the second generation.	Canada.
Pellicciari et al., 2013	To evaluate the effects of a theatre workshop "Metamorphosis Project" on improving eating behaviour and patterns.	Children with eating disorders.	A mixed method.	n=15 aged 14-19 years. 6-15 weekly sessions.	Improved obsessive thoughts and moods. Attained more knowledge about eating disorders.	Italy.
Agnihotri et al., 2012	To investigate the effects of theatre skills on social skills training.	Adolescents with childhood brain injury.	A mixed study (qualitative and quantitative inquiries). A pilot study.	n=2 female participants aged 16-17 years. 3 focus group interviews with the participants, parent and trainers at the end of the intervention. 4 hours per day, 3 weeks. 8 months post-treatment. 3 theatre artists and 3 occupational therapy students at Master level. Pre- and post-tests.	Improved social skills and self-awareness. Increased self-esteem, self-efficacy, abstract thinking and imagination, and adaptability of social environments through creative training.	USA.
Rousseau et al., 2012	To evaluate the effects of combining drama and language workshops.	Immigrant and refugee adolescents in 2 high schools (4 classes).	A mixed study. Quantitative analysis. Participant observations and interviews with students and teachers. A pilot study.	Assigned participants to the experimental group (n=27) (n=14 girls, n=13 boys), and to the comparison group (n=28) (n=16 girls, n=12 boys); a total of 55 participants (unspecified age range). 90-minute plurilingual drama weekly session, 12 weeks.	Achieved stronger feelings of empowerment, and social bonds. Improved expression of experience and feelings. Decreased impairment.	Canada.

Figure 1. (Continued).

Source	Objective(s)	Target participants	Research method	Intervention / Data collection	Results	Research location
Joronen et al., 2011	To examine the effects of a school-based drama programme on social and emotional learning.	4th-5th grades children.	A mixed study, including quantitative and qualitative methods (4 focus group interviews). A pilot study.	n=90 students aged 10-12 (n=50 girls, n=40 boys). n=16 students for interviews (n=8 girls, n=8 boys). 60-minute hour per month, 8 months, including 4-8 sessions. 1-4 home activities, plus 3 parents' evenings (13-50 participants).	Enhanced social and emotional learning. Understood diversity and consequences of bullying. Increased prosocial behaviour (friendly, positive interaction).	Finland.
Moneta & Rousseau, 2008	To explore how school-based drama therapy can facilitate emotion expression and emotional regulation.	Immigrant adolescents with behavioural disorders.	Case studies.	n=40 participants aged 13-16 years (n=20 in each of the special classes). 16 75-minute sessions, 8 weeks. A focus group with teachers after the 5th session.	Improved emotion expression (especially for anger) that facilitated emotional and social learning. Helped teachers address emotions of the students.	USA.
Rousseau et al., 2007	To evaluate a school drama therapy to prevent emotional and behavioural problems for immigrant and refugee adolescents.	Newly arrived immigrants and refugee adolescents who learned French, the official language in Quebec.	A quantitative study.	Assigned participants to the experimental group (n=66) (n=26 girls, n=40 boys), and to the control group (n=57) (n=27 girls, n=30 boys); a total of 123 aged 12-18 years in 5 integration classes; and 2 teachers. 9 weeks. Pre- and post-tests with students and teachers	Lowered the impairment level (particularly in girls). Achieved better mathematics performance (particularly in boys), and better social adjustment.	Canada.
Novy, 2005	To examine the effects of drama therapy on relation skills training.	Pre-adolescent boys with attention deficit and hyperactivity disorder.	A clinical observation.	n=2 participants (unspecific ages). 25 45-minute sessions.	Improved communication skills. Became more willingness to collaborate with other people.	USA.
Rousseau, Gauthier, et al., 2005	To look into the effects of drama therapy on reducing distress incurred by tensions of immigration.	Young immigrants and refugees.	A qualitative study.	A group of young immigrants and refugees aged 12-18 years (unspecified number of participants). 75-minute weekly sessions, 10 weeks. Participants' personal accounts, and notes jotted down by an independent	Improved behaviour and self-esteem.	Canada.

Source	Objective(s)	Target participants	Research method	Intervention / Data collection	Results	Research location
				observer.		
Perry et al., 2002	To evaluate the effects of a drama programme (All's Well That Eats Well) on eating behaviour.	Grade 1-6 students in 20 elementary schools.	A quantitative study.	n=2,893 participants aged 5-12 years randomly-assigned sequential groups. n=1,266 in 1st-3rd grades (n=633 girls, n=633 boys). n=1,627 in 4th-6th grades (n=813 girls, n=814 boys). 45-minute session. Pre- and post-tests. Follow-up activities in classroom and at home.	Learned healthier food-related knowledge. Performed food choices and food recall for fruits and vegetables.	USA.

Figure 1. Analysis of the Reviewed 33 Research Projects.

Limitations and Future Research Directions

Despite the fact that in the current literature review the expressive art based interventions exemplify how they can be used in mental care treatments pertaining to a broad range of psychological problems for children, there are only two randomised controlled trials among the 33 reviewed projects. In order to achieve more cogent results, randomised controlled studies with larger sample sizes are proposed in these creative approaches.

Although this review covers many forms of expressive art therapy, it does not include play therapy, which focuses on game-oriented activities (even though it may partly use art-related media) (Scaefer & Drewes, 2010). It is suggested that play therapy be studied separately in order to investigate how it is effective for childhood behavioural and psychological treatments (Ewing, Monsen, & Kwoka, 2014), such as those for anger management (Fischetti, 2010), posttraumatic stress disorder (Shen, 2010), and emotional problems that arise due to cancer (Adamo & De Falco, 2012) or substance abuse (Jacobus-Kantor & Emshoff, 2010).

Practical Implications

The present literature review regarding the application of different art forms to healing remarkably demonstrates positive outcomes in psychological health for adolescents (Goldstein-Roca & Crisafulli, 1994), which sheds light on implications for practices pertaining to individual and cultural suitability, a psycho-pharmaceutical model, multiple settings for both children and their parents, and enhancements in school curriculum and professional training.

While most of the reviewed interventions are carried out in group settings, four out of the 33 consist of one participant in each project, dealing with adolescents with sensory integration disorders, brain injury, mental illnesses, or abuse. These studies support effective results regarding improvements in negative behaviour, emotional regulation, self-awareness, self-esteem, and interpersonal relationships. However, a failure to draw the attention of children who have mood problems increases their resistance to treatments and lessens engagement in interventions. This reveals the importance of adaptation to individual preferences and abilities (Ritter & Low, 1996) because client-driven design (Daveson, 2008) results in effect maximisation.

Fourteen (42%) of the studies integrate different modes of expressive art, for example, music and dance (Leslie, Ojeda, & Makeig, 2014), implying an effective combination of creative therapies for children. This implication may address an extension of the use of diverse artwork; for example, the use of patchwork, needlework and embroidery (Heard, 2009; Karlsson & Malmqvist, 2013), knotting, floral arrangement (Pereira & Pereira, 2009), and calligraphy (Kwok, Bai, Kao, Li, & Ho, 2011; Zhu et al., 2014), which can cater more flexibly to person-centred planning, as discussed earlier. In emphasising individual favourites, the incorporation of such novel interventions with cultural exercises potentially strengthens their effectiveness; such as with taekwondo (He, 2015), judo (Boguszewski, Świderska, Adamczyk, & Białoszewski, 2013; Gleser & Brown, 1988), karate, martial arts (Croom, 2014; Strayhorn & Strayhorn, 2009), Tai Chi (or "taiji") (Cheng, 2015a; Song et al., 2014;

Zheng et al., 2014), Qigong (Tiwari et al., 2014; Wang et al., 2014), and Baduanjin (Cheng, 2015b; Sutherland, 2011). Meanwhile, these encouraging signs do not undermine medical methods, leading to a psycho-pharmaceutical approach in order to attain more efficient outcomes for both preventive and curative purposes.

Moreover, the integration of expressive art with other psychotherapeutic measures is becoming increasingly vogue; for example, cognitive behavioural therapy (Blacker, Watson, & Beech, 2008; Morris, 2014), psychoanalytic methods (Dosamantes-Beaudry, 2007), and animal-assisted therapy (Ford, 2013). Such eclectic means not only expand the practicality of expressive art based interventions but also develop the sophistication of available therapeutic theories and practices, offering more choices for clients.

Stress-related symptoms appear common in inpatients (Medinas-Amorós et al., 2012) which likely hinders recovery (Evagelia et al., 2001). This stress particularly impacts hospitalised children (Coyne, 2006) and their family caregivers (Van Horn & Tesh, 2000). Within the reviewed research, there is only one project dealing with inpatient adolescents, indicating insufficient studies on this population segment. Thus, more attention is required to improving the quality of life of parents and inpatient children during their hospitalisation, for which expressive art activities is a potential tool (Barrera, Rykov, & Doyle, 2002).

Employing creative therapeutic methods is not restricted to children, and is also found to be effective among adults (Johnson & Sullivan-Marx, 2006). In order to optimise intervention effectiveness, parental involvement (Regev, Kedem, & Guttmann, 2012) is strongly proposed, which benefits not only teenagers but also parents (Ponteri, 2001) who find it stressful to take care of their children with mental problems. In a practical sense, these non-conventional approaches widen its adoption from individual, group, and family perspectives (Falloon, 2003). The multiple settings (Vanderploeg, Franks, Plant, Cloud, & Tebes, 2010) explored in schools, communities, and at home allow expressive art activities to be utilised flexibly.

Research outcomes in this review likewise report the therapeutic effectiveness of expressive art activities at school, which hints at refining school curricula or extra-curriculum activities by adding such events for enhancing the mental well-being of the students. This also brings forward a discussion on appending relevant courses in the training curricula for teachers, paediatric nurses, occupational therapists, and mental health practitioners (Van Lith, Fenner, & Schofield, 2009), in order to equip them with versatility and relationship skills that are critical factors for client engagement and rapport building (Peña & Juan, 2011). Since expressive art based interventions are comparatively more economical than medicinal treatments (Porter et al., 2012), they are highly recommended for application to mental care, especially for underdeveloped countries, which will significantly save on costs.

CONCLUSION

By analysing 33 research projects on the use of expressive art based interventions in treating childhood mental illnesses, the current literature review approves the proposition that non-traditional, creative therapies are eligible for these vulnerable populations pertaining to curative, remedial, rehabilitative, and preventive purposes. It has also listed the promising indicators of such innovative body-mind approaches towards a diverse age group of adolescents across major continents, and from three to 24 years old, who suffer from emotional problems; in particular, developmental disorders and sensory integration difficulties. This review subsequently suggests the extension of the applicability and practicability of these novel and artistic techniques (that plausibly also interweave with various cultural elements) through self-expression, presenting gains in self-discovery, self-efficacy, self-assurance, and resulting in self-empowerment. It also concurs with the idea of combining art initiatives with verbal-focused therapies, which provide clients with options for catering to diverse personal needs in individual, family, and group settings. As a consequence, expressive art based approaches (such as art making, music, dance, and drama) potentially integrate into school curricula and professional training, via which these cost effective methods not only mitigate mental health expenditure burdens, but more importantly enhance individual and societal wellness. Their contributions significantly support the movement towards evidence-based, inter-disciplinary development in the health humanities, and particularly in mental care issues.

REFERENCES

Adamo, S. M. G., & De Falco, R. (2012). The role of play in the psychotherapy of a child suffering from cancer. *Psychoanalytic Social Work, 19*(1-2), 101-120. doi: 10.1080/15228878.2012.666490.

Afifi, T. O., MacMillan, H. L., Boyle, M., Taillieu, T., Cheung, K., & Sareen, J. (2014). Child abuse and mental disorders in Canada. *Canadian Medical Association Journal, Online First*. doi: 10.1503/cmaj.131792.

Afifi, T. O., Mota, N. P., Dasiewicz, P., MacMillan, H. L., & Sareen, J. (2012). Physical unishment and mental disorders. *Pediatrics, 130*(1-9). doi: 10.1542/peds.2011-2947.

Agnihotri, S., Gray, J., Colantonio, A., Polatajko, H., Cameron, D., Wiseman-Hakes, C., Rumney, P., Keightley, M. (2012). Two case study evaluations of an arts-based social skills intervention for adolescents with childhood brain disorder. *Developmental Neurorehabilitation, 15*(4), 284-297. doi: 10.3109/17518423.2012.673178.

Agnihotri, S., Gray, J., Colantonio, A., Polatajko, H., Cameron, D., Wiseman-Hakes, C., Rumney, P., Keightley, M. (2014). Arts-based social skills interventions for adolescents with acquired brain injuries: Five case reports. *Developmental Neurorehabilitation, 17*(1), 44-63. doi: 10.3109/17518423.2013.844739.

Baines, S., & Danko, G. (2010). Community mental health music therapy: A consumer-initiated song-based paradigm. *Canadian Journal of Music Therapy, 16*(1), 148-191.

Barrera, M., Rykov, M. H., & Doyle, S. L. (2002). The effects of interactive music therapy on hospitalised children with cancer: A pilot study. *Psycho-Oncology, 11*, 379-388. doi: 10.1002/pon.589.

Barrett, K. (1999). Psychiatric sequelae of acquired brain injury. *Advances in Psychiatric Treatment, 5*, 250-260.

Basso, R. (2010). Expressive arts in pediatric orientation groups. *Journal of Pediatric Nursing, 25*, 482-489. doi: 10.1016/j.pedn.2009.07.008.

Baudino, L. M. (2010). Autism spectrum disorder: A case of misdiagnosis. *American Journal of Dance Therapy, 32*, 113-129. doi: 10.1007/s10465-010-9095-x.

Ben-Avil, N., Almagor, M., & Engel-Yeger, B. (2012). Sensory processing difficulties and interpersonal relationships in adults: An exploratory study. *Psychology, 3*(1), 70-77.

Betty, A. (2013). Taming tidal waves: A dance/movement therapy approach to supporting emotion regulation in maltreated children. *American Journal of Dance Therapy, 35*, 39-59. doi: 10.1007/s10465-013-9152-3.

Birman, D., Ho, J., Pulley, E., Batia, K., Everson, M. L., Ellis, H., Betancourt, T., Gonzalez, A. (2005). *Mental health interventions for refugee children in resettlement white paper II*. Los Angeles: The National Child Traumatic Stress Network.

Bitonte, R. A., & De Santo, M. (2014). Art therapy: an underutilised, yet effective tool. *Mental Illness, 6*(5354), 18-19.

Blacker, J., Watson, A., & Beech, A. R. (2008). A combined drama-based and CBT approach to working with self-reported anger aggression. *Criminal Behaviour and Mental Health, 18*, 129-137. doi: 10.1002/cbm.686.

Boehm, K., Cramer, H., Staroszynski, T., & Ostermann, T. (2014). Arts therapies for anxiety, depression, and quality of life in breast cancer patients: A systematic review and meta-analysis. *Evidence-Based Complementary and Alternative Medicine, 2014*(Article ID 103297), 1-9. doi: 10.1155/2014/103297.

Boguszewski, D., Świderska, B., Adamczyk, J. G., & Białoszewski, D. (2013). Judo as a supplementary form of therapy for children with mental retardation. *Archives of Budo Science of Martial Arts and Extreme Sports, 9*, 85-92.

Bolwerk, A., Mack-Andrick, J., Lang, F. R., Dorfler, A., & Maihofner, C. (2014). How art changes your brain: Differential effects of visual art production and cognitive art evaluation on functional brain connectivity. *PLoS ONE, 9*(7, e101035), 1-9. doi: 10.1371/journal.pone.0101035.

Bräuninger, I. (2014). Dance movement therapy with the elderly: An international Internet-based survey undertaken with practitioners. *Body, Movement and Dance in Psychotherapy: An International Journal for Theory, Research and Practice, 9*(3), 138-153. doi: 10.1080/17432979.2014.914977.

Brauer, J. (2012). Clashes of emotions: Punk music, youth Subculture, and authority in the GDR (1978-1983). *Social Justice, 38*(4), 53-70.

Brotons, M., & Koger, S. M. (2000). The impact on music therapy on the language functioning in dementia. *Journal of Music Therapy, 37*(3), 183-195.

Brumleve, E. (2010). Expressive mask making for teens: Beginning insights. Retrieved March 1, 2015, from http://www.arttherapy.org/upload/News&Info/ExpressiveMask MakingForTeens.pdf.

Buchanan, M. (2015, January 9). Children's mental health services 'cut by £50m'. *BBC News*. Retrieved from http://www.bbc.com/news/education-30735370.

Capello, P. P. (2008). Dance/movement therapy with children throughout the world. *American Journal of Dance Therapy, 30*, 24-36. doi: 10.1007 /s10465-008-9045-z.

Cassidy, S., Turnbull, S., & Gumley, A. (2014). Exploring core processes facilitating therapeutic change in drama therapy: A grounded theory analysis of published case studies. *The Arts in Psychotherapy, 41*, 353-365.

Cattanach, A. (1995). Drama and play therapy with young children. *The Arts in Psychotherapy, 22*(3), 223-228.

Cheng, F. K. (2015a). Does movement-based Taiji contribute to mental health? A comprehensive review. *Journal of Nature and Science, 1*(5, e54), 1-10.

Cheng, F. K. (2015b). Effects of Baduanjin on mental health: A comprehensive review. *Journal of Bodywork and Movement Therapies, 19*, 138-149. doi: 10.1016/j.jbmt. 2014.11.001.

Choi, C. M. H. (2010). A pilot analysis of the psychological themes found during the CARING at Columbia-Music therapy programme with refugee adolescents from North Korea. *Journal of Music Therapy, 47*(4), 380-407.

Christie, D., Hood, D., & Griffin, A. (2006). Thinking, feeling and moving: Drama and movement therapy as an adjunct to a multidisciplinary rehabilitation approach for chronic pain in two adolescent girls. *Clinical Child Psychology and Psychiatry, 11*(4), 569-577. doi: 10.1177/ 1359104506067878.

Coqueiro, N. F., Vieira, F. R. R., & Freitas, M. M. C. (2010). Art therapy as a therapeutic tool in mental health. *Acta Paul Enferm, 23*(6), 859-862.

Couroucli-Robertson, K. (2001). Brief drama therapy of an immigrant adolescent with a speech impediment. *The Arts in Psychotherapy, 28*, 289-297.

Coyne, I. (2006). Children's experiences of hospitalization. *Journal of Child Health Care, 10*(43), 326-336. doi: 10.1177/1367493506067884.

Croom, A. M. (2014). Embodying martial arts for mental health: Cultivating psychological well-being with martial arts practice. *Archives of Budo Science of Martial Arts and Extreme Sports, 10*, 59-70.

Daveson, B. A. (2008). A description of a music therapy meta-model in neuro-disability and neuro-rehabilitation for use with children, adolescents, and adults. *The Australian Journal of Music Therapy, 19*, 70-85.

de Valenzuela, M. P. (2014). Dancing with mothers: A school-based dance/movement therapy group for Hispanic immigrant mothers. *American Journal of Dance Therapy, 36*, 92-112. doi: 10.1007/s10465-014-9166-5.

Dibbell-Hope, S. (2000). The use of dance/movement therapy in psychological adaptation to breast cancer. *The Arts in Psychotherapy, 27*(1), 51-68.

Djurichkovic, A. (2011). Art in prisons: A literature review of the philosophies and impacts of visual arts programmes for correctional populations *UTS Shopfront Student Series*. Sydney: UTSePress.

Dosamantes-Beaudry, I. (2007). Somatic transference and countertransference in psychoanalytic intersubjective dance/movement therapy. *American Journal of Dance Therapy, 29*(2), 73-89. doi: 10.1007/s10465-007-9035-6.

Erkkila, J., Punkanen, M., Fachner, J., Ala-Ruona, E., Pontio, I., Tervaniemi, M., Vanhala, M., Gold, C. (2011). Individual music therapy for depression: Randomised controlled trial. *The British Journal of Psychiatry, 199*, 132-139. doi: 10.1192/bjp.bp.110.085431.

Evagelia, K., Heleni, T., Ioanna, P., Crisoula, D., Vasilios, R., & Evagelos, K. (2001). How do patients experience stress caused by hospitalisation and how do nurses perceive this hospitalisation stress experienced by patients? A comparative study. *ICUs and Nursing Web Journal, 7*(June-October), 2-17.

Ewing, D. L., Monsen, J. J., & Kwoka, M. (2014). Behavioural and emotional well-being of children following non-directive play with school staff. *Educational Psychology in Practice: Theory, Research and Practice in Educational Psychology, 30*(2), 192-203. doi: 10.1080/ 02667363.2014.907128.

Fagen, T. S. (1982). Music therapy in the treatment of anxiety and fear in terminal pediatric patients. *Music Therapy, 2*(1), 13-21.

Falloon, I. R. H. (2003). Family interventions for mental disorders: Efficacy and effectiveness. *World Psychiatry, 2*(1), 20-28.

Farrington, Conor (2015). Music and madness: From Kontakte to the cure. *The Lancet, 2*(May), 388-390.

Finley, Susan (2014). An introduction to critical arts-based research: Demonstrating methodologies and practices of a radical ethical aesthetic. *Cultural Studies-Critical Methodologies, 14*(6) 531-532. doi: 10.1177/1532708614548123.

Fischetti, B. A. (2010). Play therapy for anger management in the schools. In A. A. Drewes & C. E. Schaefer (Eds.), *School-based play therapy* (2nd ed., pp. 283-305). New Jersey: John Wiley & Sons, Inc.

Fish, B. (1989). Addressing countertransference through image making. In H. Wadeson, J. Durkin, & D. Perach (Eds.), *Advance in art therapy* (pp. 377-389). New Jersey: John Wiley & Sons, Inc.

Flohr, J. W. (2010). Best practices for young children's music education: Guidance from brain research. *General Music Today, 23*(2), 13-19. doi: 10.1177/1048371309352344.

Ford, C. (2013). Dancing with horses: Combining dance/movement therapy and equine facilitated psychotherapy. *American Journal of Dance Therapy, 35*, 93-117. doi: 10.1007/s10465-013-9156-z.

Frank, G. K. W. (2014). Music to my brain: Could music training be used to improve adolescent brain development? *Journal of the American Academy of Child and Adolescent Psychiatry, 53*(11), 1147-1149.

Gao, T. 高. (2007). *Music therapy: Fundamental theories 音樂治療論學：基礎理論*. Beijing: World Publishing Corporation 世界圖書出版公司.

Gao, T. 高. (2008). *The introduction to music therapy 音樂治療論*. Beijing: World Publishing Corporation 世界圖書出版公司.

Gardstrom, S. C., Bartkowski, J., Willenbrink, J., & Diestelkamp, W. S. (2013). The impact of group music therapy on negative affect of people with co-occurring substance use disorders and mental illnesses. *Music Therapy Perspectives, 31*, 116-126.

Ghanizadeh, A. (2011). Sensory processing problems in children with ADHD: A systematic review. *Psychiatry Investigation, 8*(2), 89-94. doi: 10.4306/pi.2011.8.2.89.

Gilboa, A., & Ben-Shetrit, S. (2009). Sowing seeds of compassion: The case of a music therapy integration group. *The Arts in Psychotherapy, 36*, 251-260.

Gleser, J., & Brown, P. (1988). Judo principles and practices: Applications to conflict-solving strategies in psychotherapy. *American Journal of Psychotherapy, 42*(3), 437-447.

Gold, C., Mossler, K., Grocke, D., Heldal, T. O., Tjemsland, L., Aarre, T., Aaro, L., Rittmannsberger, H., Stige, B., Assmus, J., & Rolvsjord, R. (2013). Individual music therapy for mental health care clients with low therapy motivation: Multicentre randomised controlled trial. *Psychotherapy and Psychosomatics, 82*, 319-331. doi: 10.1159/ 000348452.

Goldstein-Roca, S., & Crisafulli, T. (1994). Integrative creative arts therapy: A brief treatment model. *The Arts in Psychotherapy, 21*(3), 219-222.

Groff, J. S. (2013). Expanding our "frames" of mind for education and the arts. *Harvard Educational Review, 83*(1), 15-39.

Guetin, S., Soua, B., Voiriot, G., Picot, M.-C., & Herisson, C. (2009). The effect of music therapy on mood and anxiety-depression: An observational study in institutionalised patients with traumatic brain injury. *Annals of Physical and Rehabilitation Medicine, 52*, 30-40. doi: 10.1016/ j.annrmp.2008.08.009.

Gussak, D. (2007). The effectiveness of art therapy in reducing depression in prison populations. *International Journal of Offender Therapy and Comparative Criminology, 51*(4), 444-460.

Hartshorn, K., Olds, L., Field, T., Delage, J., Cullen, C., & Escalona, A. (2001). Creative movement therapy benefits children with autism. *Early Child Development and Care, 166*(1), 1-5. doi: 10.1080/ 0300443011660101.

He, X. (2015). The influences of taekwondo of nursing school in Beihai City on the comprehensive development of health school girls. *Advances in Physical Education, 5*, 57-59.

Heard, C. (2009). Myrllen's Coat. *The Brock Review, 10*(2), 38-60.

Henley, D. (1998). Art therapy in a socialisation program for children with attention deficit hyperactivity disorder. *American Journal of Art Therapy, 37*(1), 2-12.

Henley, D. (2001). Annihilation anxiety and fantasy in the art of children with Asperger's syndrome and others on the autistic spectrum. *American Journal of Art Therapy, 39*(May), 113-121.

Henley, D. (2007). Naming the enemy: An art therapy intervention for children with bipolar and comorbid disorders. *Journal of the American Art Therapy Association, 24*(3), 104-110.

Henley, D. R. (2000). Blessings in disguise: Idiomatic expression as a stimulus in group art therapy with children. *Art Therapy: Journal of the American Art Therapy Association, 17*(4), 270-275. doi: 10.1080/07421656.2000.10129762.

Ho, R. T. H. (2000). Effects of dance movement therapy on Chinese cancer patients: A pilot study in Hong Kong. *The Arts in Psychotherapy, 32*, 337-345. doi: 10.1016/j.aip.2005.04.005.

Homann, K. B. (2010). Embodied concepts of neurobiology in dance/movement therapy practice. *American Journal of Dance Therapy, 32*, 80-99. doi: 10.1007/s10465-010-9099-6.

Jacobus-Kantor, L., & Emshoff, J. G. (2010). Play therapy for children of alcoholics. In A. A. Drewes & C. E. Schaefer (Eds.), *School-based play therapy* (2nd ed., pp. 333-357). New Jersey: John Wiley & Sons, Inc.

Jeong, Y.-J., & Hong, S.-C. (2005). Dance movement therapy improves emotional responses and modulates neurohormones in adolescents with mild depression. *International Journal of Neuroscience, 115*(12), 1711-1720. doi: 10.1080/00207450590958574.

Johnson, C. M., & Sullivan-Marx, E. M. (2006). Art therapy: Using the creative process for healing and hope among African American older adults. *Geriatric Nursing, 27*(5), 309-316. doi: 10.1016/ j.gerinurse.2006.08.010.

Johnson, D. R. (1982). Developmental approaches in drama therapy. *The Arts in Psychotherapy, 9*, 183-189.

Joronen, K., Hakamies, A., & Astedt-Kurki, P. (2011). Children's experiences of a drama programme in social and emotional learning. *Scandinavian Journal of Caring Sciences, 25*, 671-678. doi: 10.1111/j.1471-6712.2011. 00877.x.

Jung, K. H., Won, J. H., Drennan, W. R., Jameyson, E., Miyasaki, G., Norton, S. J., & Rubinstein, J. T. (2012). Psychoacoustic performance and music and speech perception in prelingually deafened children with cochlear implants. *Audiology Neurotology, 17*, 189-197. doi: 10.1159/000336407.

Kaltsatou, A. C. H., Kouidi, E. I., Anifanti, M. A., Douka, S. I., & Deligiannis, A. P. (2014). Functional and psychosocial effects of either a traditional dancing or a formal exercising training program in patients with chronic heart failure: A comparative randomised controlled study. *Clinical Rehabilitation, 28*(2), 128-138. doi: 10.1177/026921 5513492988.

Karlsson, L. B., & Malmqvist, A. (2013). “Poetry in yarn”: Making sense of life experiences in the shadow of schizophrenia. *Schizophrenia Bulletin, 39*(4), 732-736. doi: 10.1093/schbul/sbs144.

Kearns, D. (2004). Art therapy with a child experiencing sensory integration difficulty. *Art Therapy: Journal of the American Art Therapy Association, 21*(2), 95-101.

Kedem-Tahar, E., & Kellermann, P. F. (1996). Psychodrama and drama therapy. *The Arts in Psychotherapy, 23*(1), 27-36.

Khadar, M. G., Babapour, J., & Sabourimoghaddam, H. (2013). The effect of art therapy based on painting therapy in reducing symptoms of oppositional defiant disorder (ODD) in elementary school boys. *Procedia: Social and Behavioral Sciences, 84*, 1872-1878. doi: 10.1016/ j.sbspro.2013.07.051.

Kim, J. B., Kirchhoff, M., & Whitsett, S. (2011). Expressive arts group therapy with middle-school aged children from military families. *The Arts in Psychotherapy, 38*, 356-362. doi: 10.1016/j.aip.2011.08.003.

Knapp, M., Snell, T., Healey, A., Guglani, S., Evans-Lacko, S., Fernandez, J.-L., Meltzer, H., Ford, T. (2014). How do child and adolescent mental health problems influence public sector costs? Interindividual variations in a nationally representative British sample. *Journal of Child Psychology and Psychiatry, Online first*. doi: 10.1111/jcpp.12327.

Ko, K. S. (2014). Korean expressive arts therapy students' experiences with movement-based supervision: A phenomenological investigation. *American Journal of Dance Therapy, 36*, 141-159. doi: 10.1007/s10465-014-9180-7.

Koch, S., Kunz, T., Lykou, S., & Cruz, R. (2014). Effects of dance movement therapy and dance on health-related psychological outcomes: A meta-analysis. *The Arts in Psychotherapy, 41*, 46-64. doi: 10.1016/ j.aip.2013.10.004.

Koch, S. C., Morlinghaus, K., & Fuchs, T. (2007). The joy dance specific effects of a single dance intervention on psychiatric patients with depression. *The Arts in Psychotherapy, 34*, 340-349. doi: 10.1016/j.aip.2007.07.001.

Kruk, K. A., Aravich, P. F., Deaver, S. P., & deBeus, R. (2014). Comparison of brain activity during drawing and clay sculpting: A preliminary qEEG study. *Art Therapy: Journal of the American Art Therapy Association, 31*(2), 52-60. doi: 10.1080/07421656.2014. 903826.

Kwok, T. C. Y., Bai, X., Kao, H. S. R., Li, J. C. Y., & Ho, F. K. Y. (2011). Cognitive effects of calligraphy therapy for older people: A randomised controlled trial in Hong Kong. *Clinical Interventions in Aging, 6*, 269-273.

Kyaga, S., Lichtenstein, P., Boman, M., Hultman, C., Langstrom, N., & Landen, M. (2011). Creativity and mental disorder: Family study of 300000 people with severe mental disorder. *The British Journal of Psychiatry, 199*, 373-379. doi: 10.1192/ bjp.bp.110.085316.

Lai, N.-H. (2011). Expressive arts therapy for mother-child relationship (EAT-MCR): A novel model for domestic violence survivors in Chinese culture. *The Arts in Psychotherapy, 38*, 305-311. doi: 10.1016/j.aip.2011.08.001.

Lamont, S., Sutton, D., & Brunero, S. (2009). A brief report of art therapy in an inpatient mental health unit – Consumer feedback and experience. *Australia and New Zealand Journal of Art Therapy, 4*(1), 68-74.

Leslie, G., Ojeda, A., & Makeig, S. (2014). Measuring musical engagement using expressive movement and EEG brain dynamics. *Psychomusicology: Music, Mind, and Brain, 24*(1), 75-91. doi: 10.1037/pmu0000031.

Levy, F. J. (1988). *Dance/movement therapy: A healing art*. Virginia: American Alliance for Health, Physical Education, Recreation and Dance.

Lloyd, C., Wong, S. R., & Petchkovsky, L. (2007). Art and recovery in mental health: A qualitative investigation. *British Journal of Occupational Therapy, 70*(5), 207-214.

Lobban, J. (2014). The invisible wound: Veterans' art therapy. *International Journal of Art Therapy: Formerly Inscape, 19*(1), 3-18. doi: 10.1080/17454832.2012.725547.

Lorenzo-Lasa, R., Ideishi, R. I., & Ideishi, S. K. (2007). Facilitating preschool learning and movement through dance. *Early Childhood Education Journal, 35*(1), 25-31. doi: 10.1007/s10643-007-0172-9.

Mössler, K., Chen, X., Heldal, T. O., & Gold, C. (2013). Music therapy for people with schizophrenia and schizophrenia-like disorders. *Cochrane Database of Systematic Reviews, 2011*(12: CD004025), 1-70. doi: 10.1002/14651858.CD004025.pub3.

Magee, W. L., Baker, F., Daveson, B., Hitchen, H., Kennelly, J., Leung, M., & Tamplin, J. (2011). Music therapy methods with children, adolescents, and adults with severe neurobehavioural disorders due to brain injury. *Music Therapy Perspectives, 29*(1), 5-13.

Malchiodi, C. A. (2005). Expressive therapies: History, theory, and practice. In C. A. Malchiodi (Ed.), *Expressive therapies* (pp. 1-15). New York: Guilford Publications.

Mallay, J. N. (2002). Art therapy, an effective outreach intervention with traumatised children with suspected acquired brain injury. *The Arts in Psychotherapy, 29*, 159-172.

Mangerud, W. L., Bjerkeset, O., Lydersen, S., & Indredavik, M. S. (2013). Chronic pain and pain-related disability across psychiatric disorders in a clinical adolescent sample. *BMC Psychiatry, 13*(272), 1-10.

Maratos, A., Crawford, M. J., & Procter, S. (2011). Music therapy for depression: It seems to work, but how? *The British Journal of Psychiatry, 199*, 92-93. doi: 10.1192/bjp.bp.110.087494.

Mateos-Moreno, D., & Atencia-Dona, L. (2013). Effect of a combined dance/movement and music therapy on young adults diagnosed with severe autism. *The Arts in Psychotherapy, 40*, 465-472. doi: 10.1016/j.aip.2013.09.004.

McKay, M. M., Hibbert, R., Hoagwood, K., Rodriguez, J., Murray, L., Legerski, J., & Fernandez, D. (2004). Integrating evidence-based engagement interventions into 'real world' child mental health settings. *Brief Treatment and Crisis Intervention, 4*(2), 177-186. doi: 10.1093/brief-treatment/mhh014.

Medinas-Amorós, M., Montaño-Moreno, J. J., Centeno-Flores, M. J., Ferrer-Pérez, V., Renom-Sotorra, F., Martín-López, B., & Alorda-Quetglas, C. (2012). Stress associated with hospitalization in patients with COPD: The role of social support and health related quality of life. *Multidisciplinary Respiratory Medicine, 7*(51), 1-6.

Meijer-Degen, F. (2014). Art therapy for mental health workers in areas affected by violence: A rarely explored resource. *Intervention, 12*(1), 99-107.

Milia, D. (2013). Creative healing in mental health: Art and drama in assessment and therapy. *Art Therapy: Journal of the American Art Therapy Association, 30*(3), 137-138. doi: 10.1080/ 07421656.2013.819457.

Miller, A., Rubin, J., & Irwin, E. (2011). *Instructor's manual for creative healing in mental health: Art and drama in assessment and therapy*. Mill Valley: Psychotherapy.net.

Moneta, I., & Rousseau, C. (2008). Emotional expression and regulation in a school-based drama workshop for immigrant adolescents with behavioural and learning difficulties. *The Arts in Psychotherapy, 35*, 329-340. doi: 10.1016/j.aip.2008.07.001.

Morris, F. J. (2014). Should art be integrated into cognitive behavioural therapy for anxiety disorders? *The Arts in Psychotherapy, 41*, 343-352.

Morris, N. (2014). Silenced in childhood: A survivor of abuse finds her voice through group dramatherapy. *Dramatherapy, 36*(1), 3-17. doi: 10.1080/02630672.2014.926958.

Morrison, A. P. (2004). The use of imagery in cognitive therapy for psychosis: A case example. *Memory, 12*(4), 517-524.

Morrow, R. (1985). The use of art therapy in a patient with chronic schizophrenia. *Jefferson Journal of Psychiatry, 3*(1), 48-51.

Murphey, D., Barry, M., & Vaughn, B. (2013). Mental health disorders. *Child Trends, 2013*(1), 1-10.

National Research Council and Institute of Medicine. (2009). *Preventing mental, emotional, and behavioural disorders among young people: Progress and possibilities*. Washington, DC: The National Academies Press.

Novy, C. (2005). Drama therapy with pre-adolescents: A narrative perspective. *The Arts in Psychotherapy, 30*, 201-207. doi: 10.1016/S0197-4556(03)00055-8.

Odell-Miller, H. (2005). Why provide music therapy in the community for adults with mental health problems? *Voices: A World Forum for Music Therapy, 5 (1).* Retrieved March 2, 2015, from https://voices.no/ index.php/voices/article/view/220/164.

Odell-Miller, H., Hughes, P., & Westacott, M. (2006). An investigation into the effectiveness of the arts therapies for adults with continuing mental health problems. *Psychotherapy Research, 16*(1), 122-139. doi: 10.1080/10503300500268342.

Ozcan, N. K., Bilgin, H., & Eracar, N. (2011). The use of expressive methods for developing empathic skills. *Issues in Mental Health Nursing, 32*, 131-136. doi: 10.3109/01612840.2010.534575.

Padilla-Frausto, D. I., Grant, D., Aydin, M., & Aguilar-Gaxiola, S. (2014). *Three out of four children with mental health needs in California do not receive treatment despite having health care coverage*. California: UCLA Center for Health Policy Research.

Pallaro, P., & Fischlein-Rupp, A. (2002). Dance/movement therapy in a psychiatric rehabilitative day treatment setting. *The USA Body Psychotherapy Journal, 1*(2), 29-51.

Parteli, L. (1995). Aesthetic listening: Contributions of dance movement therapy to the psychic understanding of motor sterotypes and distortions in autism and psychosis in childhood and adolescence. *The Arts in Psychotherapy, 22*(3), 241-247.

Peña, A. L. N., & Juan, L. C. (2011). The experience of hospitalised children regarding their interactions with nursing professionals. *Revista Latino-Americana de Enfermagem, 19*(6), 1429-1436.

Pellicciari, A., Rossi, F., Iero, L., Di Pietro, E., Verrotti, A., & Franzoni, E. (2013). Drama therapy and eating disorders: A historical perspective and an overview of a Bolognese project for adolescents. *The Journal of Alternative and Complementary Medicine, 19*(7), 607-612. doi: 10.1089/acm.2011.0623.

Pereira, A. J., & Pereira, M. A. O. (2009). The flower workshop in psychosocial rehabilitation: A pilot study. *Issues in Mental Health Nursing, 30*, 47-50. doi: 10.1080/01612840802555216.

Perou, R., Bitsko, R. H., Blumberg, S. J., Pastor, P., Ghandour, R. M., Gfroerer, J. C., Hedden, S. L., Crosby, A. E., Visser, S. N., Schieve, L. A., Parks, S. E., Hall, J. E., Brody, D., Simile, C. M., Thompson, W. W., Baio, J., Avenevoli, S., Kogan, M. D., & Huang, L. N. (2013). Mental health surveillance among children — United States, 2005–2011. *Morbidity and Mortality Weekly Report, 62*(2), 1-35.

Perry, C. L., Zauner, M., Oakes, J. M., Taylor, G., & Bishop, D. B. (2002). Evaluation of a theatre production about eating behaviour of children. *Journal of School Health, 72*(6), 256-261.

Phelps, D. (undated). Therapeutic use of expressive arts with children. Retrieved March 1, 2015, from http://www.socialworktoday.com/archive/exc_020712.shtml.

Pinniger, R., Brown, R. F., Thorsteinsson, E. B., & McKinley, P. (2012). Argentine tango dance compared to mindfulness meditation and a waiting-list control: A randomised trial for treating depression. *Complementary Therapies in Medicine, 20*(6), 377-384. doi: 10.1016/j.ctim.2012.07.003.

Pollock, N. (2009). Sensory integration: A review of the current state of the evidence. *Occupational Therapy Now, 11*(5), 6-10.

Ponteri, A. K. (2001). The effect of group art therapy on depressed mothers and their children. *Art Therapy: Journal of the American Art Therapy Association, 18*(3), 148-157. doi: 10.1080/07421656.2001.10129729.

Porter, S., Holmes, V., McLaughlin, K., Lynn, F., Cardwell, C., Braiden, H.-J., Doran, J., & Rogan, S. (2012). Music in mind, a randomised controlled trial of music therapy for young people with behavioural and emotional problems: Study protocol. *Journal of Advanced Nursing, 68*(10), 2349-2358. doi: 10.1111/j.1365-2648.2011.05936.x.

Potash, J. S., Chen, J. Y., Lam, C. L. K., & Chau, V. T. W. (2014). Art-making in a family medicine clerkship: How does it affect medical student empathy? *BMC Medical Education, 14*(247), 1-9. doi: 10.1186/s12909-014-0247-4.

Radmall, B. (1997). Dramatherapy and eating disorders: The telling of tales: Stories about anorexia. *Dramatherapy, 19*(1), 2-4. doi: 10.1080/ 02630672.1997.9689434.

Rapp-Paglicci, L., Stewart, C., & Rowe, W. (2011). Can a self-regulation skills and cultural arts programme promote positive outcomes in mental health symptoms and academic achievement for at-risk youth? *Journal of Social Service Research, 37*(3), 309-319. doi: 10.1080/01488376. 2011.564067.

Read, J., & Bentall, R. P. (2012). Negative childhood experiences and mental health: Theoretical, clinical and primary prevention implications. *The British Journal of Psychiatry, 200*, 89-91. doi: 10.1192/bjp.bp.111.096727.

Regev, D., Kedem, D., & Guttmann, J. (2012). The effects of mothers' participation in movement therapy on the emotional functioning of their school-age children in Israel. *The Arts in Psychotherapy, 39*, 479-488.

Ren, J., & Xia, J. (2013). Dance therapy for schizophrenia. *Cochrane Database of Systematic Reviews, 2013*(10: CD006868), 1-39. doi: 10.1002/14651858.CD006868.pub3.

Richardson, P., Jones, K., Evans, C., Stevens, P., & Rowe, A. (2007). Exploratory RCT of art therapy as an adjunctive treatment in schizophrenia. *Journal of Mental Health, 16*(4), 483-491.

Riley, S. (2001). Art therapy with adolescents. *West Journal of Medicine, 175*(July), 54-57.

Ritter, M., & Low, K. G. (1996). Effects of dance/movement therapy: A meta-analysis. *The Arts in Psychotherapy, 23*(3), 249-260.

Rousseau, C., Armand, F., Laurin-Lamothe, A., Gauthier, M.-F., & Saboundjian, R. (2012). Innovations in Practice: A pilot project of school-based intervention integrating drama and language awareness. *Child and Adolescent Mental Health, 17*(3), 187-190. doi: 10.1111/j.1475-3588.2011.00629.x.

Rousseau, C., Beauregard, C., Daignault, K., Petrakos, H., Thombs, B. D., Steele, R., Vasiliadis, H.-M., & Hechtman, L. (2014). A cluster randomised-controlled trial of a classroom-based drama workshop programme to improve mental health outcomes among immigrant and refugee youth in special classes. *PLoS ONE, 9*(8, e104704), 1-10. doi: 10.1371/journal.pone.0104704.

Rousseau, C., Benoit, M., Gauthier, M.-F., Lacroix, L., Alain, N., Rojas, M. V., Moran, A., & Bourassa, B. (2007). Classroom drama therapy programme for immigrant and refugee adolescents: A pilot study. *Clinical Child Psychology and Psychiatry, 12*(3), 451-465. doi: 10.1177/1359104507078477.

Rousseau, C., Drapeau, A., Lacroix, L., Bagilishya, D., & Heusch, N. (2005). Evaluation of a classroom program of creative expression workshops for refugee and immigrant children. *Journal of Child Psychology and Psychiatry, 46*(2), 180-185. doi: 10.1111/j.1469-7610.2004.00344.x.

Rousseau, C., Gauthier, M.-F., Lacroix, L., Alain, N., Benoit, M., Moran, A., Rojas, M. V., & Bourassa, D. (2005). Playing with identities and transforming shared realities: Drama therapy workshops for adolescent immigrants and refugees. *The Arts in Psychotherapy, 32*, 13-27. doi: 10.1016/j.aip.2004.12.002.

Rousseau, C., & Guzder, J. (2008). School-based prevention programmes for refugee children. *Child and Adolescent Psychiatric Clinics of North America, 17*, 533-549. doi: 10.1016/j.chc.2008.02.002.

Scaefer, C. E., & Drewes, A. A. (2010). The Therapeutic powers of play and play therapy. In A. A. Drewes & C. E. Schaefer (Eds.), *School-based play therapy* (2nd ed., pp. 3-16). New Jersey: John Wiley & Sons, Inc.

Scharoun, S. M., Reinders, N. J., Bryden, P. J., & Fletcher, P. C. (2014). Dance/movement therapy as an intervention for children with autism spectrum disorders. *American Journal of Dance Therapy, 36*, 209-228. doi: 10.1007/s10465-014-9179-0.

Schwartz, C., Waddell, C., Barican, J., Zuberbier, O., Nightingale, L., & Gray-Grant, D. (2009). The economics of children's mental health. *Children's Mental Health Research Quarterly, 3*(1), 1-16.

Schwartzbold, M., Diaz, A., Martins, E. T., Rufino, A., Amante, L. N., Thais, M. E.,.. Walz, R. (2008). Psychiatric disorders and traumatic brain injury. *Neuropsychiatric Disease and Treatment, 4*(4), 797-816.

Shen, Y.-J. (2010). Trauma-focused group play therapy in the schools. In A. A. Drewes & C. E. Schaefer (Eds.), *School-based play therapy* (2nd ed., pp. 237-255). New Jersey: John Wiley & Sons, Inc.

Shik, A. W. Y. (2013). Integrating creative art into a community-based mental health programme for Asian American transition age youth. *Children and Youth Services Review, 35*, 377-383.

Simavli, S., Kaygusuz, I., Gumus, I., Usluogullari, B., Yildirim, M., & Kafali, H. (2014). Effect of music therapy during vaginal delivery on postpartum pain relief and mental health. *Journal of Affective Disorders, 156*, 194-199. doi: 10.1016/j.jad.2013.12.027.

Snow, S., D'Amico, M., & Tanguay, D. (2003). Therapeutic theatre and well-being. *The Arts in Psychotherapy, 30*, 73-82. doi: 10.1016/S0197-4556(03)00026-1.

Social Exclusion Unit. (2004). *Mental health and social exclusion: Social Exclusion Unit report summary*. London: Office of the Deputy Prime Minister.

Solli, H. P., & Rolvsjord, R. (2015). "The Opposite of Treatment": A qualitative study of how patients diagnosed with psychosis experience music therapy. *Nordic Journal of Music Therapy, 24*(1), 67-92. doi: 10.1080/08098131.2014.890639.

Solli, H. P., Rolvsjord, R., & Marit, B. (2013). Towards understanding music therapy as a recovery-oriented practice within mental health care: A meta-synthesis of service users' experiences. *Journal of Music Therapy, 50*(4), 244-273.

Song, Q.-H., Shen, G.-Q., Xu, R.-M., Zhang, Q.-H., Ma, M., Guo, Y.-H., Zhao, X.-P., & Han, Y.-B. (2014). Effect of Tai Chi exercise on the physical and mental health of the elder patients suffered from anxiety disorder. *International Journal of Physiology, Pathophysiology and Pharmacology, 6*(1), 55-60.

Strayhorn, J. M., & Strayhorn, J. C. (2009). Martial arts as a mental health intervention for children? Evidence from the ECLS-K. *Child and Adolescent Psychiatry and Mental Health, 3*(32), 1-9. doi: 10.1186/1753-2000-3-32.

Stuckey, H. L., & Nobel, J. (2010). The connection between art, healing, and public health: A review of current literature. *American Journal of Public Health, 100*(2), 254-263. doi: 10.2105/AJPH.2008.156497.

Sundaram, R. (1995). In focus: Art therapy with a hospitalised child. *American Journal of Art Therapy, 34*(1), 2-7.

Sussman, A. (2007). Mental illness and creativity: A neurological view of the "tortured artist." *Stanford Journal of Neuroscience, 1*(1), 21-24.

Sutherland, B. (2011). *Chi for children: A practical guide to teaching Tai Chi and Qigong in schools and the community*. London: Singing Dragon.

Sze, S., & Yu, S. (2004). *Effects of music therapy on children with disabilities*. Paper presented at the The 8th International Conference on Music Perception and Cognition, August 3-7, 2014, Evanston, USA.

Talwar, N., Crawford, M. J., Maratos, A., Nur, U., McDermott, O., & Procter, S. (2006). Music therapy for in-patients with schizophrenia: Exploratory randomised controlled trial. *British Journal of Psychiatry, 189*, 405-409. doi: 10.1192/bjp.bp.105.015073.

Taylor, C. B., Sallis, J. F., & Needle, R. (1985). The relation of physical activity and exercise to Mental Health. *Public Health Reports, 100*(2), 195-202.

Thom, L. (2010). From simple line to expressive movement: The use of creative movement to enhance socio-emotional development in the preschool curriculum. *American Journal of Dance Therapy, 32*, 100-112. doi: 10.1007/s10465-010-9090-2.

Tiwari, A., Chan, C. L. W., Ho, R. T. H., Tsao, G. S. W., Deng, W., Hong, A. W. L., Fong, D. Y. T., Fung, H., Y. K. Y., Pang, E. P. S., Cheung, D. S. T., & Ma, J. L. C. (2014). Effect of a qigong intervention program on telomerase activity and psychological stress in abused Chinese women: A randomised, wait-list controlled trial. *BMC Complementary and Alternative Medicine, 14*(300), 1-10.

Van Dyck, E., Vansteenkiste, P., Lenoir, M., Lesaffre, M., & Leman, M. (2014). Recognizing induced emotions of happiness and sadness from dance movement. *PLoS ONE, 9*(2, e89773), 1-8. doi: 10.1371/ journal.pone.0089773.

Van Horn, E., & Tesh, A. (2000). Impact of critical care hospitalisation on family members: Stress and responses. *Dimensions of Critical Care Nursing, 19*(4), 40-49.

Van Lith, T., Fenner, P., & Schofield, M. J. (2009). Towards an understanding of how art making can facilitate mental health recovery. *Australian e-Journal for the Advancement of Mental Health, 8*(2), 1-11.

Vanderploeg, J. J., Franks, R. P., Plant, R., Cloud, M., & Tebes, J. K. (2010). Extended day treatment: A comprehensive model of after school behavioural health services for youth. *Child Youth Care Forum, 38*(1), 5-18. doi: 10.1007/s10566-008-9062-6.

Wada, I., & Igarashi, A. (2014). The social costs of child abuse in Japan. *Children and Youth Services Review, 46*, 72-77. doi: 10.1016/j.childyouth. 2014.08.002.

Walter, O., & Sat, E. (2013). Dance and its influence on emotional self-control and regulation and emotional intelligence abilities among early childhood-aged children. *International Journal of Arts and Sciences, 6*(4), 77-97.

Wang, C.-W., Chan, C. H. Y., Ho, R. T. H., Chan, J. S. M., Ng, S.-M., & Chan, C. L. W. (2014). Managing stress and anxiety through qigong exercise in healthy adults: A systematic review and meta-analysis of randomised controlled trials. *BMC Complementary and Alternative Medicine, 14*(8), 1-9.

Wexler, M. (2014). A poetry programme for the very elderly: Narrative perspective on one therapeutic model. *Journal of Poetry Therapy: The Interdisciplinary Journal of Practice, Theory, Research and Education, 27*(1), 35-46. doi: 10.1080/08893675.2014.871811.

Willis, S. (1988). Group-analytic drama: A therapy for disturbed adolescents. *Group Analysis, 21*, 153-168.

World Health Organisation. (2003). *Investing in mental health*. Geneva, Switzerland: World Health Organisation.

World Health Organisation. (2012). *Adolescent mental health: Mapping actions of nongovernmental organisations and other international development organisations*. Switzerland: World Health Organisation.

World Health Organisation. (2013). *Autism spectrum disorders and other developmental disorders: From raising awareness to building capacity*. Geneva, Switzerland: World Health Organisation.

World Health Organisation. (2015). Child and adolescent mental health. Retrieved March 1 2015, from http://www.who.int/mental_health/ maternal-child/child_adolescent/en/.

Xu, M.-Y. 徐., Huang, X.-Y. 黃., Lu, Y. 陸., Xu, X.-C. 徐., Tang, Y. 唐., & Lu, P.-J. 陸. (2010). Explorative analysis on the effects of pictures and music on the attention and emotion in autistic children 圖片與音樂改善孤獨症兒童注意力與情緒的探索性分析. *Chinese Mental Health Journal 中國心理衛生雜誌, 24*(9), 696-710. doi: 10.3969/j.issn.1000-6729.2010.09.013.

Zheng, G., Lan, X., Li, M., Ling, K., Lin, H., Chen, L., Tao, J., Li, J., Zheng, X., Chen, B., & Fang, Q. (2014). The effectiveness of Tai Chi on the physical and psychological well-being of college students: A study protocol for a randomised controlled trial. *Trials, 15*(129), 1-9.

Zhu, Z., Wang, R., Kao, H. S. R., Zong, Y., Liu, Z., Tang, S., Xu, M., Liu, I. C.Y., & Lam, S. P. W. (2014). Effect of calligraphy training on hyperarousal symptoms for childhood survivors of the 2008 China earthquakes. *Neuropsychiatric Disease and Treatment, 10*, 977-985.

In: Psychological Health and Needs Research Developments ISBN: 978-1-63483-332-5
Editor: Raul Wolfe

Chapter 4

Psychological Benefits in Physical Activity and Sports

***Dr. Alejo Garcia-Naveira Vaamonde*[*1]**
***and Dr. Luz J. Locatelli Dalimier*[2]**
[1]Studies and Research Center, Club Atletico Madrid, Spain
[2]Leeds Beckett University, England

Abstract

The practice of regular and moderate Physical Activity and Sports (PAS) produces positive effects in the health, the well-being and the quality of life of the persons.

An active life benefits children, young women, adults, and disabled persons, from a well-being, preventive and rehabilitation perspective.

More, the practice of PAS helps to reduce anxiety, stress levels and depression, stimulates and supports the cognitive capacities, produces sensations of well-being and favours the establishment of other healthy associate behaviours.

Findings have demonstrated that PAS help to reduce obesity, cardiovascular problems and reduce the addictive behaviours.

The research in this field show a list of motives of the PAS practise such as the amusement, to relate to the others, the health and the competition, to keep fit. On the other hand, some factors which keep people enrolled in these activities have been found (Availability of time and facilities, social support towards the exercise, previous history of exercise, self - efficacy and positive attitude towards the exercise) and others which make people to give up the sport activities like (lack of time, smoking, no habits, no sport history), persistence give up factors (conflict between different activities, lack of time).

In summary, it is suggested to start the sport and physical activity practise since the childhood to acquire the habit to avoid sedentary behaviours and to keep good physical and psychological health levels.

---

[*] Email: alejogarcianaveira@gmail.com

INTRODUCTION

The World Health Organization (WHO, 2014) defines health as "a state of complete physical, psychological and social well-being and not merely the absence of disease" in which physical activity and sport is one of the central elements to the prevention, promotion and treatment thereof. Leading an active lifestyle can benefit children, adolescents, adulthood, late adulthood, elderly and individuals with disabilities. As Canton (2001) notes physical activity refers to exercise done in a planned, orderly, repeated and deliberate way (e.g., going to the gym two or three days a week) whereas in the case of the sport, it includes the existence of competition, the submission of relatively stable rules under structured and institutionalized organizations that regulate their practice (e.g., play in a football team where they train 2 or 3 days a week and compete on weekends). The practice of physical activity and sport regularly and moderate, but not in a high performance levels, is a factor that favours general health, while a sedentary lifestyle is associated with poor health. According to the World Health Organization (WHO, 2014), two thirds of the population is sedentary, factor responsible for 6% of deaths and the fourth between the main risks of overall mortality. It is also one of the main risk factors for many chronic diseases, diabetes, obesity, osteoporosis, certain cancers, stress and anxiety - depression. However, only a small percentage of the population meets the exercise recommendations suggested for the healthy population (see section 4). More, it is not recommended practice in certain people with certain physical or psychological pathology (see Table 1).

From this perspective, the sports physical health benefits of people is an important line of work in Science of Physical Activity, Sport and Health (doctors, psychologists, physical trainers, physiotherapists, nutritionists, etc.). There is ample scientific evidence that physically active people have higher levels of physical, psychological and social health levels and lower rates of chronic diseases (Esnaola, Infante, Goñi, & Rodriguez, 2011; Martin, Barriopedro Martinez del Castillo Jimenez -Beatty, & Rivero - Herráiz, 2014; Urrutia, Azpillaga, Luis de Cos, & Muñoz, 2010).

Table 1. Contraindications to physical activity and sports (Canton, 2001)

Severe heart desease
High blood preassure
Important presence of arrhythmias
High levels of obesity
Depressed people
People with little contact with reality
People with suicide possibilities

Active people have a lower likelihood of cardiovascular risk of oncological diseases, psychological disorders and other chronic diseases than those with sedentary lifestyles (De Miguel, Schweiger, De las Mozas, & Hernandez, 2011; Canton 2001). Moreover, physical - sporting activity is important for preventing conditions such as morbid obesity or diabetes and helps improve musculoskeletal parameters influencing the prevention of osteoporosis, arthritis, and back pain.

1. Psychological Benefits of Physical- Sport Practice

Different studies conclude that the physical activity and sport practice has significant benefits in the maintenance, enhancement and treatment of psychological health of people (Gómez- Juanes et al., 2015). Table 2 shows some representative results on this subject are presented.

Table 2. Psychological benefits of physical activity practice

Variables	References
Well-being and positive emotions	Cervelló, Peruyero, Montero, González-Cutre, Beltrán-Carrillo, & Moreno-Murcia (2014); De Miguel et al. (2011); González, Garcés de los Fayos, & García (2012); Márquez (1995); Torrents, Mateu, Planas, & Dinusôva (2011)
Depression	Herrera-Gutiérrez, Brocal-Pérez, Sánchez, & Rodríguez (2012); Ruiz and Vilella (2012)
Anxiety and stress	De Miguel et al. (2011); González-Campos, Valdivia-Moral, Zagalaz, & Romero (2015); Herrera-Gutiérrez et al. (2012); Márquez (1995); Remor & Pérez-Llantada (2007); Ruiz & Vilella (2012)
Cognitive stimulus	Cantón (2001); Márquez (1995)
Intrinsic Motivation	Cervelló et al. (2014); De Miguel et al. (2011)
Body image	Urrutia et al. (2010)
Self concept	Aróstegi, Goñi, Zubillaga, & Infante (2013); Infante, Goñi, & Villarroel (2011)
Self confidence	González-Campos et al. (2015)
Social abilities	Gil, Gutiérrez, & Madrid (2012)
Optimism	Cantón (2001); De Miguel et al. (2011); Márquez (1995).
Life quality	Martín et al. (2014)
Work productivity	De Miguel et al. (2011)
Sleep quality	Cervelló et al. (2014); De Miguel et al. (2011).

1.1. Well-Being and Psychological Health in Physical Activity and Sport

As it noted in the previous section, the physical activity and sports practice affect positively on psychological well-being and people health. Psychological variables have received special attention in recent years by sport psychology, in a positive and non-therapeutic perspective (Canton, 2010), in which besides these aspects are related directly or indirectly on the conduct sports and achieving results (Garcia - Naveira, 2010). Therefore, assessment and intervention of psychological well-being and health of people are important issues for study in the sport context.

On the one hand, we must highlight the growing importance of the perception of well – being that people have nowadays. This well-being is the personal perception that life is proceeding satisfactorily, and that the person is also aware of their personal development (Ryff & Singer, 1998). This proposal, called eudemonic, opposes the concept of happiness or simple vitality and is based on the existence of six dimensions repeatedly validated in empirical research (Van Dierendock, 2004): self-acceptance, positive relationships, autonomy, environmental mastery, growth staff and purpose in life. Direct, and previous research experience have clearly established the validity of this construct to assess favourable conditions of perception of personal well-being, in all situations, as well as physical - sport

(Romero Garcia –Mas, & Brustad, 2009; Romero, Zapata, Letelier, Lopez, & Garcia -Mas, 2013; Van Dierendock, Diaz, Rodriguez - Carvajal, White, & Moreno -Jiménez, 2008).

This model of psychological well-being has demonstrated to be useful in the field of physical activity and sport whereas sport and the sporting life are activities that require robust, high volitional capacity, autonomy, own challenges, set goals, achieve goals, grow as person, adapting to different environments and changes and for that positively interact with the environment, be healthy and maintain control over what he does (Romero, Brustad, Zapata, Aguayo, & Garcia - Ucha, 2013; Romero et al., 2009). Also be noted that persons performing physical - sport usually have a positive perception of their psychological well-being (Rivas et al., 2012; Romero et al., 2013).

On the other hand, to analyse the perception of health problems, it is necessary to resort to another framework, in order to complement the assessment athlete's state. Thus, the concept most used today is the empirical evaluation of the psychological distress associated with perceived by the general health of the people (Hilllierd & Goldberg, 1979; Hammer, Stamatakis & Septoe, 2009). Furthermore, in the field of sport performance results indicate that athletes have a perceived poor general health (Rivas et al., 2012), although it does not exactly correspond with other data, in which people who practice physical activity or amateur sports perceive a good health (De la Cruz-Sanchez, Moreno- Contreras, Pino –Ortega, & Martinez -Santos, 2011; Mota; Santos, Silva, Aires, Martins, & Vale, 2012).

Therefore, not all sports can be considered healthy (Canton & Czech, 2010). Perhaps the sport performance, sometimes doubt their high dedication and athletic demands, while the presence of injuries and pain more intensely, could affect negatively in the positive health feeling, so the development and promotion of the perception of psychological well-being and health during the career should be a fundamental principle of action of the sports psychologists (Rivas et al., 2012).

2. Sport, Adolescence, Elderly and Disable People

Once you know the psychological benefits of physical activity and sports in the general population, it is necessary to focus on three types of specific populations such as adolescents, the elderly and people with disabilities, because they tend to have special needs.

2.1. Adolescence

Adolescence is a stage on the essentially complex life cycle in which the young faces numerous obstacles and challenges and where substantial changes in personality are produced, while identity is defined, and developing a life project (Romero, Zapata Garcia - More, Brustad, Garrido, & Letelier, 2010). The adolescent period comes marked by a series of physical, social, psychological, moral and emotional changes, which suppose several variations and modifications to adolescents daiily habits, lifestyle and the way of occupying leisure time (Gonzalez & Portolés, 2013).

In general, physically active adolescents have a positive appreciation of life, they rely in other people and can establish good relationship with them, they have goals and projects, and they have personal resources to cope with the various facts or normal situations posed by the stage through which pass, looking for potentially successful situations, strengthening their self-concept and body image, achieving greater acceptance of others, gaining prestige and enhancing their self-esteem (Romero et al., 2010). And on the other hand, those who are inactive are dissatisfied with themselves have few links, have a gap between their expectations, achievements and a negative perception of the demands that the medium presents them to solve and have more personal limitations to cope with the events of everyday life.

It should be noted that there is a progressive decrease in physical activities and sports from the school stage, which is accentuated significantly in adolescence, coinciding with the pre-university period (Gonzalez et al., 2012; Herrera - Gutierrez et al., 2012). Numerous studies indicate an increase in sedentary behaviours among adolescents, taking their leisure time watching television, surfing the net, playing consoles or using mobile, reaching exist many diseases related to addiction new technologies. (Gonzalez & Portolés, 2013). The increase in hours that teens spend at the computer and television are two fundamental reasons as favouring sedentary behaviours. In addition, practice sport and physical activity in adolescents is associated with lower levels of substance abuse (e.g., alcohol, snuff and cannabis), better health habits (e.g., food and rest), as well as higher performance academic and educational motivation. Therefore, adolescence is a time to serve between the different professionals in the field, analysing the factors that enhance adhesion promotion and physical sport at this age. For example, it is important to establish good exercise habits during the early stages of life, as people keep those habits in the future, and also noted as the coach coaching style (leadership, communication, etc.) also affects psychological well-being of young people and their sport habits (Gonzalez et al., 2012), so the promotion of physical and sporting activity at an early age and the selection of specialized coaches to work with this population are a relevant issue managed by public and private institutions.

2.2. Elderly People

In recent years, in most developed countries it is emphasizing a demographic process called “aging “(Campos, Huertas, Colado, Lopez Pablos, & Pablos, 2003). Aging is a complex process involving variables genetic characteristics, lifestyles, diseases that interact with each other, and that affects all structures of the individual. As a first premise should be taken into account that aging is not only identified as a biological process (changes in cellular and organizational structures), but is also modulated by anthropological and ecological factors in certain psychological and social aspects play an important role (Pont, 2014).

In any case, without prejudice to the differences that performs dynamic individual involution of people, usually it observed 60 years as the age at which the entry is recognized in this evolutionary phase "third age" (Choque & Choque, 2015). In fact, it is from this age when the losses suffered by these people in the workplace increases, status (no longer productive assets- subject), the affective environment (loss of family and friends), or time busy. In the specific case of women and as a result of the effects of menopause, a number of characteristic symptoms such as headache, insomnia, anxiety, distress, hot flashes, sweating, weight gain, memory loss is suffered, depression, lack of concentration, flushing, palpitations, etc.

There are therefore a number of consequences of the entry into this phase of elderly who manifest both physically and psychologically. Psychologically, such a decline of physical self (body tired, rundown, slower, more awkward and less pretty than they would like to retain for life) occurs, there is a decrease in self-esteem to feel lacking in critical perspectives or denial of the body, certain disinterest in things or new objects, tendency to introversion, feelings of inferiority to the youngers, sometimes expresses itself in the form of aggression, envy and intransigence towards them is observed, or feeling disabled or useless.

Numerous studies have shown that physical exercise produces positive effects on the state of physical and psychological health of older people. Different studies have already described relationships between variables such as physical exercise and mental health, quality of life, happiness, stress, mood, anxiety, depression, self-concept and self-efficacy (Arostegi et al., 2013; Bohorquez, Lorenzo, & Garcia, 2014; Campos et al., 2003). Hence, more often they arise fitness programs and sporting activities aimed at older people promoted by public and private institutions and patterns of social intervention aimed at motivating older towards physical exercise adapted to the evolving features and adaptive for this population.

2.3. The Disability

People with disabilities are a population that requires special attention in relation to the physical - sport (Orsatti, 2004). If for the general population are obvious benefits of physical and sport, activity for specific populations as it is, the benefit and the need to practice are even greater. Inclusion - Integration is the opportunity for people with disabilities to participate openly in all activities: sports, leisure, culture, etc., that typifies today's society. Adapted sports can have different forms: physical, sensory (visual / auditory), intellectual and cerebral palsy (Reina & Sanz, 2014) disabilities. In these populations entertainment programs (sport continuous) helps improve physical health (healthy, not sedentary), improves mental health (communication and social - emotional state) and improves quality of life (standardization and welfare).

As Rocha (2012) points out, these collective sport in general is an excellent way to educate (enhanced capacity), stimulate (helps achieve new goals), entertaining (occupies leisure time), integrated (developed together or another person) and normalize (with anyone else). And in particular, the physical and psychological sport level help to improve self-esteem, personal autonomy, image, motivation, enjoy – fun, cooperation, equality, social inclusion, competitiveness, teamwork and improves mental functioning, among others.

Despite these benefits and social policies have progressed in recent years, the sports opportunities are not the same for people with disabilities, which must be respected and valued as an issue of basic human rights (Pérez, 2010). Everyone adds value to society and is in its variety where the values that define society lie. There is a right to sport, physical education which involves removal of barriers (physical and psychological), an accessible, sustainable and inclusive world (solidarity, participation and accountability).

Therefore, institutions are required to perform a wide range of sports for this group, as well as the activity is quality (adapted and resources) and organized and taught by specialist disability (Reina & Sanz, 2014) professionals.

3. Psychosocial Analysis of Physical Activity and Sports Practice

After establishing the psychological benefits of physical- sports practice for the general population, adolescents, the elderly and disabled, then a brief psychosocial and psychological analysis of physical activity and sports practice is presented, based on the nature socio- and motivational sports practice, as well as background factors / maintenance and abandonment of sportsmanship.

3.1. Social-Sport Analysis

For the understanding, promotion, prediction and intervention of behaviour in this context it is necessary to know the socio- sports population trends in general. Moreover, from a gender perspective a number of differences in the ratio of adult men and women with physical and sporting activities, which seems to indicate two sports cultures, male and female, largely of adults materialize. For reference, we note the findings of Martin et al. (2014):

- 57% of men and 50.3% of weekly practice some form of physical activity, exercise or sport adult women.
- Among women 30.4% but not practiced, you would like to do and 19.3% or practice or want to practice, while among men 25.4% but not practice, I do it and 15.6% did not practice and is interested in practicing.
- The practice of self-organized activities are the majority in both genders (80.3% men and 63.7% women), with important only practice (62.7% in men and 50.5% women) and outdoor (60.4% in men and 46.6% women). Among the most popular activities for both genders are perceived as spaces shared practice walking, bicycling and swimming.
- Men (6.69 hours) weekly practice more hours than women (4.64 hours).
- Women spend more money on monthly activity practiced (17.69 euros and 7.96 euros in women in men).
- Women (67.8%) move to the space where they practice walking more than men (42.9%).
- With regard to activities, they prefer to practice greater extent (37.4%) than men (5.9%) group activities aimed at improving health and welfare and activities of expressive character with musical support (yoga, Pilates, cycling Indoor, variants aerobics, dance or fitness training), while they prefer to practice more than women autonomous intense activities such as running (20.2% in men and 8.8% women), and soccer, competitive sports confrontational orientation (9.8% in men and 2.2% for women).

3.2. Psychological Analysis of Sports Behaviour

3.2.1. Reasons for Practice of Physical Activity and Sport

Being motivated is to have some important goals or objectives for the person that their behaviours are directed towards achieving them (Cox, 2009; Weinberg & Gould, 2010). This motivation in sport is given by a number of reasons why universal practice it, such as prescription, maintain physical fitness, psychological health, social relationships, physical appearance, racing and fun.

What matters is that each person find their motivation in the physical activity and sport practice and the benefits. Therefore, knowledge of the reasons for the physical activity and the sport practice, serve the different professionals in the field to know, explain and predict the sports behaviour.

3.2.2. Maintenance Factors, Neglect and Abandonment Persistence in Physical Activity and Sport

As Marquez (1995) stated 50% of people who start physical activity and sport leave within the first 6 months of practice due to personal, environmental and situational factors. In it, antecedents and consequences of sportsmanship as factors that make up the service or giving it are observed (Devis, 2000). Table 2 summarizes these issues:

Factor	Antecedent	Consequent
Manintenance	- Time availability - Availability of facilities - Social support toward excercise. - Previous physical activity history. - Self-efficacy and self – confidence. - Positive attitude toward excercise.	- Social support during excercise. - Moderate intensity program. - Enjoy the excercise. - Reinforcement fitness effect. - Good health perception.
Abandonment	- Lack of time. - Work or family obligations. - Smoking/overweight - Lack of previous exercise history. - Non realistic expectations. - Physical pains.	- Lack of social supoort during the excercise. - High intensity program. - Do not enjoy exercise/absence of reinforcements.

Additionally, there are some factors of persistence of drop such as lack of time, fatigue and lack of resources (Weineck, 2000). Examples include job responsibilities, family obligations, use of public or private transport, long commutes, loss of social support, alternative leisure activities, unclear motivation or objectives, inability to find new activities, lack of alternative facilities, loss physical form, etc.

These issues are important to know for the physical activity and sport and healthy activity habits among the population and to plan sports programs that enhance factors and minimize maintenance of sport dropout.

4. Guidelines to Benefit from Physical Sport

One series of suggestions or recommendations regarding proper physical activity and sports will be presented at the end of this chapter. In the last 25 years, they have proliferated exercise programs that properly designed and implemented, affect the maintenance and improvement of overall health. To do this, you should organize physical and sports activities adapted user (age, gender, special needs, etc.) profile.

As a starting point it is necessary to obtain relevant information regarding the individual, personal circumstances and context in which it operates. Therefore, a sports interview could be the first step to collect and analyse information regarding the practice of physical activity and sport, in order to establish strengths / weaknesses and an action plan for its development (Cox, 2009; Weinberg & Gould, 2010). For example, meet the psychosocial profile of the individual motivations, personal current situation, social support, sport background, medical history, physical examination, psychological diagnosis, attitudes towards sport, etc. It is also important to know sports and logistical aspects as physical offers local sports programs distance from the centre, transportation, etc.

As general guidelines for the practice of physical and sporting activities, some aspects to be considered as selecting an enjoyable exercise, adjust the intensity, duration and frequency of exercise, promote the practice of group exercises, set targets short, medium and long term, reinforce success, using music as a supplement if required, find a nearby home to practice exercise place, etc. (Devis, 2000).

Therefore, professionals in the field recommend that physical and sport activities must have certain characteristics to health benefits (Campos, Huertas, Colado, Lopez, Pablos, & Pablos, 2003; Gómez- Juanes et al., 2015; Weineck, 2000). Some representative examples:

1. Training programs longer time is more effective than shorter (e.g., 6 months vs. 1 month).
2. The greatest effects occur with aerobic activities (e.g., continuous running) than anaerobic (e.g., do strenuous sports such a squash).
3. Initially low-intensity aerobic exercise is recommended and today will give greater importance to work involving force with over 60% of maximum strength levels in order to also impact on bone density and mainly on the fast fibres that are most likely to atrophy.
4. It is estimated that aerobic exercise at the traditionally recommended doses (17 kcal / kg / week, carried out 3-5 times a week) improves health, while exercise at low doses (7 kcal / kg / week). It has no effect, in which you have to customize the dose (type, intensity, duration, frequency) for each person and increase it if necessary in stages, and to track practice to improve long-term adherence.
5. For reference, it is suggested physical exercise 2-3 days a week, with an intensity of 50-70% of heart rate and lasts between 30-45 minutes the session.
6. There is a need for monitoring and gradual adaptation of the physical activity and sport subject to the possibilities of activity, where the lack of supervision is negative for the proper adherence of the exercise.
7. Supervised exercise programs and recommend from childhood with the aim of encouraging the habit to the sport, one of the most suitable to occupy the leisure time and, simultaneously, improve health status measures.
8. It is necessary to increase physical activity in schools and in the workplace.
9. And finally, before each session should follow good stretch after and regularly visit a physical therapists, physicians, nutritionists and sports psychologists.

REFERENCES

Aróstegi, B., Goñi, A., Zubillaga, A., & Infante, G. (2013). El autoconcepto físico de jóvenes futbolistas de alto rendimiento. *Cuadernos de Psicología del Deporte*, *13*(1), 9-14.

Bohórquez, M. R., Lorenzo, M., & García, A. J. (2014). Actividad física como promotor del autoconcepto y la independencia personal en personas mayores. *Revista Iberoamericana de Psicología del Ejercicio y del Deporte*, 9(2), 533-546.

Campos, J., Huertas, F., Colado, J. C., López, A. L., Pablos, A., & Pablos, C. (2003). Efectos de un programa de ejercicio físico sobre el bienestar psicológico de mujeres mayores de 55 años. *Revista de Psicología del Deporte, 12*(1), 7-26.

Cantón, E. (2001). Deporte, salud, bienestar y calidad de vida. *Cuadernos de Psicología del Deporte, 1*(1), 27-38.

Cantón, E. (2010). La psicología del deporte como profesión especializada. *Papeles del Psicólogo, 31*(3), 237-245.

Cantón y Checa (2010). La psicología del deporte y la psicología de la salud: dos campos profesionales y un objetivo común. *Apuntes de Psicología, 28*(2), 307-314.

Cervelló, E., Peruyero, F., Montero, C., González-Cutre, D., Beltrán-Carrillo, V. J., & Moreno-Murcia, J. A. (2014). Ejercicio, bienestar psicológico, calidad de sueño y motivación situacional en estudiantes de educación física. *Cuadernos de Psicología del Deporte*, *14*(3), 31-38.

Choque, J. & Choque, S. (2015). *Actividades de animación para la tercera edad.* Editorial Paidotribo.

Cox, R. H. (2009). *Psicología del deporte: conceptos y sus aplicaciones* (6ª ed.). Madrid: Editorial.

De la Cruz-Sánchez, E., Moreno-Contreras, M.I., Pino-Ortega, J., & Martínez-Santos, R. (2011). Actividad física durante el tiempo libre y su relación con algunos indicadores de salud mental en España. *Salud Mental, 34*, 45-52.

De Miguel, J. M., Schweiger, I., De las Mozas, O., & Hernández, J. M. (2011). Efecto del ejercicio físico en la productividad laboral y el bienestar. *Revista de Psicología del Deporte, 20*(2), 589-604.

Devis, J. (2000). *Actividad física, deporte y salud.* Inde Publicaciones.

Esnaola, I., Infante, G., Goñi, E., & Rodríguez, A. (2011). Relación entre variables psicosociales y la salud percibida. *Revista de Psicología del Deporte,* 20 (2), 413-427.

García-Naveira, A. (2010). El psicólogo del deporte en el alto rendimiento: aportaciones y retos futuros. *Papeles del Psicólogo, 31*(3), 143-154.

Gil, P., Gutiérrez, E. C., & Madrid, P. D. (2012). Incrementos de las habilidades sociales a través de la expresión corporal: la experiencia en clases de iniciación al baile. *Cuadernos de Psicología del Deporte*, 12 (2), 83-88.

Goldberg, D.P. & Hillier, V.F. (1979). A scale version of the General Health Questionnaire. *Psychological Medicine, 9*, 139-145.

González, J., Garcés de los Fayos, E. J., & García, A. (2012). Indicadores de bienestar psicológico percibido en alumnos de Educación Física. *Revista de Psicología del Deporte*, *21*(1), 183-187.

Gonzalez, J. & Portolés, A. (2013). Actividad física extraescolar: relaciones con la motivación educativa, rendimiento académico y conductas asociadas a la salud. *Revista Iberoamericana de Psicología del Ejercicio y el Deporte, 9*(1), 51-65.

González-Campos, G., Valdivia-Moral, P., Zagalaz, M. L., & Romero, S. (2015). La autoconfianza y el control del estrés en futbolistas: revisión de estudios. *Revista Iberoamericana de Psicología del Ejercicio y el Deporte*, 10 (1), 95-101.

Gómez-Juanes, R., Gili, M., Roca, R., Castro, A., Lopez-Navarro, E., Crespí, C., Calafat, A., Oliván, B., Sarasa, C., Vicens, C., & Garcia-Toro, M. (2015). Prescripción de ejercicio físico en la depresión por parte de médicos de familia. factores involucrados. *Revista de Psicología del Deporte, 24*(1), 61-69.

Hammer, M., Stamatakis, E., & Steptoe, A. (2009). Dose-response relationship between physical activity and mental health: the Scotish Health Survey. *British Journal of Sports Medicine, 34*(14), 1111-1114.

Herrera-Gutiérrez, E., Brocal-Pérez, D., Sánchez, D. J., & Rodríguez, J. M. (2012). Relación entre actividad física, depresión y ansiedad en adolescentes. *Cuadernos de Psicología del Deporte*, *12*(2), 31-38.

Infante, G., Goñi, A., & Villarroel, J. D. (2011). Actividad física y autoconcepto, físico y general, a lo largo de la edad adulta. *Revista de Psicología del Deporte*, *20*(2), 429-444.

Márquez, S. (1995). Beneficios psicológicos de la actividad física. *Revista de Psicología General y Aplicada, 48*(1), 185-206.

Martín, M., Barriopedro, M. I., Martínez del Castillo, J., Jiménez-Beatty, J. E., & Rivero-Herráiz, A. (2014). Diferencias de género en los hábitos de actividad física de la población adulta en la Comunidad de Madrid. *Revista internacional de ciencias del deporte, 38*(10), 319-335.

Mota, J., Santos, R.M., Silva, P., Aires, L., Martins, C., & Vale, S. (2012). Associations between self-rated health with cardiorespiratory fitness and obesity status among adolescents girls. *Journal of Physical Activity and Health, 9*(3), 378-381.

Organización Mundial de la Salud (OMS, 2014). *Estadísticas sanitarias mundiales 2014*. Extraído el 07 de mayo de 2015 de http://apps.who.int/iris/bitstream/10665/112817/1 /WHO_HIS_HSI_14.1_spa.pdf?ua=1&ua=1&ua=1

Orsatti, L. (2004). *Deporte para discapacitados mentales*. Buenos Aires: Stadium.

Pérez, L. (2010). *Discapacidad, derecho y políticas de inclusión*. Madrid: Ediciones Cinca.

Pont, P. (2014). *Tercera edad. Actividad física y salud*. Editorial Paidotribo.

Remor, E. & Pérez-Llantada, M. (2007). La relación entre niveles de la actividad física y la experiencia de estrés y de síntomas de malestar físico. *Interamerican Journal of Psychology*, *41*(3), 313-322.

Reina, R. & Sanz, D. (2014). *Actividad física y deporte adaptado para personas con discapacidad*. Editorial Paidotribo

Rivas, C., Romero, A., Pérez-Llantada, M.C., López, A., Portau, M., Molina, I., González, J. & García-Mas, A. (2012). Bienestar psicológico, salud general, autonomía percibida y lesiones en futbolistas. *Revista de Psicología del Deporte, 21*(2), 365-371.

Rocha, M. (2012). *Discapacidad y deporte*. Lugar Editorial.

Romero, A., Brustad, R., Zapata, R., Aguayo, C., & García-Ucha, F. (2013). Bienestar psicológico y psicopatología: estudio de un caso de intervención en el equipo técnico y deportistas en un club de tenis. *Revista de Psicología del Deporte, 22* (2), 387-394.

Romero, A., García-Mas, A., & Brustad, R. (2009). Estado del arte, y perspectiva actual del concepto de bienestar psicológico en psicología del deporte. *Revista Iberoamericana de Psicología, 41*(2), 335-347.

Romero, A., Zapata, R., García-Mas, A., Brustad, R., Garrido, R., & Letelier, A. (2010). Estrategias de afrontamiento y bienestar psicológico en jóvenes tenistas de competición. *Revista de Psicología del Deporte, 19*(1), 117-133.

Romero, A., Zapata, R., Letelier, A., López, I., & Garcia-Mas, A. (2013). Autonomy, coping strategies and psychological well-being in young professional tennis players. *Spanish Journal of Psychology, 16*(e75), 1-11.

Ruiz, M. A. & Vilella, S. B. (2012). Efectos del tipo y cantidad de actividad física en la salud psicosocial de profesoras. Revista Iberoamericana de Psicología del Ejercicio y el Deporte, *7*(1), 149-162.

Ryff, C. & Singer, B. (1998). The contours of positive human health. *Journal of Psychological Inquiries, 9*(11), 1-28.

Torrents, C., Mateu, M., Planas, A., & Dinusôva, M. (2011). Posibilidades de las tareas de expresión corporal para suscitar emociones en el alumnado. *Revista de Psicología del Deporte*, *20*(2), 401-412.

Urrutia, S., Azpillaga, I., Luis de Cos, G., & Muñoz, D. (2010). Relación entre la percepción de estado de salud con la práctica físicodeportiva y la imagen corporal en adolescentes. *Cuadernos de Psicología del Deporte*, *10*(2), 51-56.

Van Dierendonck, D. (2004). The construct validity of Ryff's Scale of Psychological well-being and its extension with spiritual well-being. *Personality and Individual Differences, 36*(3), 629-644.

Van Dierendock, D., Díaz, D., Rodríguez-Carvajal, R., Blanco, A., & Moreno-Jiménez, B. (2008). Ryff's Six factor model of Psychological Well-being. A Spanish exploration. *Social Indicators Research, 87*, 473-479.

Weinberg, R. & Gould, D. (2010). *Fundamentos de Psicología del Deporte y del Ejercicio Físico*. Madrid: Editorial Médica Panamericana.

Weineck, J. (2000). *Salud, ejercicio y deporte*. Editorial Paidotribo.

In: Psychological Health and Needs Research Developments ISBN: 978-1-63483-332-5
Editor: Raul Wolfe

Chapter 5

Do Group Comparisons of Psychological Health Reveal Real Differences? The Issue of Measurement Invariance Across Groups

Fengsong Gao ***and Peter Newcombe***
University of Queensland, Brisbane, Australia

Abstract

Psychological health researchers often explore population heterogeneity regarding unobservable latent variables. The presence of substantial non-equivalence of measurement instruments across different populations creates problems. Often, measurement invariance is just ignored rather than tested. This chapter aims to highlight the importance of testing measurement invariance for Psychological health research, and to clarify biases generated from traditional comparative procedures. We designed a sample study to test mean differences of Psychological health constructs between two groups using traditional statistical procedures and multi-group confirmatory factor analysis (CFA) model with structural equation modeling (SEM). The results of the statistical analysis suggested that ignoring measurement invariance across groups may produce invalid findings. It further confirmed that measurement invariance should be tested before any mean difference comparisons of latent constructs across groups. The authors discuss an available remedy option if full measurement invariance does not hold, and propose a new approach. Implications for Psychological health research are suggested.

Introduction

Psychological health researchers often test mean differences of unobservable latent constructs across different populations (e.g., comparing social functioning between females

* Address correspondence to: Fengsong Gao, Email: annie.gao@uqconnect.edu.au

and males). In these Group comparisons, the presence of substantial non-equivalence of measurement instruments across different populations creates problems (Mellenbergh, 1989; Meredith, 1993; Schmitt & Kuljanin, 2008; Vandenberg & Lance, 2000), and hence should be understood and handled properly. However, many Psychological health studies have ignored measurement equivalence (also called measurement invariance), and applied traditional parametric statistical tests (e.g., *t*-test and ANOVA) to compare mean differences of latent constructs across diverse populations, resulting in potentially misleading findings. The significance and impact of this problem and the assumption of measurement invariance associated with relevant parametric statistical tests (e.g., ANOVA and *t* test) remain elusive in the textbooks of social and behavioural science.

This chapter aims to highlight the importance of testing measurement invariance for Psychological health research, and to clarify biases generated from traditional comparative procedures. To this end, we first introduce the concept of measurement invariance and invalid results produced by traditional comparative procedures. Then, for the purpose of illustrating that measurement invariance cannot be assumed, we designed a sample study to test mean differences of Psychological health constructs between two groups using traditional statistical procedures and multi-group confirmatory factor analysis (CFA) model with structural equation modeling (SEM).

BACKGROUND

Researchers have explored the concept of measurement invariance for more than 50 years. Mellenbergh (1989) formally stated that a measurement item is invariant if and only if

$$f(X|\ A=a,\ B=b)=f(X|\ B=b) \quad \text{(Formula 1)}$$

where X is an item response, a and b are the values of variables A and B, and function f is a conditional distribution of X. *Formula 1* implies that this conditional distribution of X given a and b are equal to given only b. Variable A can be used to represent either group memberships or time, but group memberships are the focus of this chapter. Suppose we would like to measure vitality scores (variable B) among nurses from different work settings (variable A). If and only if the distribution of item responses only rely on individual nurses' vitality scores, and work setting has no influences on item responses, the measurement of vitality is invariant across subgroups of nurses. Otherwise, measurement invariance is violated in terms of work setting; that is, the observed scores of vitality do not measure the same theoretical construct in nurses from different work settings. If measurement invariance cannot be established, mean differences between groups are not comparable (Vandenberg & Lance, 2000), thus, findings might represent a Type I or Type II error.

Since Mellenbergh's early work (1989), measurement invariance has been extensively investigated in different areas, with a focus on exploring statistical methods and procedures that can be used to assess measurement invariance. There is a general consensus that measurement invariance is testable, and it must be validated before any Group comparisons in spite of whether the instrument demonstrates excellent reliability (Mellenbergh, 1989; Meredith, 1993; Vandenberg & Lance, 2000). However, surprisingly, in practice, when comparing group mean differences, much Psychological health research has assumed measurement invariance without testing it, and this has rarely been acknowledged as a study limitation.

Measurement invariance presents many challenges for Psychological health researchers. One challenge is to understand why it matters. Psychological health research often examines population heterogeneity regarding unobservable latent variables (e.g., gender differences in the level of vitality), using self-administered questionnaires. For example, researchers have frequently used a Job Demand-Control-Support (JDCS) model (Johnson & Hall, 1988; Karasek, 1979) to investigate employees' Psychological health. The JDCS model proposes that employees experiencing excessive job demands along with inadequate coping resources (i.e., job control and support) are vulnerable to poor Psychological health. The JDCS model is still valid to study employee's Psychological health in today's working environments, although it was developed about 30 years ago (Häusser, Mojzisch, Niesel, & Schulz-Hardt, 2010). Studies applying this model often utilize self-report questionnaires to measure the latent constructs (i.e., job demands, coping resources, and Psychological health). Many of these studies made substantive cross-Group comparisons without first validating measurement invariance.

In the Group comparisons analysis of latent constructs, simply assuming measurement invariance without testing it, has led to mixed findings. For instance, in a Norwegian study, Burke and Mikkelsen (2005) compared job demands, coping resources, burnout, indicators of Psychological health, and other variables between female police officers (n=99) and male police officers (n=352). Based on findings solely from one-way ANOVA, they found very few differences on the above variables between female and male police officers. This was inconsistent with previous findings that have shown gender pervasive differences (e.g., Pancheri et al., 2002). Burke and Mikkelsen (2005) attributed this inconsistency to the cultural context of police in Norway. Another possibility may contribute to this inconsistency. It is possible that female police officers interpreted the questionnaires differently than male police officers. For example, the study used Maslach Burnout Inventory (MBI: Maslach, Jackson, & Leiter, 1996) to measure burnout. One domain of burnout, exhaustion, was assessed by five items, with 7-point Likert-type scales from 0 "never" to 6 "everyday." Higher scores indicated greater exhaustion. An example question was "I feel emotionally drained from my work." The female police officers might conceptualize the underlying meanings of exhaustion very differently from the male police officers. As a consequence, the values of "1" for exhaustion from the female respondents may not be equivalent to those from the male respondents.

Many studies have applied traditional comparative procedures (e.g., ANOVA and independent samples *t*-test) to conduct cross-Group comparisons of Psychological health (e.g., Burke & Mikkelsen, 2005; Liang, Famakin, Bowen, & Leung, 2015). Do these tests address the concern of measurement invariance? For parsimony, we use independent samples *t*-test as an example. The independent samples *t*-test (also called student *t*-test) aims to compare means between two independent groups of observations (Moore & McCabe, 2006). The test procedures involve calculating a *t*-statistic and comparing it with a critical value for the *t* distribution. If it is greater than the critical value, we reject the null hypothesis of no differences in mean scores between the two groups. The independent samples *t*-statistic is calculated based on the following formula:

$$t = \frac{\overline{x_1} - \overline{x_2}}{\sqrt{\frac{s_1^2}{n_1} + \frac{s_2^2}{n_2}}} \quad \text{(Formula 2)}$$

where $\overline{x_1}$ and $\overline{x_2}$ are the means of each group; s_1 and s_2 are standard deviations for each sample; and n_1 and n_2 are the sample sizes of each group. *Formula 2* does not account for item response bias across groups. That is, the independent samples *t* procedures assume item response equivalently across groups. Similar to the independent samples *t*-test, other traditional parametric statistical comparison procedures, for example, ANOVA and MANOVA, also assume invariance of measurement instruments across different groups.

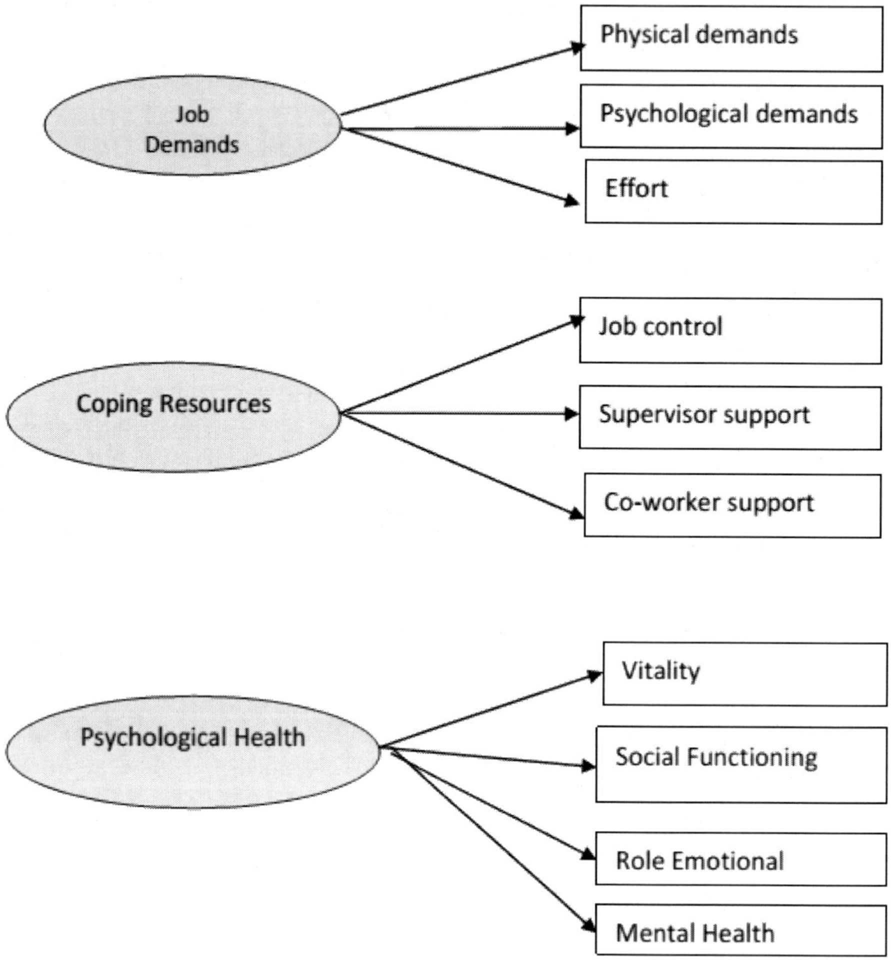

Figure 1. CFA model.

To evaluate measurement invariance across different populations, methodologists recommend using multi-group CFA models with SEM, where the equivalence of a number of measurement parameters (i.e., factor loadings, item intercepts or indicator intercepts, and error variance) are assessed (Schmitt & Kuljanin, 2008; Vandenberg & Lance, 2000; Wang &

Wang, 2012). In the following section, we applied this method with a first order multi-group CFA model (Figure 1) including three latent constructs (i.e., Job Demands, Coping Resources, and Psychological health) to demonstrate that measurement invariance is testable. In addition, traditional statistical procedures were performed to illustrate that assuming measurement invariance is inappropriate.

METHODS

Data

Data presented in this paper was derived from the Nurses and Midwives e-cohort Study (NMeS), a three-wave longitudinal survey study exploring health and work life balance among nurses and midwives in Australia, New Zealand, and the United Kingdom (Turner et al., 2009). The NMeS is particularly suitable for this study, given that it included the three variables of interest (i.e., Psychological health, Job Demands, and Coping Resources), and sampled nurses from a number of health care settings. This study was a cross-sectional analysis of baseline Australian samples of residential aged care (RAC) nurses and acute care (AC) nurses, excluding samples from New Zealand and the United Kingdom. At baseline, there were 254 nurses who indicated working in Australian RAC facilities, and 2496 nurses who reported working in Australian AC hospitals. Those who reported pregnant and/or not working at baseline and cases with extreme values and missing values across all items were eliminated from the analysis. Consequently, the samples included 244 RAC nurses and 2362 AC nurses in Australia. Due to the large discrepancy between the sample sizes of the two groups, a random subsample of 470 participants from the total AC nurses were selected for comparison with the RAC nurses (about one fifth of the total AC sample).

Variables and Measures

In line with previous research (e.g.Fillion et al., 2007; Gao, Newcombe, Tilse, Wilson, & Tuckett, 2014), the Job Content Questionnaire (JCQ: Karasek et al., 1998) and the Effort Reward Imbalance Questionnaire (ERI: Siegrist, 1996) were used to assess the latent constructs Job Demands and Coping Resources. Psychological health was measured with the Psychological health dimensions of the SF-36 Health Survey (Ware, 2000). Specifically, Job Demands were assessed by Psychological Demands and Physical Demands from the JCQ, and Effort from the ERI. Coping Resources were measured by Job Control, Supervisor Support, and Co-worker Support of the JCQ. Psychological health was indicated by Vitality, Social Functioning, Role Emotional, and Mental Health from the SF-36. Higher scores represented higher levels of job demands, greater coping resources, and better Psychological health. For a detailed description of the measurements, please refer to Gao et al. (2014). In this study, the Cronbach's alpha coefficient for each indicator ranged from.70 to.88 for RAC nurses, and from.68 to.90 for AC nurses, suggesting acceptable to good reliability (Table 1).

Table 1. Mean scores and Cronbach's α of observed indicators along with t-test analyses of Work Setting differences

Variables	Residential aged care nurses (n=244)			Acute care nurses (n=470)			t-value(df)	p-value [a]
	Mean	SD	Cronbach's α	Mean	SD	Cronbach's α		
Job Demands [b]								
Physical demands	5.01	1.58	.82	5.42	1.48	.81	3.41 (712)	.001***
Psychological demands	16.86	3.65	.73	16.86	3.54	.77	-.01(712)	.994
Effort	16.29	4.94	.81	15.94	4.83	.79	-.92(712)	.358
Coping Resources [b]								
Job control	71.88	11.14	.82	71.63	9.76	.76	-.30 (439.154) [f]	.761
Co-worker support	5.95	.99	.70	6.02	.98	.68	.88(712)	.377
Supervisor support	5.98	1.46	.88	5.76	1.55	.90	-1.82(712)	.069
Psychological health [b]								
Mental health [c]	-5.25	1.61	.83	-5.44	1.46	.82	-1.55(712)	.121
Role emotional [d]	-.82	.75	.86	-.89	.72	.86	-1.10 (474.197) [f]	.270
Social functioning [e]	-.74	.75	.81	-.67	.75	.80	1.17(712)	.242
Vitality	49.97	19.11	.85	49.43	18.49	.83	-.37(712)	.712

Notes: a.*p<.05, **p<.01, ***p<.001.

b. Higher scores represented higher levels of job demands, greater coping resources, and better Psychological health.

c. transformed mental health (MH)=-sqrt(101-MH).

d. transformed role emotional (RE)=-log(101-RE).

e. transformed social functioning (SF) =-log(101-SF).

f. t-test was run with df corrections due to heterogeneity of variance.

Analytical Strategy

To achieve normality of distribution, Role Emotional and Social Functioning were reversed reciprocal log transformed, and Mental Health was reversed reciprocal squared root transformed.

t-test and MANOVA Three sets of multivariate analysis of variance (MANOVA) were performed. Dependent variables were the indicators of each latent construct. The independent variable was Work Setting (RAC vs. AC). Then, *t*-tests were conducted to compare the mean differences for the indicators of the three latent constructs between RAC and AC nurses. *t*-tests and MANOVA were performed using SPSS 22 (IBM Corporation, 2011).

Multi-group structural equation modeling Multi-group structural equation modeling (SEM) was conducted with Mplus 7.11 statistical software (Muthén &Muthén, 2012). Work Setting was used as a grouping variable (coded 1 for RAC, and 0 for AC) in the multi-group SEM analysis.

The analysis followed procedures recommended by Wang and Wang (2012). To begin with, the first-order CFA model was used to fit RAC and AC samples separately to validate the three-factor structure for each sample. The validated models are called baseline models. If the baseline models demonstrate similar patterns of factor loadings, measurement invariance tests can be performed.That is, the two baseline models were tested simultaneously in a configural model without any parameter constraints. Then, restrictions on factor loadings and indicator intercepts were sequentially added to the measurement model by first testing metric invariance (also called weak measurement invariance, i.e., factor loadings are set equal across samples), then investigating scalar invariance (also called strong measurement invariance, i.e., both factor loadings and indicator intercepts are set equal across samples). The measurement invariance was assessed by inspecting the changes in model fit between the least-restricted model (i.e., configural model) and more restricted models (i.e., metric invariance model and scalar invariance model).

Both a non-significant p-value of likelihood ratio test (LRT) and a less than or equal to.01 change in CFI were used as indicators of measurement invariance across groups (Cheung & Rensvold, 2002). It should be noted that the more restricted models can only be tested after the less restricted models fit data well.

When examining the overall model fit, this research followed recommendations suggested by Hu and Bentler(1999) that a model is evaluated as a close fit of the data when fit indices meet the following cut-off criteria: both the Comparative Fit Index (CFI) and the Tucker-Lewis Index (TLI)$\geq$.95, the Root Mean Square Error of Approximation (RMSEA)$\leq$.06, and the Standardized Root Mean Square Residual (SRMR)$\leq$.08.

RESULTS

MANOVA

Findings from the MANOVA test indicated that there was a statistically significant difference in Job Demands between the RAC and AC nurses ($F=5.92$ (3,710), $p=.001$,Wilk's $\Lambda=.98$, and partial $\eta^2=.02$). There were no significant differences between RAC and AC nurses on Coping Resources and Psychological health.

Independent Samples *t*-Test

Table 1 shows mean scores of observed indicators by work setting. Compared with RAC nurses, AC nurses experienced statistically significant higher level of Physical Demands ($p<.001$). In terms of mean scores of other observed indicators, there were no statistically significant differences between the two groups.

Multi-Group Structural Equation Modelling

In both baseline models, indicators were significantly loaded to their latent constructs, with similar patterns of factor loadings (Table 2). Based on modification indices and theoretical justifications, one error covariance (Job Control with Physical Demands) was specified in baseline model for the RAC sample to improve model fit. The model fit indices of the two baseline models indicated that both models were a close fit of the data. Therefore, in the separate samples of AC and RAC nurses, the indicators adequately measured Job Demands, Coping Resources and Psychological health.

Table 2. Standardized estimates and model fit indices for the fitted baseline measurement models

	Residential aged care nurses (n=244)		Acute care nurses (n=470)	
Model fit indices				
RMSEA (90% CI)	.000 (.000 -.047)		.050 (.034 -.066)	
Close-fit test p-value	.966		.461	
CFI	1.000		.964	
TLI	1.001		.949	
SRMR	.037		.038	
	factor loading	R^2	factor loading	R^2
Job Demands				
Physical Demands	.35***	.12**	.44***	.19***
Psychological Demands	.62***	.38***	.55***	.30***
Effort	.93***	.86***	.98***	.97***
Coping Resources				
Control	.64***	.41***	.47***	.22***
Supervisor Support	.58***	.66***	.73***	.53***
Co-worker Support	.81***	.38***	.65***	.43***
Psychological health				
Vitality	.74***	.55***	.69***	.48***
Social Functioning [a]	.62***	.38 ***	.59***	.34***
Role Emotional [b]	.66***	.43***	.58***	.34***
Mental Health [c]	.85***	.72***	.86***	.73***
Modified path				
Physical Demands correlated with Job Control	-.37***	-	-	-

Notes: *p<.05,**p<.01, ***p<.001.

a. transformed social functioning (SF) =-log(101-SF).

b. transformed role emotional (RE)=-log(101-RE).

c. transformed mental health (MH)=-sqrt(101-MH).

Then, the measurement model was tested for configural invariance. The configural model achieved a close fit to the data (χ^2(df=63)=100.68, close-fit test p-value=.839, CFI=.98, TLI=.97, RMSEA=.04 with [90% CI=.025-.055], and SRMR=.04), suggesting that indicators were loading on the same factors in both groups. The model χ^2 statistic for the configural model was used as a baseline value for subsequent comparisons. Thereafter, metric invariance was assessed. The metric invariance model fit data well (χ^2(df=70)=111.78, close-fit test p-value=.854, CFI=.98, TLI=.97, RMSEA=.04 with [90% CI=.026-.055], and SRMR=.05). Compared with the configural model, the metric invariance model χ^2 statistic rose 11.10, with an increase of 7 df, which was not statistically significant (p=.134); with the change in CFI =.003. Therefore, the null hypothesis of metric invariance was retained, indicating that factor loadings of the first order CFA model were not significantly different between the RAC and AC nurse samples.

Finally, the model was evaluated for scalar invariance. The scalar invariance model fit data well (χ^2(df=80)= 145.41, close-fit test p-value=.597, CFI=.96, TLI=.96, RMSEA=.05 with [90% CI=.035-.060], and SRMR=.05). The difference in model χ^2 statistic between the scalar invariance model and the configural model was 44.73, with a change of 17 df, which was statistically significant (p<.001). Additionally, there was.02 change in CFI. Given that significant p-value of LRT and a greater than.01 change in CFI are indicators of measurement non-invariance across groups (Cheung & Rensvold, 2002), the measurement model failed tests of scalar measurement invariance by Work Setting.

In summary, MANOVA results indicated that Job Demands were statistically significantly different between the two groups. The independent samples *t*-test results indicated that there was a statistically significant difference between RAC and AC nurse samples in the indicator of Physical Demands. Results from the multi-group SEM analysis indicated that the factor loading of each indicator was invariant across the two groups; however, indicator intercepts were not equivalent in the two groups. That is, the indicators of the three latent constructs (i.e., Psychological health, Job Demands, and Coping Resources) did not perform equivalently in both RAC and AC nurse samples. If the latent constructs were not equivalent across the two groups, then finding a significant difference for Job Demands and not finding a significant difference for Psychological health and Coping Resources may represent errors.

Discussion

The results of the statistical analysis suggested that ignoring measurement invariance across groups may produce invalid findings. It further confirmed that measurement invariance should be tested before any mean difference comparisons of latent constructs across groups (Vandenberg & Lance, 2000).

In the more traditional procedures (i.e., independent samples *t*-test and MANOVA), the mean differences of Job Demands, Coping Resources, and Psychological health between RAC and AC nurses were tested under an assumption of measurement invariance across the two groups. However, this assumption was rejected by the multi-group CFA model with SEM, which demonstrated that there was substantial measurement non-invariance across RAC and AC groups. The test of configural invariance showed that the measurement model had the same pattern for both groups; that is, AC and RAC nurses applied similar references when responding to Job Demands, Coping Resources and Psychological health (Vandenberg & Lance, 2000). The test of metric invariance suggested that the indicators had the same scales in the two samples (Vandenberg & Lance, 2000). However, the test of scalar invariance indicated that the thresholds for these indicators were unequal in the two groups (Vandenberg & Lance, 2000). Only when metric invariance and scalar invariance are demonstrated, can further group mean differences be tested (Mellenbergh, 1989). Therefore, the analysis of mean differences of Job Demands, Coping Resources, and Psychological health between RAC and AC nurses using the independent samples *t*-test and MANOVA is not reliable and may be misleading.

If the full measurement invariance is violated, some methodologists recommend evaluating partial measurement invariance, that is, testing a subset of the measurement items, with elimination of problematic items; if the partial measurement invariance exists, Group comparisons of latent variables can be performed (Byrne, Shavelson, & Muthén, 1989). However, this approach requires theoretical justification, and potential bias should be accounted for (Vandenberg & Lance, 2000). Thus, findings based on the partial invariance model should be interpreted with caution.

Rather than excluding a subset of measurement items, we propose investigating measurement invariance by subsamples, if the full measurement invariance does not hold for the full sample. In Mellenbergh (1989)'s statistical framework (i.e., Formula 1), some other variables (e.g., age) may confound the conditional distribution. For example, respondents in one group may be significantly older than the other group and it may be age that affects the relationships between item responses and latent constructs rather than group membership. Testing the full measurement invariance by age group may eliminate the effect of age, and achieve full measurement invariance. This process involves identification of potential confounding variables and repeating the tests of measurement invariance. It allows for retention of all measurement items in line with the theoretical constructs; meanwhile, it may remedy the non-invariance of parameters, and make Group comparisons of latent variables possible. Given that this study used a secondary dataset which was not specifically designed to compare Psychological health between AC and RAC nurses, variables of interest and the sample size of RAC nurses were limited. We were unable to explore potential confounding variables with adequate sub-sample sizes. Future research could further explore this strategy to remedy the violation of measurement invariance.

Psychological health researchers are likely to encounter measurement invariance problems in Group comparisons of means, because variables of interest are often unobservable. It is important for Psychological health researchers to understand the existence of measurement invariance, and the procedures to test the measurement invariance. When designing cross-group Psychological health comparative studies, researchers should carefully choose valid instruments, and pilot test measurement invariance with target groups of interest. There is a need to provide demonstration studies to guide Psychological health researchers to conduct valid comparative studies.

Given that measurement invariance is a universal concern in all cross-Group comparisons of latent constructs in Psychological health research, it should be addressed in such research. In order for other researchers to replicate the study, researchers should report whether and how measurement invariance has been tested. If the researchers are unable to test measurement invariance for some reasons (e.g., limited skills or inability to obtain adequate sample sizes), implications of the potential biased estimates should be addressed.

In conclusion, this chapter aimed to alert Psychological health researchers to the existence of measurement non-invariance and its potential impact on identifying group differences. Psychological health researchers can test measurement invariance using modern statistical techniques (e.g., multi-group CFA model with SEM). If full measurement invariance does not hold, partial measurement invariance may be tested on the basis of theoretical justification. Alternatively, we propose that researchers may consider identifying confounding variables and testing full measurement invariance by sub samples. Much of the information on measurement invariance has been developed theoretically, but not fully articulated in the textbooks of social and behavioral science. When introducing traditional statistical comparative procedures, the textbooks should address the underlying assumption of measurement invariance. Moreover, the textbooks should provide a guide regarding how to conduct valid comparative studies in Psychological health research.

ACKNOWLEDGMENTS

The data set used in this paper was derived from a project supported by grants from the Australian Research Council (LP0562102), Australian National Health and Medical Research Council (2005002108) and New Zealand Health Research Council (456163). Industry partners providing additional funding include: Queensland Health, the South Australian Department of Health, Injury Prevention and Control Australia (Pty Ltd), Nursing Council of New Zealand and the Macquarie Bank Foundation. Industry partners providing in-kind support for the project include: Queensland Nursing Council, Nurses and Midwives Board of New South Wales, Nurses Board of Tasmania, Nurses Board of Western Australia, Nurses Board of the Australian Capital Territory and Nursing Council of New Zealand. Corporate sponsors include Virgin Blue, Virgin Atlantic and MessageNet.

Ethical approval: The University of Queensland's Behavioural and Social Science Ethical Review Committee (No. 2005000696) and Massey University Human Ethics Committee (Wellington: No. 05/71).

Conflict of interest: The authors have nothing to disclose.

REFERENCES

Burke, R. J., & Mikkelsen, A. (2005). Gender differences in policing: signs of progress? *Employee Relations, 27*(4), 425-436.

Byrne, B. M., Shavelson, R. J., & Muthén, B. (1989). Testing for the Equivalence of Factor Covariance and Mean Structures: The Issue of Partial Measurement Invariance. *Psychological Bulletin, 105*(3), 456-466.

Cheung, G. W., & Rensvold, R. B. (2002). Evaluating Goodness-of-Fit Indexes for Testing Measurement Invariance. *Structural Equation Modeling: A Multidisciplinary Journal, 9*(2), 233-255.

Fillion, L., Tremblay, I., Struthers, C. W., Dupuis, R., Côté, D., & Truchon, M. (2007). Job Satisfaction and Emotional Distress Among Nurses Providing Palliative Care: Empirical Evidence for an Integrative Occupational Stress-Model. *International Journal of Stress Management, 14*(1), 1-25.

Gao, F., Newcombe, P., Tilse, C., Wilson, J., & Tuckett, A. (2014). Models for predicting turnover of residential aged care nurses: a structural equation modelling analysis of secondary data. *International Journal of Nursing Studies, 51*(9), 1258-1270.

Häusser, J. A., Mojzisch, A., Niesel, M., & Schulz-Hardt, S. (2010). Ten years on: A review of recent research on the job demand-control (-support) model and psychological well-being. *Work & Stress, 24*(1), 1-35.

Hu, L.-t., & Bentler, P. M. (1999). Cutoff Criteria for Fit Indexes in Covariance Structure Analysis: Conventional Criteria versus New Alternatives. *Structural Equation Modeling, 6*(1), 1-55.

IBM Corporation. (2011). IBM SPSS Statistics for Windows, Version 20.0. (Version 20.0). Armonk, NY: IBM Corporation.

Johnson, J. V., & Hall, E. M. (1988). Job strain, work place social support, and cardiovascular disease: a cross-sectional study of a random sample of the Swedish working population. *American journal of public health, 78*(10), 1336-1342.

Karasek, R., Brisson, C., Kawakami, N., Houtman, I., Bongers, P., & Amick, B. (1998). The Job Content Questionnaire (JCQ): an instrument for internationally comparative assessments of psychosocial job characteristics. *Journal of Occupational Health Psychology, 3*(4), 322-355.

Karasek, R. A., Jr. (1979). Job Demands, Job Decision Latitude, and Mental Strain: Implications for Job Redesign. *Administrative Science Quarterly, 24*(2), 285-308.

Liang, Q., Famakin, I., Bowen, P., & Leung, M.-y. (2015). Development of a Job-Stress Model for Construction Professionals in South Africa and Hong Kong. *Journal of Construction Engineering and Management, 141*(2), 4014077.

Maslach, C., Jackson, S. E., & Leiter, M. P. (1996). *Maslach burnout inventory manual*. Palo Alto, Calif. (577 College Ave., Palo Alto 94306): Consulting Psychologists Press.

Mellenbergh, G. J. (1989). Item bias and item response theory. *International Journal of Educational Research, 13*(2), 127-143.

Meredith, W. (1993). Measurement invariance, factor analysis and factorial invariance. *Psychometrika, 58*(4), 525-543.

Moore, D. S., & McCabe, G. P. (2006). *Introduction to the practice of statistics*. New York: W.H. Freeman.

Muthén, L. K., & Muthén, B. O. (2012). *Mplus Statistical Analysis With Latent Variables: User's Guide* (Seventh ed.). Los Angeles, CA: Muthén & Muthén.

Pancheri, P., Martini, A., Tarsitani, L., Rosati, M. V., Biondi, M., & Tomei, F. (2002). Assessment of subjective stress in the municipal police force of the city of Rome. *Stress and Health, 18*(3), 127-132.

Schmitt, N., & Kuljanin, G. (2008). Measurement invariance: Review of practice and implications. *Human Resource Management Review, 18*(4), 210-222.

Siegrist, J. (1996). Adverse Health Effects of High-Effort/Low-Reward Conditions. *Journal of Occupational Health Psychology, 1*(1), 27-27.

Turner, C., Bain, C., Schluter, P. J., Yorkston, E., Bogossian, F., McClure, R., & Huntington, A. (2009). Cohort profile: The nurses and midwives e-cohort study - A novel electronic longitudinal study. *International Journal of Epidemiology, 38*(1), 53-60.

Vandenberg, R. J., & Lance, C. E. (2000). A Review and Synthesis of the Measurement Invariance Literature: Suggestions, Practices, and Recommendations for Organizational Research. *Organizational Research Methods, 3*(1), 4-70.

Wang, J., & Wang, X. (2012). *Structural equation modeling: applications using Mplus*. Chichester, West Sussex: Wiley.

Ware, J. J. E. (2000). SF-36 health survey update. *Spine, 25*(24), 3130-3139.

In: Psychological Health and Needs Research Developments ISBN: 978-1-63483-332-5
Editor: Raul Wolfe

Chapter 6

THE INFLUENCES OF SPIRITUAL WELL-BEING, PARENTAL REARING ATTITUDE, AND COPING STRATEGIES ON USA COLLEGE STUDENTS' ANXIETY AND DEPRESSION

Pi-Ming Yeh,*[*,1] RN, PhD
***and Cheng-Huei Chiao*[2], PhD**
[1]Associate Professor, Department of Nursing and Allied Health, Missouri Western State University, US
[2]Associate Professor, Craig School of Business, Missouri Western State University, US

ABSTRACT

Purpose: The purpose of this study was to exam the relationships between college student's spiritual well-being, parental rearing attitude, and coping strategies with their anxiety and depression.

Methods: This was a cross-sectional descriptive research design. There were 330 college students recruited from a state university in the central USA including 79 male (23.9%) and 251 female (76.1%). The mean age was 25.20 (SD = 6.83). The data were collected by structured questionnaires. The SPSS 20 was used to do the data analysis.

Results: The statistical significant factors related to Anxiety included Spiritual well-being ($r = -0.262, p \leq 0.001$), Positive Parental Rearing Attitude including *Inductive Reasoning* ($r = -0.16, p \leq 0.01$), *Communication* ($r = -0.154, p \leq 0.01$), and *Involvement* ($r = -0.132, p \leq 0.05$) as well as Negative Parental Rearing Attitude ($r = 0.22, p \leq 0.001$), *Inconsistent Discipline* ($r = 0.18, p \leq 0.001$) and *Harsh Discipline* ($r = 0.163, p \leq 0.01$). Coping strategies including *Problem Focused Disengagement* ($r = -0.316, p \leq 0.001$), *Emotion Focused Engagement* ($r = 0.29, p \leq 0.001$), and *Emotion Focused Disengagement* ($r = 0.304, p \leq 0.001$) had significant relationships with college students' anxiety. Same as Anxiety, Depression had significant relationships with those variables.

[*] Phone number: 816-271-4250, Email: pimingyeh@yahoo.com

Depression also had a significant relationship with Positive Parental Rearing Attitude ($r = -0.164, p \leq 0.01$).

Conclusion: Increasing the scores of Spiritual well-being, Positive Parental Rearing Attitude, and using Problem Focused Disengagement coping strategies decreased college students' Anxiety and Depression. Decreasing scores of Negative Parental Rearing Attitude and emotional coping strategies also decreased college students' Anxiety and Depression.

Keywords: College student, spiritual well-being, parental rearing attitude, coping strategies, anxiety and depression

INTRODUCTION

Suicidal ideation is related to the depression and anxiety that are caused by stressors in the life (Altangerel, Liou, & Yeh, 2014; Yeh & Chiao, 2013). Anxiety and depression among college students are important mental health issues to be concerned (ADAA, 2015). Anxiety disorders are one of the most common mental health problems on college campuses. Forty million U.S. adults suffer from an anxiety disorder, and 75 percent of them experience their first episode of anxiety by age 22 and most of them feel stressed and depressed (ADAA, 2015). Anxiety disorders are highly treatable, but only about one-third of those suffering receive treatment (ADAA, 2015). Anxiety disorders cost the U.S. more than $42 billion a year, almost one-third of the country's $148 billion total mental health bill (ADAA, 2015).

About 30 percent of college students reported feeling "so depressed that it was difficult to function" (NIMH, 2015). Depression is also a major risk factor for suicide (Garlow et al., 2008). More than 6 percent of college students reported seriously considering suicide, and about 1 percent reported attempting suicide in the previous year (ACHA, 2012). Suicide is the third leading cause of death for teens and young adults ages 15 to 24 (NCHS, 2012).

Although college students' anxiety and depression are important topics to discussed, but few studies examine the influences of spiritual well-being, parental rearing attitude, and coping strategies on the college students' anxiety and depression. Therefore, the purpose of this study was to exam the influences of college student's spiritual well-being, parental rearing attitude, and coping strategies on their anxiety and depression.

LITERATURE REVIEW

The research framework used for this study is the Development of Personality and Psychological Well-Being Model developed by Yeh and Chiao (2013) according to literature reviews. This framework indicates that a person's personality is developed by biological temper, parental rearing attitude, and cognitive learning. When people have stressors, people with different personalities use different coping strategies that will cause them have a good psychological well-being or anxiety and depression. During this process, spiritual well-being plays a mediator to influence the outcome variables (Yeh & Chiao, 2013). In this study, the influences of the spiritual well-being, parental rearing attitude, and coping strategies on anxiety and depression were examined.

Theoretical Framework

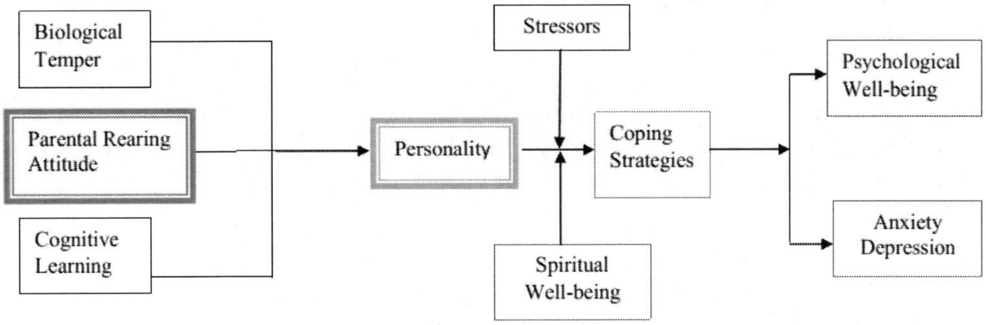

Figure 1. Development of Personality and Psychological Well-being Model (Yeh & Chiao, 2013).

The Relationships between Spiritual Well-Being with Anxiety and Depression

Most of previous studies focus on the relationship between cancer patients' spiritual well-being and their anxiety and depression. There is a positively significant relationship between spiritual well-being and hope for cancer patients (Rawdin, Evans, & Rabow, 2013). Spiritual well-being also is significantly negatively correlated with anxiety and depression (Kandasamy, Chaturvedi, & Desai, 2011). Therefore, if a cancer patient has a better spiritual well-being, he/she has higher level of hope, and lower level of anxiety and depression.

The Relationships between Parental Rearing Attitudes with Anxiety and Depression

Parental rearing attitudes are important factors to shape a person's personality (Yeh & Chiao, 2013). Parental rearing attitudes include positive rearing attitudes including child monitoring, inductive reasoning, communication, positive reinforcement, and involvement subscales and negative rearing attitudes including inconsistent discipline and harsh discipline (Melby et al., 1998). Negative family interaction is significantly and positively associated with the chances of having a mood disorder and anxiety disorder (Lincoln et al., 2010). People with the experiences of anxious and ambivalent family interaction have more obvious expression of depression and anxiety (Leveridge, Stoltenberg, & Beesley, 2005). Family interaction patterns mediated the relationship between poorer pulmonary function and child separation anxiety symptoms (Fiese, Winter, Wamboldt, Anbar, & Wamboldt, 2010). Positive daily family interactions reduce females' emotional distress and eliminate gender differences in internalizing symptoms at high levels of positive interactions (Telzer & Fuligni, 2013).

Depressive symptoms in girls were more linked to the lack of protective family factors, while depressive symptoms in boys were more linked to the existence of harmful family factors (Smojveri-Ažič & Bezinovič, 2011). Family activities and the father's warmth and affection have a higher significance for girls than for boys, while destructive parental conflict and the mother's aggression and hostility are equally significant for both girls and boys (Smojveri-Ažič & Bezinovič, 2011).

The Relationships among Coping Strategies, Anxiety, and Depression

Coping strategies include problem focus coping strategies, emotional coping strategies (Addison et al., 2007), religious and spiritual coping strategies, as well as escape and avoidance coping strategies (Manzi, 1986). Active avoidance and religious/ denial coping strategies are positively associated with state and trait anxiety (Fatima & Tahir, 2013). Problem-focused and positive coping strategies are negatively associated with state and trait anxiety (Fatima & Tahir, 2013).

Over 50% of family caregivers of patients with moderate to severe dementia had significant depression or anxiety (García-Alberca et al., 2013). Family caregivers' coping strategies were associated with care receivers' behavioral and psychological symptoms. Care receivers whose caregivers used disengagement coping strategies showed more frequent and severe behavioral and psychological symptoms than those whose caregivers used engagement coping strategies (García-Alberca et al., 2013).

METHODS

Design

A cross-sectional descriptive research design was used to examine the influences of college students' spiritual well-being, coping strategies, and their parents' rearing attitude on their anxiety and depression in the USA. Structured questionnaires were used to do the data collection.

Data Collection and Analysis

A convenience sample of 330 USA college students was recruited in this study including 253 nursing students and 77 business students. The mean age was 25.20 (*SD* = 6.83). After the researchers' explanation, if the students were willing to participate this study, they filled out the questionnaires voluntarily. After they completed the questionnaires, they got a pack of chocolate (about worthy $2). It took about 20-25 minutes to complete the questionnaires. They could stop to participate this study at any time. If they did not finish the questionnaire, they would not get the pack of chocolate. The investigators collected data from the class rooms.

The analyses were conducted using the Statistic Package for the Social Sciences (SPSS) PC Version 20.0. Descriptive statistics (mean, SD, range, frequency, and percent) were used to describe the study sample. Pearson Correlations was used to examine the relationships between independent variables (spiritual well-being, parents' rearing attitude, and coping strategies) and dependent variables (anxiety and depression). Stepwise Multiple Regression was used to examine how much of anxiety and depression were predicted by spiritual well-being, parents' rearing attitude, and coping strategies.

Instruments

Data were collected using five instruments to measure participants' spiritual well-being, parents' rearing attitude, coping strategies, anxiety, and depression. All instruments were selected for their reliability and validity.

Spiritual Well-Being Participants' spiritual well-being was measured by the 21 item *Jarel Spiritual Well-Being Scale* (Hungelmann, Kenkel-Rossi, Klassen, & Stollenwerk, 1996). Three concepts (Faith/belief dimension, Life/self-responsibility, and Life satisfaction/Self-actualization) were assessed by this questionnaire. The items were scored on a six point Likert-type scale ranging from (1) strongly disagree to (6) strongly agree. Higher scores indicate better spiritual well-being. The maximum total score is 126, and the minimum score is 21.

Evidence for the validity and reliability of the scale were examined by Hungelmann et al., 1996. The Cronbach's alpha (internal consistency reliability) was 0.84 in this study. *Parental Rearing Attitude* was measured by Iowa Family Interaction Rating Scales (Melby et al., 1998). It was used to measure parents' rearing attitude to college students in this study. There were twenty- nine questions including positive rearing attitude subscales: 21 questions (Child Monitoring, Inductive Reasoning, Communication, Positive Reinforcement, and Involvement subscales) and negative rearing attitude: 8 questions (Inconsistent Discipline and Harsh Discipline subscales). The items were scored on a five point Likert-type scale ranging from (1) Never, (2) Once in a while, (3) Sometimes, (4) A lot of time, and (5) Always. For positive rearing attitude subscales, higher scores indicate more positive rearing attitude. The maximum was 105 points, and minimum was 21 point for positive rearing attitude subscales. The Cronbach's alpha was 0.95 for positive rearing attitude subscales in this study. For negative rearing attitude subscales, higher scores indicate more negative rearing attitude. The maximum was 40 points, and minimum was 8 point for negative rearing attitude subscales. The Cronbach's alpha was 0.71 for negative rearing attitude subscales in this study.

Coping strategies Coping Strategies Inventory Short-Form (*CSI-SF*) (Addison et al., 2007) was used to measure college students' coping strategies including four subscales: Problem-Focused Engagement, Problem-Focused Disengagement, Emotion-Focused Engagement, and Emotion-Focused Disengagement subscales. There were total 16 items. The items were scored on a five point Likert-type scale ranging from (1) never to (5) almost always. Higher scores of the subscale indicated the coping strategies have been used more frequently. The Cronbach's alpha for Problem-Focused Engagement subscale was 0.83; for Problem-Focused Disengagement subscale was 0.63, for Emotion-Focused Engagement subscale was 0.58; and for Emotion-Focused Disengagement subscales 0.49 in this study.

Anxiety was measured by Hamilton Anxiety Scale (Hamilton, 1959). There were forty-two questions. The items were scored on a five point Likert-type scale ranging from (0) Not present, (1) mild, (2) Moderate, (3) Severe, and (4) Very severe. Higher scores indicate higher level of anxiety. The maximum was 168 points, and minimum was 0 point. The Cronbach's alpha was 0.92 in this study.

Depression was measured by Zung Depression Scale (Zung, 1976). There were twenty questions. The items were scored on a four point Likert-type scale ranging from (1) None or Little, (2) Some, (3) Good Part, and (4) Most or All. Higher scores indicate feeling more depressive. The maximum was 80 points, and minimum was 20 point. The Cronbach's alpha was 0.79 in this study.

RESULTS

Participants' Characteristics

The sample for this study consisted of 330 college students from a mid-west state University with 253 students coming from the Nursing department and 77 students coming from the Business department. The participants' mean age was 25.2 (SD = 6.83; range = 19-56 years) which included 23.9% males and 76.1% females. The majority of participants were white (n = 302, 91.5%), single (n = 225, 68.2%), believe in Jesus Christ (n = 270, 81.8%), had a part time job (n = 217, 65.8%), income below $1000 ($n$ = 209, 63.3%) (Table 1). Their mean anxiety level was 31.49 (SD = 18.2; range = 2-124). Their mean depression level was 34.94 (SD = 7.41; range = 21-60).

Table 1. Demographic Data Description of College Students (*N* = 330)

Variable	*n*	%	*M*	*SD*
Gender				
Male	79	23.9		
Female	251	76.1		
Age (19-56 years)			25.20	6.83
Anxiety (2-124)			31.49	18.20
Depression(21-60)			34.94	7.41
Race: White	302	91.5		
Black	14	4.2		
Asian	5	1.5		
Other	6	1.8		
Marriage				
Single	225	68.2		
Married	84	25.5		
Divorced	16	4.8		
Religion				
Believe in Jesus Christ	270	81.8		
No Religion	35	10.6		
Others	20	6.1		
Work				
Full Time	28	8.5		
Part Time	217	65.8		
Retired	4	1.2		
Unemployed	81	24.5		
Income per month				
Below $1000	209	63.3		
1000-1999	57	17.3		
2000-2999	32	9.7		
3000-3999	11	3.3		
4000-4999	6	1.8		
5000-5999	5	1.5		
6000-6999	2	0.6		
above 7000	8	2.4		

The Relationships between Spiritual Well-Being and Anxiety

In this study, spiritual well-being included 3 subscales: (1) Faith/belief, (2) Life/self responsibility, and (3) Life Satisfaction/ self-actulization. According to the Pearson Correlation, the statistical significant factors related to Anxiety included total scores of the Spiritual well-being (r = -0.262, $p \leq 0.001$), Faith/belief (r = -0.166, $p \leq 0.01$), Life/self responsibility (r = -0.259, $p \leq 0.001$), and Life Satisfaction/ self-actulization (r = -0.175, $p \leq 0.001$) (Table 2). Increasing the total scores of the Spiritual well-being and its three subscales, college students had lower level of anxiety.

Table 2. Pearson's Correlation: The influences of college students' Spiritual Well-being, Parental Rearing Attitude, and Coping Strategies with their Anxiety and Depression (*N* = 330) (r value in the box)

Variable	Anxiety	Depression
Depression	0.705***	
Spiritual Well-being	-0.262***	-0.281***
1. Faith/belief	-0.166**	-0.133*
2. Life/self responsibility	-0.259***	-0.261***
3. Life Satisfaction/ self-actulization	-0.175***	-0.265***
Positive Parental Rearing Attitude	-0.106	-0.164**
1. Child monitor	-0.037	-0.093
2. Inductive Reasoning	-0.160**	-0.212***
3. Communication	-0.154**	-0.202***
4. Positive Reinforcement	-0.032	-0.086
5. Involvement	-0.132*	-0.132*
Negative Parental Rearing Attitude	0.220***	0.211***
1. Inconsistent Discipline	0.180***	0.182***
2. Harsh Discipline	0.163**	0.146**
Coping Strategies		
Problem Focused Engagement	0.003	-0.058
Problem Focused Disengagement	-0.316***	-0.368***
Emotion Focused Engagement	0.290***	0.282***
Emotion Focused Disengagement	0.304***	0.297***

r value in the box, * $p \leq 0.05$, **$p \leq 0.01$, ***$p \leq 0.001$.

The Relationships between Spiritual Well-Being and Depression

According to the Pearson Correlation, the statistical significant factors related to Depression include total scores of the Spiritual well-being (r = -0.281, $p \leq 0.001$), Faith/belief (r = -0.133, $p \leq 0.05$), Life/self responsibility (r = -0.261, $p \leq 0.001$), and Life Satisfaction/ self-actulization (r = -0.265, $p \leq 0.001$) (Table 2). Increasing the total scores of the Spiritual well-being and its three subscales, college students had lower level of depression (Table 2).

The Relationships between Parental Rearing Attitude and Anxiety

Parental rearing attitudes included positive rearing attitude and negative rearing attitude. The positive rearing attitudes included Child Monitoring, Inductive Reasoning, Communication, Positive Reinforcement, and Involvement subscales. The negative rearing attitudes included Inconsistent Discipline and Harsh Discipline subscales. According to the Pearson Correlation, Positive Parental Rearing Attitude including *Inductive Reasoning* (r = -0.16, $p \leq 0.01$), *Communication* (r = -0.154, $p \leq 0.01$), and *Involvement* (r = -0.132, $p \leq 0.05$) as well as the total scores of Negative Parental Rearing Attitude (r = 0.22, $p \leq 0.001$), *Inconsistent Discipline* (r = 0.18, $p \leq 0.001$) and *Harsh Discipline* (r = 0.163, $p \leq 0.01$) were the statistical significant factors related to Anxiety (Table 2). When college students' parents had higher scores of using *Inductive Reasoning*, *Communication*, and *Involvement*, college students had lower level of anxiety. When college students' parents had higher scores of using Negative Parental Rearing Attitude, *Inconsistent Discipline* and *Harsh Discipline*, college students had higher level of anxiety (Table 2).

The Relationships between Parental Rearing Attitude and Depression

According to the Pearson Correlation, total scores of Positive Parental Rearing Attitude (r = -0.164, $p \leq 0.01$), *Inductive Reasoning* (r = -0.212, $p \leq 0.001$), *Communication* (r = -0.201, $p \leq 0.001$), and *Involvement* (r = -0.132, $p \leq 0.05$) as well as the total scores of Negative Parental Rearing Attitude (r = 0.211, $p \leq 0.001$), *Inconsistent Discipline* (r = 0.182, $p \leq 0.001$) and *Harsh Discipline* (r = 0.146, $p \leq 0.01$) were the statistical significant factors related to Depression (Table 2).

When college students' parents had higher scores of using Positive Parental Rearing Attitude, *Inductive Reasoning*, *Communication*, and *Involvement*, college students had lower level of depression. When college students' parents had higher scores of using Negative Parental Rearing Attitude, *Inconsistent Discipline* and *Harsh Discipline*, college students had higher level of depression (Table 2).

The Relationships between Coping Strategies and Anxiety

In this study, Coping strategies including four subscales: Problem Focused Engagement, Problem Focused Disengagement, Emotion Focused Engagement, and Emotion Focused Disengagement subscales. According to the Pearson Correlation, Problem Focused Disengagement (r = -0.316, p ≤ 0.001), Emotion Focused Engagement (r = 0.29, p ≤ 0.001), and Emotion Focused Disengagement (r = 0.304, p ≤ 0.001) had statistically significant relationships with college students' anxiety (Table 2).

When college students had higher scores of using Problem Focused Disengagement, they had lower scores of anxiety. When college students had higher scores of using Emotion Focused Engagement and Emotion Focused Disengagement coping strategies, they had higher scores of anxiety (Table 2).

The Relationships between Coping Strategies and Depression

According to the Pearson Correlation, *Problem Focused Disengagement* (r = -0.368, $p \le 0.001$), *Emotion Focused Engagement* (r = 0.282, $p \le 0.001$), and *Emotion Focused Disengagement* (r = 0.297, $p \le 0.001$) had statistically significant relationships with college students' depression (Table 2). When college students had higher scores of using *Problem Focused Disengagement*, they had lower scores of depression. When college students had higher scores of using *Emotion Focused Engagement* and *Emotion Focused Disengagement* coping strategies, they had higher scores of depression (Table 2).

Predictors of College Students' Anxiety

Stepwise Multiple Regression was used to analyze how much college students' anxiety was predicted by the independent variables (spiritual well-being, parental rearing attitude, and coping strategies). As shown in table 3, the model variables accounted for 24.4% of the anxiety variance. Lower scores of Life/self responsibility (β= -0.123, $p < 0.05$), lower scores of Problem Focused Disengagement (β = -0.225, $p < 0.001$), increasing Negative Parental Rearing Attitude (β= 0.172, $p < 0.001$), Problem *Focused Engagement* (β= 0.134, $p < 0.01$), *Emotion Focused Engagement* (β = 0.117, $p < 0.05$), *Emotion Focused Disengagement* (β= 0.226, $p < 0.001$) were found to predict significantly greater increasing anxiety (Table 3).

Table 3. Multiple Regression: The Predictors of College Students' Anxiety and Depression (N = 330) (β and t value in the box)

Variable	Anxiety		Depression	
	Beta	t	Beta	t
Spiritual Well-being				
Life/self responsibility	-0.123	-2.390*	-0.107	-2.100*
Positive Parental Rearing Attitude				
Inductive Reasoning			-0.106	-2.038*
Negative Parental Rearing Attitude	0.172	3.475***	0.119	2.302*
Coping Strategies				
Problem Focused Engagement	0.134	2.611**		
Problem Focused Disengagement	-0.225	-4.181***	-0.246	-4.679***
Emotion Focused Engagement	0.117	2.198*	0.126	2.395*
Emotion Focused Disengagement	0.226	4.296***	0.176	3.457***
R^2	0.244		0.254	
F (*d.f.*= 6, 323)	17.261***		18.328***	

* $p \le 0.05$, ** $p \le 0.01$, *** $p \le 0.001$.

Predictors of College Students' Depression

Stepwise Multiple Regression was used to analyze how much college students' depression was predicted by the independent variables (spiritual well-being, parental rearing attitude, and coping strategies). As shown in table 3, the model variables accounted for 25.4%

of the depression variance. Lower scores of Life/self responsibility (β = -0.107, $p < 0.05$), lower scores of parents using inductive reasoning (β = -0.106, $p < 0.05$), lower scores of Problem Focused Disengagement (β = -0.246, $p < 0.001$), increasing Negative Parental Rearing Attitude (β = 0.119, $p < 0.05$), higher scores of *Emotion Focused Engagement* (β = 0.126, $p < 0.05$), higher scores of *Emotion Focused Disengagement* (β = 0.176, $p < 0.001$) were found to predict significantly greater increasing the level of depression (Table 3).

Discussion

The Relationships among Spiritual Well-Being, Anxiety, and Depression

In this study, the statistical significant factors related to Anxiety include total scores of the Spiritual well-being, Faith/belief, Life/self responsibility, and Life Satisfaction/ self-actulization (Table 2). Increasing the total scores of the Spiritual well-being and its three subscales, college students had lower level of anxiety. The results are similar to the study of Mann, McKeown, Bacon, Vesselinov and Bush in 2008. Mann et al. (2008) indicated that religiosity and spirituality were significantly related to reducing anxiety in pregnant women. Overall religiosity or spirituality and social support were significantly related to significantly lower anxiety.

The possible reason of this result was that spiritual well-being played an important role of coping mechanism to resolve the stressors. Spirituality provides a way to understand the meaning of life when face difficult circumstances (Mann et al., 2008). While religiosity provides people with a belief in a superpower that ultimate control over life's uncertainties (Mann et al., 2008).

Musarezaie, Naji Esfahani, Momeni Ghaleghasemi, Karimian, and Ebrahimi (2012) examined the relationship between spiritual wellbeing and stress, anxiety, and depression in patients with breast cancer. They indicated that there were reversed statistically significant relationships between spiritual well-being and stress, anxiety, and depression in patients with breast cancer (Musarezaie et al., 2012). Their results were similar to the results in this study. Although their participants were cancer patients, in study, the participants were college students. The results in this study indicated that there were significant inverse relationships between depression and total scores of the Spiritual well-being, Faith/belief, Life/self responsibility, and Life Satisfaction/ self-actulization. Increasing the total scores of the Spiritual well-being and its three subscales, college students had lower level of depression.

The Relationships among Parental Rearing Attitudes, Anxiety, and Depression

In this study, when college students' parents had higher scores of using Inductive Reasoning, Communication, and Involvement, college students had lower level of anxiety. When college students' parents had higher scores of using Negative Parental Rearing

Attitude, Inconsistent Discipline and Harsh Discipline, college students had higher level of anxiety. The results of this study are similar to Yoshihiro's results in 2014.

Yoshihiro (2014) examined adolescents' internal working models of attachment as a mediator between their social adjustment and parental child-Rearing Attitudes. The results of Yoshihiro's study indicated that adolescents who lacked their maternal care showed highly avoidant attachment, while those who felt overprotected by their mother showed highly anxious attachment.

Yoshihiro (2014) also indicated that higher" anxiety" resulted in lower self-esteem (an index of intrapersonal adjustment) and higher "avoidance of being injured" (an index of interpersonal adjustment), while higher "avoidance" resulted in lower self-esteem and higher "surficial relationship" and "avoidance of being injured" (indices of interpersonal adjustment) (Yoshihiro, 2014). Therefore, negative recognition of parental child-rearing attitudes led to insecure attachment, and that insecure attachment led to social adjustment difficulties (Yoshihiro, 2014).

In this study, when college students' parents had higher scores of using Positive Parental Rearing Attitude, Inductive Reasoning, Communication, and Involvement, college students had lower level of depression. When college students' parents had higher scores of using Negative Parental Rearing Attitude, Inconsistent Discipline and Harsh Discipline, college students had higher level of depression. The results of this study are similar to the study of Telzer and Fuligni, in 2013. Telzer and Fuligni (2013) indicated that negative daily family interactions increased adolescent girls' experiences of increasing internalizing symptoms (Telzer & Fuligni, 2013). Positive daily family interactions reduce adolescent girls' emotional distress and eliminating gender differences in internalizing symptoms (Telzer & Fuligni, 2013). Therefore, it is importance of positive family interactions for adolescent girls' mental health.

The Relationships among Coping Strategies, Anxiety, and Depression

According to the results of this study, when college students had higher scores of using Problem Focused Disengagement, they had lower scores of anxiety and depression. When college students had higher scores of using Emotion Focused Engagement and Emotion Focused Disengagement coping strategies, they had higher scores of anxiety and depression. These results are similar to Yeh's study results in 2013. Yeh and Chiao (2013) indicated that higher scores of problem-focused engagement, higher scores of problem-focused disengagement and lower scores of emotion-focused disengagement were found to predict significantly higher scores of psychological well-being (Yeh & Chiao, 2013).

Although stressors influenced the level of psychological well-being directly, coping self-efficacy still mediates significantly between distress and psychological well-being (Wissing et al., 2011). Self-efficacy, dispositional control and support are important predictors of psychological well-being, and avoidance coping is the strongest predictor of adverse psychological well-being (Gibbons, Dempster, & Moutray, 2011). Therefore, initiatives to promote support and self-efficacy are likely to have immediate benefits for students' psychological well-being (Gibbons et al., 2011). Jaser, Champion, Dharamsi, Riesing, and Compas (2011) indicated that coping as a protective factor, related to higher levels of positive affect and fewer depressive symptoms, in adolescents exposed to maternal depressive symptoms (Jaser et al., 2011).

REFERENCES

Addison, C.C., Campbell-Jenkins, B. W., Sarpong, D. F., Kibler, J., Singh, M., Dubbert, P., Wilson, G., Payne, T., Taylor, H. (2007). Psychometric evaluation of a Coping Strategies Inventory Short-Form (CSI-SF) in the Jackson Heart Study cohort. *International Journal of Environmental Research and Public Health, 4*(4), 289-295.

Altangerel, U., Liou, J. C., & Yeh, P. M. (2014). Prevalence and Predictors of Suicidal Behavior among Mongolian High School Students. *Community Mental Health Journal. 50(3),* 362-372.

American College Health Association (ACHA) (2012). *American College Health Association-National College Health Assessment II: Reference Group Executive Summary Fall 2011.* Hanover, MD: American College Health Association.

Anxiety and Depression Association of America (ADAA) (2015). USA College Students' Anxiety and Depression. Cited on 04/30/2015, http://www.adaa.org/living-with-anxiety/college-students

Fatima, S., & Tahir, S. (2013). Comparison of Coping Strategies Used by Adolescents on State and Trait Anxiety. *FWU Journal of Social Sciences, 7*(2), 165-174.

Fiese, B. H., Winter, M. A., Wamboldt, F. S., Anbar, R. D., & Wamboldt, M. Z. (2010). Do family mealtime interactions mediate the association between asthma symptoms and separation anxiety? *Journal of Child Psychology & Psychiatry, 51*(2), 144-151. DOI: 10.1111/j.1469-7610.2009.02138.x.

García-Alberca, J. M., Cruz, B., Lara, J. P., Garrido, V., Lara, A., Gris, E., & Gonzalez-Herero, V. (2013). The experience of caregiving: the influence of coping strategies on behavioral and psychological symptoms in patients with Alzheimer's disease. *Aging & Mental Health,* 17(5), 615-622. DOI: 10.1080/13607863.2013.765833.

Garlow, S. J., Rosenberg, J., Moore, J. D., Haas, A. P., Koestner, B., Hendin, H., & Nemeroff, C. B. (2008). Depression, desperation, and suicidal ideation in college students: results from the American Foundation for Suicide Prevention College Screening Project at Emory University. *Depress Anxiety*, *25*(6), 482–488.

Gibbons, C., Dempster, M., & Moutray, M. (2011). Stress, coping and satisfaction in nursing students. *Journal of Advanced Nursing, 67* (3), 621-632.

Hamilton, M. (1959).The assessment of anxiety states by rating. *British Journal of Medical Psychology, 32*, 50–55.

Hungelmann, J., Kenkel-Rossi, E., Klassen, L., & Stollenwerk, R. (1996). Focus on spiritual well-being: Harmonious Interconnectedness of Mind-Body-Spirit-Use of the JAREL Spiritual Well-Being Scale. *Geriatric Nursing, 17*(6), 262-266.

Kandasamy, A., Chaturvedi, S. K., & Desai, G. (2011). Spirituality, distress, depression, anxiety, and quality of life in patients with advanced cancer. *Indian Journal of Cancer,* 48(1), 55-59. DOI: 10.4103/0019-509X.75828.

Leveridge, M., Stoltenberg, C., & Beesley, D. (2005). Relationship of attachment style to personality factors and family interaction patterns. *Contemporary Family Therapy: An International Journal, 27*(4), 577-597. DOI: 10.1007/s10591-005-8243-9.

Lincoln, K. D., Taylor, R. J., Bullard, K. M., Chatters, L. M., Woodward, A. T., Himle, J. A., & Jackson, J. S. (2010). Emotional support, negative interaction and DSM IV lifetime disorders among older African Americans: findings from the National Survey of American life (NSAL). *International Journal of Geriatric Psychiatry, 25*(6), 612-21.

Mann, J. R., McKeown, R. E., Bacon, J., Vesselinov, R., & Bush, F. (2008). Religiosity, spirituality and antenatal anxiety in Southern U.S. women. *Archives of Women's Mental Health,* 11(1), 19-26. DOI: 10.1007/s00737-008-0218-z.

Manzi, P. A. (1986). Cognitive appraisal, stress and coping in teenage employment. *Vocational Guidance, 34*(3), 160-170.

Melby, J., Conger, R., Book, R., Rueter, M., Lucy, L., Repinski, D., Rogers, S., Rogers, B., & Scaramella (1998). *The Iowa Family Interaction Rating Scales.* Institute for social and behavior research Iowa State University, Ames, IA.

Musarezaie, A., Naji Esfahani, H., Momeni Ghaleghasemi, T., Karimian, J., Ebrahimi, A. (2012). The Relationship between Spiritual Wellbeing and Stress, Anxiety, and Depression in Patients with Breast Cancer. *Journal of Isfahan Medical School, 30*(195), 1-10.

National Center for Health Statistics (NCHS) (2012). *Health, United States, 2011: With Special Feature on Socioeconomic Status and Health*. Hyattsville, MD.

National Institute of Mental Health (NIMH) (2015). *USA College Students' Depression*. Cited on 4/30/2015 http://www.nimh.nih.gov/health/ publications/depression-and-college-students/index.shtml

Rawdin, B., Evans, C., & Rabow, M. W. (2013). The Relationships among Hope, Pain, Psychological Distress, and Spiritual Well-Being in Oncology Outpatients. *Journal of Palliative Medicine, 16*(2), 167-172. DOI: 10.1089/jpm.2012.0223.

Smojveri-Ažič, S., & Bezinovič, P. (2011). Sex differences in patterns of relations between family interactions and depressive symptoms in adolescents. *Croatian Medical Journal, 52*(4), 469-477. DOI: 10.3325/cmj.2011.52.469.

Telzer, E., & Fuligni, A. (2013). Positive Daily Family Interactions Eliminate Gender Differences in Internalizing Symptoms Among Adolescents. *Journal of Youth & Adolescence, 42*(10), 1498-1511. DOI: 10.1007/s10964-013-9964-y.

Wissing, M. P., Khumalo, I. P., Oosthuizen, T. M., Nlenaber, A., Kruger, A., Potgleter, J. C., & Temane, Q. M. (2011). Coping Self-Efficacy as Mediator in the Dynamics of Psychological Well-Being in Various Contexts. *Journal of Psychology in Africa, 21*(2), 165-172.

Yeh, P. M., & Chiao, C. H. (2013). The influences of parents' rearing Attitude, personality and coping Strategies on psychological well-being and suicidal ideation among college students. In book: *Psychology of Well-Being: Theory, Perspectives and Practice.* Chapter 1, pp. 1-18. Nova Science Publishers: Hauppauge, NY.

Yoshihiro, S. (2014). Adolescents' Internal Working Models of Attachment as a Mediator between Their Social Adjustment and Parental Child-Rearing Attitudes. *Japanese Journal of Developmental Psychology*, 25(3), 260-267.

Zung, W.W.K. (1965). A self-rating depression scale. *Archives of General Psychiatry, 12*, 63-70.

In: Psychological Health and Needs Research Developments ISBN: 978-1-63483-332-5
Editor: Raul Wolfe

Chapter 7

Older Adults and Health Related Quality of Life: A Conceptual Model Based on Dynamic Systems

Mattia Roppolo[1-2], Saskia Kunnen[2], Anna Mulasso[1], Emanuela Rabaglietti[1] and Paul van Geert[2]
[1] Department of Psychology, University of Torino, Italy
[2] Department of Developmental Psychology, Rijksuniversiteit of Groningen, the Netherlands

Abstract

Ageing process involves the entire western world and in particular Europe. The analysis of demographic and health changes of the aged population is increasingly urgent in order to answer to the new individual and societal requests. An important concept in this regard is Health Related Quality of Life (HRQOL) during ageing, on which this paper will focus. Firstly, a general framework on demographics and health changes is provided. Secondly, the concept of HRQOL is analyzed, highlighting its strengths as well as its potential limitations. Thirdly, an analysis of HRQOL developmental trends, processes and mechanisms related to these processes is given. Finally, a conceptual dynamic systems model of HRQOL is delineated, in order to summarize the path taken in the paper and to propose new insights in the study of HRQOL in the aged population.

Keywords: Health related quality of life; dynamic systems; conceptual model; ageing

1. Demographic and Health Changes: A General Framework

Europe is sometimes called "the old continent." This statement becomes increasingly true, due to the ageing of the European population, which will have major effects on the global economical and societal systems and especially on public health, social needs, welfare state and economic policies. For this reason, it is important to analyze demographic and health changes of the ageing population in order to answer to the new needs of individuals and society.

In the lasts decades the concept of Health Related Quality of Life (HRQOL) became more and more used, due to its ability to focus on self-rated health status and perceptions, instead of simply using mortality and morbidity indicators. The concept HRQOL allows for a more encompassing and person-centered conceptualization of health outcome. However, currently it is not clear how HRQOL evolves during the ageing process.

This question can be answered by a comprehensive theoretical model that can structure the empirical data on the relevant health processes during ageing, and, by doing so, can form the basis for further studies on health prevention and promotion.

A comprehensive model of HRQOL has to: (i) include various domains of functioning; (ii) take into account the interconnections among domains; (iii) include predictable as well as unpredictable life events; and (iv) consider the variety of developmental processes, including stability, decline or improvement.

The paper will first describe the emergent ageing process, analyze the latest data on ageing-related changes, and highlight the relevant characteristics of HRQOL and its domains. As a next step, it gives an overview of what models we already have, and in what ways these models still lack the necessary characteristics. Finally, it will present a model that meets the requirements just mentioned, namely a model focusing on HRQOL from the perspective of Dynamic Systems theory.

Such an approach enables us to focus on processes acting on health status and perceptions during ageing, which is hardly possible with traditional approaches.

1.1. Demographic Changes

According to the World Health Organization and Eurostat, the aged population (65 years and over) will have a growth rate of 57% between 2008 and 2035, and of 80% between 2008 and 2060, rising from 84.2 to 151.7 million of older adults against a general EU population of 495.4 million of people in 2008 and 505.7 million in 2060 (Eurostat, 2011). Projections claim that, in 2060, almost 30% of European population will be over 65 years (Eurostat, 2008).

Longitudinal European data from 1990 to 2010 (Eurostat, 2011) describe an increase of 5.3% (20.6% in 1990 – 23.2% in 2000 – 25.9% in 2010) of the old-dependency ratio, defined as the proportion between the number of seniors economically inactive and the number of persons in a working age. This means that in 1990 in the European zone, for any inactive aged person, five were economically active. Currently (2010) this proportion is 1 versus 4. Eurostat projections (Giannakouris, 2008) estimate an old-age dependency ratio of 52.5% in 2060.

Over the years, life expectancy (LE - the expected numbers of years remaining at a given age) increased considerably. Currently, LE at birth in Europe is 79.6 years (min 68 for Latvia - max 85 for France; Eurostat, 2011), with a strong increase from 76.5 years in 1999 (73 years for men and 80 for women) to 79.6 in 2009 (77 for men and 83 for women; Eurostat, 2011).

Unfortunately, the increase in LE is not accompanied by an increase in the Healthy Life Years (HLY), defined as the healthy life expectancy at a certain age. The European HLY followed a negative trend from 2004 to 2010 for both genders. In particular, HLY at birth was

63.7 years for women and 62.2 years for men in 2004. In six years, it decreased with 1.1 years for women (62.6 years) and 0.5 years for men (61.7 years). If compared with LE data at birth the values highlight an average of 20 unhealthy years for women (82.6 – 62.6) and 15 years for men (76.7 – 61.7).

The WHO General Director, Dr. Hiroshi Nakajima, in 1997, said: "Increased longevity without quality of life is an empty prize. Health expectancy is more important than life expectancy." The widening gap between quality of life and longevity is paid on an individual level in terms of loss of autonomy and institutionalization, and on a societal level with a higher demand for care and increasing of National Health Systems costs.

To cope with these demographic and social changes and to try to add life to years (and not only years to life), the objectives of both researchers and clinicians are: (i) to identify processes and mechanisms underlying changes of health status and quality of life in the older adults population; and (ii) to implement effective preventive interventions in seniors, in order to maintain health status and autonomy as long as possible. In the next sections, we will give a short overview of what is known about age related changes in health.

1.2. Age-Related Health Changes

At first sight, data discussed in the previous section, confirm the expansion of morbidity theory (Manton, 1982). According to this theory, increase in LE is caused by a lower death rate for chronic diseases rather than by a decline in the incidence of these diseases. This view highlights that increasing longevity is related to increasing number of unhealthy-years.

Conversely, the dynamic equilibrium theory is based on the decrease of the impact of diseases on the health of older adults (Manton, Gu, & Lamb, 2006, Manton, 1982). This theory assumes that the lower mortality is linked to a less deterioration of the vital organs, and that diseases have a lower severity (Crimmins, 2004), however do not assume a lower incidence of pathological conditions.

The reduced impact in terms of disability (Crimmins, 2004) is not accompanied by a decrease of incidence and prevalence of chronic diseases in the seniors (Eurostat, 2011; Marengoni, Winblad, Karp, & Fratiglioni, 2008). In fact, statistics from Eurostat (2011) show that the percentage of people having an enduring illness or health problems in the European area is higher with the increase of age: 30.9% in the whole population, 54.8% in the population aged 65-74, 66.1% in the 75-84 years population and 69.5% in the over 85 years. This trend is increasing from 2004 to 2010, proportional to age: 3.2% in the whole population, 4.5% in the population aged between 65-74, 5.4% in the 75-84 age group and 6.1% in over 85 years (Eurostat, 2011). The high prevalence of non-communicable and other chronic conditions in the aged population is the most relevant cause of unhealthy years in later life.

Starting from the WHO definition of Health (1946): *''Health is a state of complete physical, mental and social well-being and not merely the absence of disease or infirmity''*, it is possible to analyze health changes typical of ageing process in each of the three domains (physical, mental and social) proposed by WHO.

Physical health changes are related to muscle-skeletal (Cummings, 1993; Doherty, 2001; Frontera, et al., 2000; Hannan, et al., 2000; Janssen, Heymsfield, Wang, & Ross, 2000; Johnell & Kanis, 2004; Lexell, 1995; Rogers & Evans, 1993), cardiorespiratory (Janssens,

Pache, & Nicod, 1999; Kitzman, 2000; Kitzman & Edwards, 1990; Rossi, Ganassini, Tantucci, & Grassi, 1996; Rossi, et al., 1996; Sharma & Goodwin, 2006), and nervous systems (Albert & Janice E. Knoefel, 1994; Rivner, Swift, & Malik, 2001; Salat, et al., 2004), that may have negative impact on health outcomes, autonomy of daily living and HRQOL (Chien, Huang, & Wu, 2008; Janssen, Baumgartner, Ross, Rosenberg, & Roubenoff, 2004; Janssen, Heymsfield, & Ross, 2002; Roubenoff & Hughes, 2000).

In the mental domain, changes were found on cognitive (Mebane-Sims & Association, 2009; Small, Stern, Tang, & Mayeux, 1999) and psychological adjustments (Beekman, Copeland, & Prince, 1999; Beekman, et al., 1998; Blazer, Burchett, Service, & George, 1991; McAvay, Seeman, & Rodin, 1996).

Finally, the social domain shows changes in and disengagement from social activities during the ageing process (Bennet, 2002; Cumming & Henry, 1961).

1.3. Successful Ageing

On the one hand the physical, mental and social changes are described as decline and disengagement from usual activities (this view is generally called usual ageing, see Atchley, 1989), on the other hand, the new and more positive thinking (successful ageing, see Baltes & Baltes, 1993)) proposes an increase or maintenance of health status in the older adult population due to changes that occur in daily habits and lifestyle (i.e., participation in activities). A recent study (Haskell, et al., 2007) shows that an active lifestyle and/or a participation in physical exercises may lead to an improvement in physical fitness, health status and diseases prevention.

An active lifestyle is also correlated with a better cognitive and psychological health (Floel, et al., 2008; Netz, Wu, Becker, & Tenenbaum, 2005), with important consequences for prevention of health decline, functional loss and disability (Fratiglioni, Paillard-Borg, & Winblad, 2004; Keysor, 2003). In contradiction with disengagement theory, activity theory (Lemon, Bengtson, & Peterson, 1972), supports the active participation of seniors in social life. This participation can be beneficial to health, with a consequent reduction of mortality (Bennett, 2002; Sabin, 1993).

Finally, the Selection, Compensation and Optimization Theory (SOC) proposed by Freund and Baltes (1998) explains in a positive view on the ageing process. SOC theory expresses ageing as a complex, multifactorial process, not understandable from a linear perspective (Baltes & Smith, 2003). In addition, the approach of Baltes identifies ageing not only as a period of decline but also as a life-phase in which individuals can find new ways and strategies to maintain their normal life.

1.4. Interplay among Domains

In order to understand age related health change, one of the most important aspects that emerged in the literature is the strong connection between the physical, psychological and social domain. It was demonstrated that changes in one of the health components affect the other domains directly or indirectly. Interconnections among health domains were found between (i) physical and mental (Bouchard & Shephard, 1994; Kramer, et al., 2003; Wang,

Larson, Bowen, & van Belle, 2006); (ii) psychological and social (Glass, De Leon, Bassuk, & Berkman, 2006; Kawachi & Berkman, 2001); and (iii) physical and social components (Bennett, 2005; Bennett, 2002). These relations, which require further investigation, reflect the complex interplay among health components, confirming the basic assumptions of the biopsychosocial model (Engel, 1977). The biopsychosocial model is in contrast with the classical biomedical model, in which "health" is a category opposite to the category "infirmity." Furthermore, the biopsychosocial model considers interconnections and mutual influences among health domains, with the use of a systemic approach, based on systems theory (Engel, 1977). The biopsychosocial model allowed to study health and health-related topics as systems of interconnected elements, that may vary and change over time in a continuous way.

In order to understand the complex interplay among health domains, a model that considers mutual relationships, focusing on changes and non-linarites, is needed. A dynamic systems approach can be very helpful to conceptualize and study such a complex, non-linear process. It offers possibilities to analyze the mutual connections and development of HRQOL over time that are not possible with more classical approaches. Dynamic systems focus on the components of the system and their mutual influences (Kunnen, 2012).

2. The Concept of Health Related Quality of Life: Definition and Limitations

The construct of HRQOL is suitable for the purpose of studying health process during ageing, because it addresses self-rated health, and because it is a predictive measure of health decline, mortality and institutionalization in the aged population (Bilotta, et al., 2011; Dorr, et al., 2006).

HRQOL is a concept deriving from two sources. The first is the definition of health previously cited (Age-related health changes section). The second is the definition of quality of life (QOL) as -"the subjective perception that an individual has of his own existence, in the context of culture and of a set of values in which he lives, even in relation to his objectives, expectations and concerns") proposed by WHO (1997).

2.1. A definition of HRQOL

HRQOL is a person centered measure that can be modified in a complex way from (i) perceptions of physical and psychological-emotional health; (ii) level of independence; (iii) social role; (iv) relationships; (v) context; and (vi) environmental and working interactions (Testa & Simonnnson, 1996). HRQOL refers to physical, mental and social domains of health that are seen as distinct areas influenced by a person's experiences, beliefs, expectations, and perceptions (Testa & Simonson, 1996). HRQOL narrows the focus to the effects of health, illness, and treatment on QOL, and excludes aspects of QOL that are not related to health, such as cultural, political, or societal attributes (Ferrans, Zerwic, Wilbur, & Larson, 2005).

2.2. Limitations of the Current Conceptualization

The distinction between health-related and non-health-related quality of life is not always simple, and for this reason many models exist that include different aspects of HRQOL. For instance, Wilson and Cleary (1995) created a model based on biological/physical variables, symptoms, functional status, health perceptions and overall QOL, with the addition of individual and environmental characteristics. Other scholars suggest six fundamental dimensions of HRQOL: physical functioning, psychological functioning, social functioning, role activities, overall life satisfaction, and perceptions of health status (Berzon, Hays, & Shumaker, 1993). Patrick and Erikson (in Aaronson, 1993) use a model composed by five concepts: life span, symptoms, physical functions, health perceptions and opportunity. Ware and Dewey (2000) analyzed HRQOL as a series of concentric circles that spread from biological functions to HRQOL via physical/mental health and social role. Other models include physical problems, psychological problems, sexual functions, activity of daily living and perceptions of wellbeing. The only common point among these models is the multidimensional nature of the concept.

Furthermore, for model building and comparison, also the modes to assess HRQOL have to be taken into consideration. Bury and Holme (1991) and Testa and Simonson (1996) argue that each dimension can be measured in an objective and subjective way. While the objective measurement refers to health status, the subjective evaluation is related to the perceptions of health, implying that two persons with the same health status may have different HRQOL's. This implication is supported by Henchoz et al. (2008), who found differences between health status and health perceptions among older adults, confirming the importance to assess both aspects.

The most used and detailed conceptual model of HRQOL is the one proposed by Wilson & Cleary (1995). This model conceptualizes HRQOL as a continuous and linear path from the biological functions to the overall QoL (via symptoms, functional status and general health perceptions). Furthermore, each concept included in the Wilson & Cleary model has a direct influence from the individual and the environmental characteristics. This model represents a uni-directional causal approach, based on the biomedical model (opposite than the biopsychosocial model, that allow a nonlinear multidirectional causal approach) to the analysis of HRQOL.

Although the model gives important information about the elements acting on the HRQOL, there are various limitations. The first regards the concepts of development and changes of the construct under examination. HRQOL is a concept that arises from the match between health-status and health-perceptions factors and this procedure can be seen as an ongoing, iterative process, in which a subsequent state is strongly connected with the previous one. The conceptualization of the development of HRQOL as linear is theoretically not plausible, and it does not fit in with empirical findings. It is therefore necessary to emphasize the role of time and the iterative process in self-assessment of HRQOL. Second, the Wilson & Cleary model shows limitations regarding the interconnections among domains/variables, which it primarily conceptualizes as a structure of uni-directional links. A single direction for the links among the elements can lead to neglecting the possible interconnections and the complexity of the structure. Third, the causal model of Wilson & Cleary (1995) insufficiently accounts for the particular influences of random events. Casual events can act on each component of the models and are not presented in the conceptualization. To avoid the loss of a source of information that acts directly on HRQOL domains, the inclusion in the conceptual model of random influences is necessary.

2.3. A Step Forward in the Definition of HRQOL

Due to the lack of consensus among models, we think that it is useful to formulate the conditions and sketch the outlines of a new and more comprehensive conceptual model of HRQOL. In particular, our aim is to adopt a three dimensional structure, using physical, mental and social domains (starting from the WHO definitions of Health). The three dimensional structure is to make the model consistent with the WHO definition, but also because we need a simply, understandable and comprehensive definition and conceptualization of HRQOL and its their main domains. Moreover, we aim to use a double way of assessment (as proposed by Testa and Simonson, 1996) in order to capture both status and perceptions of each dimension.

The advantage of this theoretical structure is based on the usefulness and easiness to adopt the tripartite nature of health as proposed by WHO, thus avoiding the use of many different domains that hinder the comparison of the results based on assessment instruments using a more complicated definition of HRQOL (Murdaugh, 1997). Furthermore, the adoption of Testa and Simonson's distinction between the health-status and health-perceptions components of HRQOL, offers the possibility to understand differences in HRQOL, and to provide new ways of explanation of changes and intra- and inter-individual variability.

2.4. Strengths of the Concept

Despite the lack of consensus on HRQOL definitions, the usefulness of a HRQOL measure in clinical and research fields is widely recognized.

HRQOL provides a patient point of view on effects of interventions, diseases and processes acting on people. It is a person-centered outcome measure, which is more specific and indicative, then the traditional measures of mortality and morbidity (Idler & Benyamini, 1997; Tsai, Chi, Lee & Chou, 2007). HRQOL is important on both the individual and the societal level. On the one hand, it is important to assess HRQOL, with the goal to enhance the healthy life expectancy (Theofilou, 2011). On the other hand, measure HRQOL is recognized as an objective that must be reached by the US program Healthy People 2020 (U.S. Department of Health and Social Services), and will help nations in monitoring to what extent health objectives have been achieved (Theofilou, 2011).

3. Developmental Trends of HRQOL in the Aged Population

In previous research, HRQOL is mainly used as an outcome measurement that indicates the impact of processes (i.e., pathological processes) on self-rated health. Specifically, previous literature reports two types of studies on HRQOL and aged people, about: (i) the impact of diseases, (ii) the impact of activities/behaviors/interventions. In the first case, scholars reported the negative impact that different kind of diseases have on HRQOL.

In particular, chronic diseases, such as hypertension, osteoarthritis, diabetes, depression, asthma are the most studied (among other: Kempen, Ormel, Brilman, & Relyveld, 1997; Lam & Lauder, 2000). Research reveals the general negative trend that diseases and comorbidity have on HRQOL of older adults (Hopman, et al., 2009). Furthermore, the mental component was seen as the most stable, that seems to maintain its level also in the presence of various diseases (Hopman, et al., 2009; Kempen, Ormel, Brilman, & Relyveld, 1997).

Other studies (Lam & Lauder, 2000; Lima, et al., 2009) show that some diseases may affect a variety of aspects: hypertension affects the physical component in particular, asthma and joint diseases are negatively associated with autonomy in activities of daily living. Depression is a condition that highly affects the whole HRQOL (Lam & Lauder, 2000).

Secondly, evidence on the effects of various types of independent variables on HRQOL affirms that there is a strong relation between active lifestyle (i.e., active leisure time, hobbies, participation in specific interventions) and HRQOL. In particular, previous studies highlight that people who are physically active during leisure time have a higher level of HRQOL in comparison with sedentary older adults (Balboa-Castillo, Leon-Munoz, Graciani, Rodriguez-Artalejo, & Guallar-Castillon, 2011; Drageset, et al., 2009; Jenkins, Pienta, & Horgas, 2002; Lee & Russell, 2003; Thompson, Zack, Krahn, Andresen, & Barile, 2012).

Recently, various interventions were compared on their effectiveness for HRQOL. Excluding drug trials, the most common are physical and psychological/cognitive interventions.

Cognitive interventions, based on memory, reasoning or speed of processing exercises, (among others: Wolinsky, Unverzagt, Smith, Jones, Stoddard, et al., 2006; Wolinsky, Unverzagt, Smith, Jones, Wright, et al., 2006) demonstrated their efficacy in terms of maintenance of HRQOL.

Various types of physical training showed beneficial effects; in particular, scholars reported the effectiveness on HRQOL of: strength exercises (Kimura, et al., 2010), combined strength and endurance exercises (Sillanpaa, Hakkinen, Holviala, & Hakkinen, 2012), and aerobic exercises (Ciairano, Liubicich & Rabaglietti, 2010; Deschamps, Onifade, Decamps, & Bourdel-Marchasson, 2009). All interventions have positive effects on HRQOL, compared with non-participants groups. In sum, the literature provides strong evidence for positive effects of general physical activity interventions on HRQOL (Acree, et al., 2006; Elavsky, et al., 2005; Inaba, Obuchi, Arai, Satake, & Takahira, 2008; Lee, Lee, & Woo, 2009; Penedo & Dahn, 2005; Shephard, 1993; Sillanpaa, et al., 2012; Yasunaga, et al., 2006).

Moreover, a study of Deschamps et al. (2009) compared a physical training based on Tai Chi exercises and a cognitive training, emphasizing that both interventions directly and positively act on HRQOL of participants. Another study, based on Shintaido discipline, combining mental and physical activities, demonstrated the ability to act directly and indirectly on physical and psychological health of older adults (Roppolo, Mulasso, Magistro, Roggero, Andreoli, & Liubicich, 2012).

Thus, there is a lot of research showing that HRQOL can be affected by a variety of processes. However, little attention has been paid to the developmental changes of HRQOL itself.

In our view, HRQOL is not just an outcome, but it is a process itself, resulting from iterations and interconnections among domains.

It seems that HRQOL is a construct characterized by complex variability, modifications and variations caused by individual characteristics, activities, behaviors and social interactions. Currently, scientific evidence clearly showing developmental trends of HRQOL in the ageing process is inconsistent. Moreover, no models take into account the role of time with regard to changes in HRQOL.

Longitudinal studies are needed to explain the role of time. Cross-sectional data reported a general decrease of the physical component with the increasing of age, while the mental component seems to remain stable (Hopman, et al., 2000). Nowadays, due to the lack of studies exploring trends of HRQOL over time, it is fundamental to build a theoretical framework in order to conceptualize HRQOL as a person-centered system composed by a set of interconnected elements, that develop during time as results of the iterations and internal/external influences. The resulting conceptual model will be useful to: (i) better understand processes and mechanisms of changes in HRQOL during the ageing process; and (ii) analyze individual developmental trajectories. This approach may allow a better comprehension of the process modifying HRQOL, and may provide effective and individualized interventions for health promotion in seniors.

4. HRQOL and Dynamic Systems

The main objective of this paper is to present a new conceptual model of HRQOL that allows for understanding the change processes in the aged population. Currently, models use a large variety of components that do not allow comparability among them. Interconnections among domains, role of time and life events are not considered. Finally, the current models are linear and confine themselves to uni-directional causal relationships.

In our view, HRQOL is a system, and as a system has to be studied as a whole, in order to understand its development over time. To delineate such a system, dynamic systems represent a solid basis.

The new conceptual model aims to take into account the development of the construct and the individual trajectories of HRQOL over time. In particular, the new HRQOL conceptual model will consider the role of time, the causal interconnections among variables/domains and the influences of random effects.

The dynamic systems approach has been already applied in the field of social sciences and developmental psychology in the analysis of psychological characteristics, mainly in childhood and adolescence (Bassano & van Geert, 2007; Kunnen, 2009; Kunnen, 2012; Lichtwarck-Aschoff, Kunnen, & van Geert, 2009; Steenbeek & van Geert, 2008; van Geert, 1994). The present article aims to extend this literature, applying a dynamic systems approach on the construct of HRQOL in a population of seniors (generally not considered in the psychological dynamic systems studies). Before doing so, we will describe the most important features of dynamic systems and discuss how the concept of HRQOL fits in with these features.

4.1. General Characteristics of Dynamic Systems

A dynamic system is composed by a set of interconnected interacting elements that affect each other. These interactions provide the causal ground for the development of the system during the course of time (van Geert, 1994; Weisstein, 2003). The dynamic systems approach to human development is based on the view that humans are complex and interactive systems that change (or develop) their state (for instance, their emotional state) during time. Development derives from interactions among environmental and individual variables and inter-individual characteristics (Kunnen, 2012; Kunnen & Bosma, 2000). In particular, the focus of a dynamic systems perspective is the analysis of individual changes and trajectories over time (Thelen & Ulrich, 1991), emphasizing the role of intra-individual variability and stability as fundamental notions to understand the development of the systems (Thelen & Smith, 1996; Thelen & Ulrich, 1991; van Geert & van Dijk, 2002). Development may emerge on a long-term time scale (changes that occur over the course of months or years), and on a short-term time scale (short time period representing actions on a real time basis; Kunnen, 2012). Furthermore, the process of individual changes, that represents the main objective of the dynamic systems studies, is complex and multivariate (Kunnen, 2012). Complexity involves mutual causality among interconnected components, which results in self-organization and emergent phenomena. Self-organization is defined as the emergence of a stable higher order characteristic in the system (Kunnen, 2012).

4.2. Can HRQOL Be Viewed As a Dynamic System?

Starting from dynamic systems theory and the current conceptualization of HRQOL, it is plausible to assume that the latter shares important characteristics with the former.

4.2.1. Developmental Process

HRQOL is assumed to show intra-indiviudal change over time (Bernhard, Lowy, Mathys, Herrmann, & Hurny, 2004; Sprangers & Schwartz, 2008). Especially, it tends to show a decline in the ageing period. The decline may be gradual or by sudden steps. Furthermore, HRQOL may show temporary increase or fluctuations. For these reasons, it is possible to hypothesize that HRQOL is a developmental process described as a sequence of states over time. Each state of the system in any time is described by the position of the relevant dimensions of the system itself (Kunnen, 2012). The position of the system in the space of relevant dimensions changes over time, and the sequence of such positions draws a path through the developmental space. The path described by the relevant dimensions over time represents the developmental process. Development, in this sense, is an iterative process. Iterative means that each step in the developmental path is related to its previous state (the starting value of a step is the outcome of the previous one).

4.2.2. Interconnected Elements

Existing definitions and conceptual models agree that HRQOL is a multidimensional construct (Lipscomb, Gotay, & Snyder, 2004). Interconnections among elements are a typical characteristic of systems in the human and social sciences. Each HRQOL component can influence, change or act on the other. As an example, mental health can influence both the physical and the social functions (i.e., the case of depressive symptoms). The interconnections among elements represent another similarity between HRQOL and dynamic systems theory.

4.2.3. Non linearity

Living systems are in general nonlinear (Kunnen, 2012; van Geert, 2008). This statement is mainly attributable to the impossibility for a human system to always proceed along continuous and stable trends (e.g., continuous and constant growth of health perception), assumption related to linear systems and their additive nature of the contribution of distinct variables. In HRQOL many factors (i.e., diagnosis of a disease, administration of a new drug) can reverse or change the growth rate of the health status. Nonlinearity is also related to the number and types of influences (internal and external) to which every person is subject. In particular, mutual influences, including iterativity causes processes to become nonlinear. A very important source of nonlinearity is the fact that many processes are time dependent, (i.e., dependent on their own history) which is a major feature of an iterative process.

HRQOL, conceptualized as a system of interconnected elements that develop during time, can be expected to show nonlinear behavior over time. The interconnections among elements imply that changes in the trend of one component can influence the trends in other domains, which can feed back onto the first component.

4.2.4. Mutual Causality

An important characteristic of complex and non-linear systems is that unidirectional and proportional (linear) causal relations between two variables are relatively rare or unlikely. Sometimes, a small change in one variable may cause a big change in the whole system. Other times, repeated and strong attempts to modify the system are without effect. Human systems are, characterized by the impossibility to predict the sequence of outputs, knowing the sequence of inputs and the initial state of the system. In non-deterministic systems, each initial state and inputs value correspond with lots of possible output states. As an example, the therapeutic effect of the same intervention may have different level of efficacy in two comparable individuals, with strongly beneficial effects for one of those and completely inefficacy for the second one.

Initial conditions, mutual causality and randomness play a strong role in these relationships making the prediction almost impossible.

For these reasons, health status and in particular HRQOL may be treated as non-deterministic systems.

4.2.5. Transitions

Transitions are important phases in the development of a Dynamic System. A transition phase is a period in which the system changes from one stable state to another stable state. The change can be attributable to modifications in its components or in their interconnections, or to the emergence of new relevant variables (Kunnen, 2012). In particular, in a transition phase, the components of a system can become more or less influential to the whole system. Some of these variables could be excluded and other variables could be added into the system. However, it is important to notice that not all the dynamic systems shows transition phases in their development.

Referring to HRQOL in the older adults population, the loss of a specific ability (e.g., walking autonomously) or the changes of habits due to health conditions (e.g., institutionalization) could be seen as transition phase, in which the whole system modifies its nature, and in which the person need to modifies his habits, lifestyle and activities. These changes may disturb the whole system before the creation of a new phase of equilibrium (different from the previous one).

Transition periods are accompanied by increased or uncommon variability that can be followed by a new and generally different stable condition (Kunnen, 2012).

4.2.6. Variability

Transitional phases are usually preceded by period with high and strange variability (van der Maas & Molenaar, 1992). Real and living systems are open and unstable systems, due to their interactions with the environment. Interactions with the environment and with other open systems (e.g., people) produce variability in the state of a system (Kunnen, 2012; van Geert & van Dijk, 2002). However, variability is not linearly related to the strength of the influences from the environment and open systems. Instead, it is dependent of the state of the system, regarding the vicinity to a stable self-sustaining state (attractor).

Also in this case, the concept of HRQOL, in particular in the older adults population (highly influenced by internal and external sources), fits in with this feature. It is an example of a system that may show high intra and inter individual variability (Wyrwich, 2000; Browne, 1994). The amount of variability provides important information about the developmental behavior and the state of a system. In particular, too high or too low variability may results in catastrophe or indicate problems within the system (Hollestein, 2004; van der Maas & Molenaar, 1992).

Summarizing, HRQOL seems to meet the features of a dynamic system. A dynamic systems concetualization may solve the limitations of the existing models.

4.3. A Conceptual Model of HRQOL Based on Dynamic Systems

The dynamic systems conceptual model of HRQOL (DSCM-HRQOL) aims: first, to apply theories and methodologies typical of dynamic systems; second, to employ the specific terminology proposed by WHO to define health, in order to create uniformity between the official definition of health and the modeling of theories; third, to apply the conceptualization proposed by Testa and Simonson (1996) for the evaluation of health-status and health-perceptions of each component of HRQOL. The use of the double evaluation dimension solves the limitation that the conceptualization and measurement of HRQOL health status and perceptions follow an increasing gap during the ageing process, and that people aged over 80 tend to underestimate the HRQOL decline (Henchoz, et al., 2008). In this way, a more comprehensive assessment may be more precise.is either a person's health and functional status or his perception of wellbeing, giving it a more complex and systematic quality. In our view, Tthe two components of each domain may be collected separately, offering the opportunity to explore dynamic relations between these components. However, since HRQOL is mainly oriented to the subjective and individual judgement of its own health, it was decided that both the health-status and health-perceptions dimensions will be detected by self-report indicators.

The DSCM-HRQOL will focus primarily on the aged population, with the aim to tackle loss of health and functionality. Nevertheless, the feasibility of the new model of HRQOL may be extended to the whole population or to specific sub-groups.

This section will move firstly with the definition, operationalization and assessments of the principal domains of the model, secondly, it will proceed with the definition of the other components of the model and finally, the structure of the whole conceptualization will be defined.

4.3.1. Domains of DSCM-HRQOL

Physical Domain - Definition

The physical domain of HRQOL refers to the ability of performing physical efforts and carrying out work, in order to have autonomy in ADLs and to maintain a state of physical functioning appropriate for social and environmental demands. Our view of physical health emphasizes functions, (such as walking, climbing stairs, bathing etc.). By doing so, we follow the key concepts proposed by the International Classification of Functioning, Disability and Health (ICF) by WHO, instead of focusing mainly on limitations, as previously conceptualized (Kaplan, Bush, & Berry, 1976; Katz, Ford, Moskowitz, Jackson, & Jaffe, 1963; Ware, 1987).

Physical Domain – Operationalization

The physical health-status assessment with the use of self-report questionnaire must to be centered on physical performance (total amount of activities performed; Leidy, 1994), because it is impossible to measure physical capacity with such instruments. One of the most reliable instrument is the International Physical Activity Questionnaire (Booth, et al., 2003) previously used in aged sample (Tomioka, Iwamoto, Saeki, Okamoto, 2011).

The health-perceptions component of physical domain may be assessed with self-report questionnaires. The physical well-being scale of the Quality of Life Questionnaire (Evans, Burns, Robinson, & Garrett; 1985) is an example.

Finally, some validated questionnaires (i.e., the Short Form-36, Physical Composite Score) allow to assess a composite score of the physical domain. These questionnaires can be used to obtain general information about the physical domain, however, they do not capture the objective and subjective component separately.

Mental Domain - Definition

WHO (2011) defines mental health as: "*a state of well-being in which every individual realizes his or her own potential, can cope with the normal stresses of life, can work productively and fruitfully, and is able to make a contribution to her or his community.*" Furthermore, MedLine Plus (U.S. National Library of Medicine, National Institute of Health) highlights that mental health "*affects how we think, feel and act as we cope with life. It also helps determine how we handle stress, relate to others, and make choices. Mental health is important at every stage of life, from childhood and adolescence through adulthood.*"

Referring to the older adults population, the evaluation of the mental domain can be subdivided in: (i) psychological; (ii) and cognitive assessment.

Mental Domain – Operationalization

As previously cited (section Age-related health changes), the most important mental characteristics are related to the cognitive and psychological area.

In order to measure the health-status component of the mental domain, instruments of cognitive and psychological assessment may be done with the Mini Mental State Examination (Folstein, Folstein & McHugh, 1975), mainly used in the aged population. In the psychological area, the focus may be oriented on the measurement of depression (i.e., Geriatric Depression Scale; Yesavage et al., 1983), anxiety (i.e., Geriatric Anxiety Inventory; Pachana et al., 2007) and, self-efficacy (i.e., General Self-Efficacy Scale; Bosscher & Smit, 1998). Moreover, the health-perceptions component can be measured with scales for the assessment of mental well-being (i.e., Warwick-Edinburgh Mental Well-being Scale; Tennant et al., 2007), previously used among older adults (Gale, Dennison, Cooper, Sayer, 2011).

Finally, also for the mental domain, some instruments (i.e., Short Form-36, Mental Composite Score) generate a composite score including health-status and health-perceptions oriented questions.

Social Domain - Definition

The social domain of our model refers to the ability of a subject to maintain his social engagement despite the ageing process. The maintenance of engagement with social life represents a protective factor (Bath & Deeg, 2005; Garcia, Banegas, Perez-Regadera, Cabrera, & Rodriguez-Artalejo, 2005) for the decline in health status and should be included in the assessment. This ability could be assessed with measurement of social network (size) and relationships (frequency and intensity).

Social Domain – Operationalization

The social domain may be divided in an objective component, seen here as the size of the social network, and a subjective component, intended as the quality of social relations.

In particular, the health-status oriented component (social health status) may be measured with questionnaires that analyze the social network size, as the Lubben Social Network Scale (Lubben, 1988).

In addition, the health-perceptions component may be evaluated with questionnaires built to analyze the quality of the social relations, such as the Friendship Quality Scale (Hawthorne, 2006), also previously used in ageing-related studies.

4.3.2. Assessments of the Domains

If we assume that HRQOL is a dynamic system that develops during time, it is necessary, after the definition and operationalization of its domain, to define how to assess and how capture the dynamic nature of such a construct.

The dynamic systems approach assumes that time is a core characteristic of the system itself (Kunnen, 2012), and in this view it is possible to observe how the system develops at different and interconnected time levels (Kunnen, 2012). Specifically, dynamic trends are detectable from very short time scales (microlevels) to very long time scales (macrolevels), all related each other, in the sense that dynamic characteristics at the microlevel influence the development at the macrolevel. The analysis of development at different time scales was previously studied and analyzed in other areas of research, defining how long-term development shapes and is shaped by everyday events (Lichtwarck-Aschoff, van Geert, Bosma, & Kunnen, 2008; Kunnen, 2012).

The use of an assessment at different time levels may be suitable also in the case of HRQOL. Specifically, such an approach gives us the possibility to match the long-term trends (i.e., the analysis of data points month away from each other) with the analysis of short-term trends. The analysis at microlevel of the indicators of the three main domains, measured very often, or sufficiently often, (i.e., day-to-day assessments) allows to detect a time series of data with which we can specify individual trajectories, including intra-individual variability. The use of such an approach may lead to a better understand of the short-term changes in the HRQOL, with the possibility to better understand also long-term trends and outcomes. In other words, a dynamic systems approach helps us to understand how long-term development of HRQOL, important indicator and predictor of negative health outcomes, emerges out of short-term (day-to-day) interactions. The assessment of HRQOL at a short-time level, will need the set-up of a series of indicators (covering both the health-status and the health-perceptions components) that allow an easy collection and in the meanwhile, that may be representative of the construct.

4.3.3. Additional Components

The three domains form the core of the dynamic systems model of HRQOL. However, to formulate a complete model, we need to specify several additional components.

Stable individual parameters

Individual parameters are essential information in complex and dynamic systems (Smith & Thelen, 2003). In particular, also weak differences in the initial condition of a system can cause a great discrepancy in the developmental trajectories or in the final state (De Toni & Comello, 2005; Kunnen, 2012). For these reasons, in addition to the baseline evaluations of the three HRQOL domains, we include in our model indicators of individual parameters, which can have a considerable impact on the trend of the construct under investigation, as it unfolds in a particular individual person.

More specifically, the indicators inserted in the model are: (i) age, due to high correlation between ageing process and health decline; (ii) presence and type of morbidity, directly affecting HRQOL; (iii) lifestyle habits (protective and risk factors).

These indicators can be aggregated to create a general index of stable individual parameters, which will have a direct influence on the baseline assessment of each domain.

Random Influences

In the model, we included also a stochastic influence that can act on physical, mental and social domains of HRQOL. As previously cited (see section Non causality), living systems are subject to unpredictable and uncontrollable effects of random events (Kunnen, 2012). Random influences are a fundamental source of information in modeling of reality, especially in dynamic systems models, because in such a models the idiosyncratic nature of the random influences is a central feature, since every system is conceived as a network of interacting components, and the interaction rules are typical of the individual subjects. Furthermore, the inclusion of random influences can be useful for future translations of the conceptual model into a mathematical model. In our DSCM, random influences may affect each of the three domains of HRQOL, and are seen as unpredictable events of everyday life. Some examples are the onset of a disease, an adverse physical situation (i.e., a fall) but also the consolidation of a friendship relation, the birth of a grandson or a new interest/hobby. All these aspects, completely unpredictable, nonlinear and idiosyncratic, influence the whole system and can explain trends and transitions.

4.3.4. Architecture of DSCM-HRQOL

After the explanations of domains included in the model, the next step in designing a conceptual model is to depict its relations during time and among components.

Developmental Process (Role of Time)

The DSCM-HRQOL is a developmental model. The aim is to delineate the evolving patterns and trends of HRQOL during time as they occur in individual subjects. As mentioned previously, developmental systems are iterative, following a process which takes place step by step and in which the outcome of a previous step is the input value for the next step (van Geert, 1994). In our conceptualization, the three central domains of HRQOL follow these rules, evolving during time in the form of an iterative process. Iterativity implies interdependency among measures (e.g., A depends on B and B depends on A, or, physical health depends on mental health, and mental health depends on physical health).

As a simple exemplification of the iterative behaviors, we can imagine an older adult who one day by chance meets one old friend. The unexpected social contact might have an immediate short-term positive effect on the persons feeling of social well-being. This temporal increase might result in the person's decision to increase the intensity of these social contacts, which might lead to consolidation of the short-term increase in social well-being. Other examples could imply the reduction of the daily physical activity after a fall, with a consequent decrease of the HRQOL in the physical domain, or an increase in performing memory games after becoming aware of a decline in cognitive functions.

This example shows that the connections between different domains occur on the microlevel of one iteration. The dynamic development starts with the events on the microlevel. Most of these events at the microlevel consolidate the person's stable state (attractor), but some may lead to other attractor states. Our model describes how the different domains affect each other on the level of one iteration. However, one iteration leads to a set of consequent iterative steps that lead to changes in the person's attractor state.

The basic structure of a dynamic systems model consists of iteration descriptions (in a mathematical model these are translated into differential equations) between the domains. The iterative character implies that these connections or equations are repeated again and again, and in this way, they describe the development of the different domains over time.

Interconnections

The upper box included in the model (see Figure 1) is the stable individual parameters of each of the three domains. In other words, it is the condition from where the model starts to simulate further behaviors. The three domains of HRQOL, representing the central body of the model, are fully interconnected. Arrows connecting the same domain at different times represent the influence of the previous condition of that domain on the condition in the next iteration.

Influences are delayed, meaning that arrows do not link two domains at the same time because, in our vision, the effect of one domain on another domain will be visible in the next situation. Regarding HRQOL among seniors, we hypothesize that process of change can be seen from a daily basis. Finally, each domain at every time level is connected with a random influence (R) that represents the casual and unpredictable part of the model.

The model that is presented here is a theoretical model. It is built upon existing knowledge, and it aims to integrate the merits of existing models, adding the developmental perspective. Contrary to earlier models, it allows to study and analyze changes in the construct as a result of the iterations among domains, explicating the possible mechanisms acting during the development of the construct. The model described here meets the basic requirements described in the beginning; it takes into account: (i) the different domains that are relevant in HRQOL; (ii) the developmental processes that result in stability or change in HRQOL; (iii) the influences of each domain on the others; and (iv) the influence of unpredictable events. The model may serve as a basis, firstly, to carry out empirical research into the HRQOL of life of individuals over time and secondly, it will be the basis of a quantitative dynamic systems model. The translation of the DCSM-HRQOL into a quantitative model permits to test the theoretical assumptions and to compare simulated data with empirical ones. This approach may contribute to enhance knowledge of the phenomenon under study, confirming (or not) the system structure presented here.

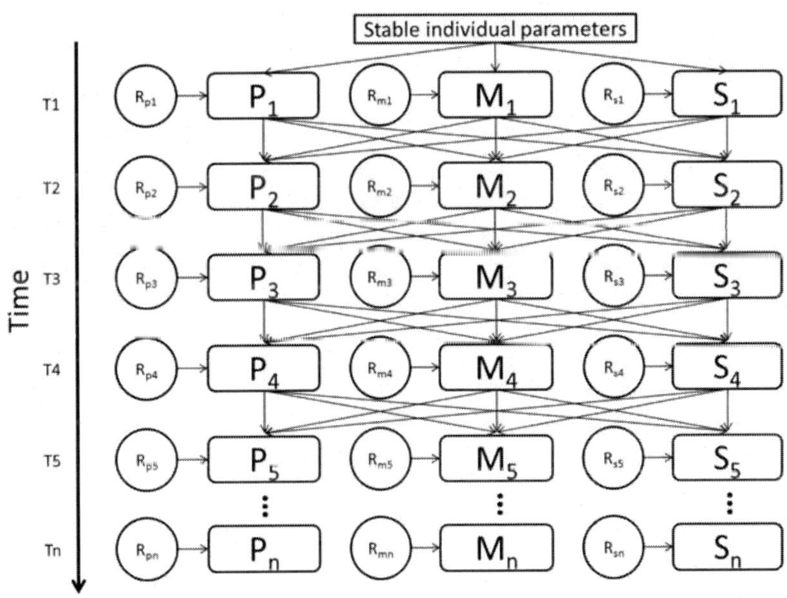

Figure 1. The Dynamic Systems conceptual model of HRQOL

Stable individual parameters is an indicator of age, comorbidity and lifestyle, directly influencing the three main domains of HRQOL.
P= physical domain
M= mental domain
S= social domain
R= random influence
The model shows 6 iterations (from T1 to a generic Tn), each arrow is a connection between domains during time

CONCLUSION

In order to analyze, understand and intervene in people's health status, reducing negative outcomes of ageing process, the construct of HRQOL was placed in a developmental perspective, following the dynamic systems theory. The conceptual model presented here could: provide new explanations about the processes acting in the ageing, generate new hypotheses and empirical questions about mechanisms and processes of changes of HRQOL during ageing, and generate new ways of measuring HRQOL, in particular in the form of repeated multivariate time serial measurements.

The general aim of the paper was to formulate the conditions and sketch the outlines of a model that enables us to study the developmental process of HRQOL in seniors. The DSCM-HRQOL employs terminology of the health definition (WHO, 1948) and the conceptualization of Testa and Simonson (1996) for the double evaluation of the inserted domains. The use of dynamic systems theory, applied to model development in old age (Schroots, 2012), seems to be a good basis to model HRQOL in the older adults, giving possible solutions and suggestions to some open questions as, in example, how HRQOL evolves during time, how the domains interact with each other, and, how life events act on HRQOL.

Future steps, starting from the conceptualization presented here, foresee the translation of the DSCM-HRQOL model in a mathematical dynamic system model that could provide additional indications about development and trends of HRQOL in the older adults population. The usefulness of a dynamic systems mathematical model can contribute to our understanding of the underlying developmental process, as previously demonstrated in the study of development in other area of research (Kunnen, 2012; Kunnen & Bosma, 2000; Steenbeek & Van Geert, 2008). The mathematical model can be used as a simulation tool (if previously validated) to analyze trends, starting from different conditions, or to simulate interventions for the maintenance/increase of HRQOL. Finally, a specific designed study is necessary to evaluate and quantify the real dynamic trend of HRQOL construct delineated here.

REFERENCES

Aaronson, N. (1993). Quality-of-Life Assessment - Key Issues in the 1990s - Walker,Sr, Rosser,Rm. *Quality of Life Research*, *2*, 305–306. doi:10.1007/Bf00434802

Acree, L. S., Longfors, J., Fjeldstad, A. S., Fjeldstad, C., Schank, B., Nickel, K. J., Gardner, A. W. (2006). Physical activity is related to quality of life in older adults. *Health Qual Life Outcomes*, *4*, 37. doi:10.1186/1477-7525-4-37

Albert, M. L., & Janice E. Knoefel, M. D. (1994). *Clinical Neurology of Aging*. Oxford University Press.

Atchley, R. C. (1989). A continuity theory of normal aging. *Gerontologist*, *29*, 183–90.

Balboa-Castillo, T., Leon-Munoz, L. M., Graciani, A., Rodriguez-Artalejo, F., & Guallar-Castillon, P. (2011). Longitudinal association of physical activity and sedentary behavior during leisure time with health-related quality of life in community-dwelling older adults. *Health Qual Life Outcomes*, *9*, 47. doi:10.1186/1477-7525-9-47

Baltes, P. B., & Baltes, M. M. (1993). *Successful Aging: Perspectives from the Behavioral Sciences*. Cambridge University Press.

Baltes, P. B., & Smith, J. (2003). New frontiers in the future of aging: from successful aging of the young old to the dilemmas of the fourth age. *Gerontology*, *49*, 123–35.

Bassano, D., & van Geert, P. (2007). Modeling continuity and discontinuity in utterance length: a quantitative approach to changes, transitions and intra-individual variability in early grammatical development. *Dev Sci*, *10*, 588–612. doi:10.1111/j.1467-7687.2007.00629.x

Bath, P. A., & Deeg, D. (2005). Social engagement and health outcomes among older people: introduction to a special section. *European Journal of Ageing*, *2*(1), 24–30. doi:10.1007/s10433-005-0019-4

Beekman, A. T. F., Bremmer, M. A., Deeg, D. J. H., van Balkom, A. J. L. M., Smit, J. H., de Beurs, E., van Dyck, R.., van Tilburg, W. (1998). Anxiety disorders in later life: A report from the longitudinal aging study Amsterdam. *International Journal of Geriatric Psychiatry*, *13*, 717–726. doi:10.1002/(Sici)1099-1166(1998100)13:10<717::Aid-Gps857>3.0.Co;2-M

Beekman, A. T. F., Copeland, J. R. M., & Prince, M. J. (1999). Review of community prevalence of depression in later life. *British Journal of Psychiatry*, *174*, 307–311. doi:10.1192/bjp.174.4.307

Bennett, K. (2005). Social engagement as a longitudinal predictor of objective and subjective health. *European Journal of Ageing*, *2*, 48–55. doi:10.1007/s10433-005-0501-z

Bennett, K. M. (2002). Low level social engagement as a precursor of mortality among people in later life. *Age and Ageing*, *31*, 165–168. doi:10.1093/ageing/31.3.165

Bernhard, J., Lowy, A., Mathys, N., Herrmann, R., & Hurny, C. (2004). Health related quality of life: a changing construct? *Qual Life Res*, *13*, 1187–97.

Berzon, R., Hays, R. D., & Shumaker, S. A. (1993). International Use, Application and Performance of Health-Related Quality-of-Life Instruments - Preface. *Quality of Life Research*, *2*, 367–368. doi:10.1007/Bf00422214

Bilotta, C., Bowling, A., Nicolini, P., Case, A., Pina, G., Rossi, S. V., & Vergani, C. (2011). Older People's Quality of Life (OPQOL) scores and adverse health outcomes at a one-year follow-up. A prospective cohort study on older outpatients living in the community in Italy. *Health Qual Life Outcomes*, *9*, 72. doi:10.1186/1477-7525-9-72

Blazer, D., Burchett, B., Service, C., & George, L. K. (1991). The Association of Age and Depression among the Elderly - an Epidemiologic Exploration. *Journals of Gerontology*, *46*, M210–M215.

Bosscher, R. J., & Smit, J. H. (1998). Confirmatory factor analysis of the General Self-Efficacy Scale. *Behaviour Research and Therapy*, *36*(3), 339–343. doi:10.1016/S0005-7967(98)00025-4

Bouchard, C., & Shephard, R. J. (1994). *Physical activity, fitness, and health: international proceedings and consensus statement*. Human Kinetics Publishers

Browne, J. P., O'Boyle, C. A., McGee, H. M., Joyce, C. R., McDonald, N. J., O'Malley, K., & Hiltbrunner, B. (1994). Individual quality of life in the healthy elderly. *Qual Life Res*, *3*, 235–44.

Chien, M. Y., Huang, T. Y., & Wu, Y. T. (2008). Prevalence of sarcopenia estimated using a bioelectrical impedance analysis prediction equation in community-dwelling elderly people in Taiwan. *Journal of the American Geriatrics Society*, *56*, 1710–1715. doi:10.1111/j.1532-5415.2008.01854.x

Ciairano, S., Liubicich, M. E., & Rabaglietti, E. (2010). The effects of a physical activity programme on the psychological wellbeing of older people in a residential care facility: an experimental study. *Ageing and Society*, *30*(04), 609–626. doi:10.1017/S014468 6X09990614

Craig, C., Marshall, A., Sjöström, M., Bauman, A., Booth, M., Ainsworth, B., Pratt, M., Ekelund, U., Yngve, A., Sallis, J. F., Oja, P. (2003). International physical activity questionnaire: 12-country reliability and validity. *Medicine and Science in Sports and Exercise*, *35*(8), 1381–1395.

Crimmins, E. M. (2004). Trends in the health of the elderly. *Annual Review of Public Health*, *25*, 79–98. doi:10.1146/annurev.publhealth. 25.102802. 124401

Cumming, E., & Henry, W. E. (1961). *Growing old, the process of disengagement*. Basic Books.

Cummings, S. R. (1993). Bone mass and bone loss in the elderly: a special case? *Int J Fertil Menopausal Stud*, *38 Suppl 2*, 92–7.

De Toni, A. F., & Comello, L. (2005). *Prede o ragni: uomini e organizzazioni nella ragnatela della complessità*. Torino: UTET universitaria.

Deschamps, A., Onifade, C., Decamps, A., & Bourdel-Marchasson, I. (2009). Health-related quality of life in frail institutionalized elderly: effects of a cognition-action intervention and Tai Chi. *J Aging Phys Act*, *17*, 236–48.

Doherty, T. J. (2001). The influence of aging and sex on skeletal muscle mass and strength. *Curr Opin Clin Nutr Metab Care*, *4*, 503–8.

Dorr, D. A., Jones, S. S., Burns, L., Donnelly, S. M., Brunker, C. P., Wilcox, A., & Clayton, P. D. (2006). Use of health-related, quality-of-life metrics to predict mortality and hospitalizations in community-dwelling seniors. *Journal of the American Geriatrics Society*, *54*, 667–673. doi:10.1111/j.1532-5415.2006.00681.x

Drageset, J., Natvig, G. K., Eide, G. E., Bondevik, M., Nortvedt, M. W., & Nygaard, H. A. (2009). Health-related quality of life among old residents of nursing homes in Norway. *International Journal of Nursing Practice*, *15*, 455–466. doi:10.1111/j.1440-172X.2009.01794.x

Elavsky, S., McAuley, E., Motl, R. W., Konopack, J. F., Marquez, D. X., Hu, L., Jerome, G. J., Diener, E. (2005). Physical activity enhances long-term quality of life in older adults: efficacy, esteem, and affective influences. *Ann Behav Med*, *30*, 138–45. doi:10.1207/s15324796abm3002_6

Engel, G. L. (1977). The need for a new medical model: a challenge for biomedicine. *Science*, *196*, 129–36.

Eurostat. (2008). *Population projections 2008-2060* (No. 119/2008) (pp. 1–4). Luxemburg.

Eurostat. (2011). *Active ageing and solidarity between generations. A statistical portrait of the European Union 2012* (Satatistica books., Vol. 1). Luxemburg: Eurostat.

Evans, D. R., Burns, J. E., Robinson, W. E., & Garrett, O. J. (1985). The quality of life questionnaire: A multidimensional measure. *American Journal of Community Psychology*, *13*(3), 305–322. doi:10.1007/BF00914935

Ferrans, C. E., Zerwic, J. J., Wilbur, J. E., & Larson, J. L. (2005). Conceptual model of health-related quality of life. *Journal of Nursing Scholarship*, *37*, 336–342. doi:10.1111/j.1547-5069.2005.00058.x

Floel, A., Witte, A. V., Lohmann, H., Wersching, H., Ringelstein, E. B., Berger, K., & Knecht, S. (2008). Lifestyle and memory in the elderly. *Neuroepidemiology*, *31*, 39–47. doi:10.1159/000137378

Folstein, M. F., Folstein, S. E., & McHugh, P. R. (1975). Mini-mental state: A practical method for grading the cognitive state of patients for the clinician. *Journal of Psychiatric Research*, *12*(3), 189–198. doi:10.1016/0022-3956(75)90026-6

Fratiglioni, L., Paillard-Borg, S., & Winblad, B. (2004). An active and socially integrated lifestyle in late life might protect against dementia. *Lancet Neurology*, *3*, 343–353. doi:10.1016/S1474-4422(04)00767-7

Freund, A. M., & Baltes, P. B. (1998). Selection, optimization, and compensation as strategies of life management: correlations with subjective indicators of successful aging. *Psychol Aging*, *13*, 531–43.

Frontera, W. R., Hughes, V. A., Fielding, R. A., Fiatarone, M. A., Evans, W. J., & Roubenoff, R. (2000). Aging of skeletal muscle: a 12-yr longitudinal study. *Journal of Applied Physiology*, *88*, 1321–1326.

Gale, C. R., Dennison, E. M., Cooper, C., & Sayer, A. A. (2011). Neighbourhood environment and positive mental health in older people: The Hertfordshire Cohort Study. *Health & Place*, *17*(4), 867–874. doi:10.1016/j.healthplace.2011.05.003

García, E. L., Banegas, J. R., Pérez-Regadera, A. G., Cabrera, R. H., & Rodríguez-Artalejo, F. (2005). Social network and health-related quality of life in older adults: A population-based study in Spain. *Quality of Life Research*, *14*(2), 511–520. doi:10.1007/s11136-004-5329-z

Gaugler, J. E., Duval, S., Anderson, K. A., & Kane, R. L. (2007). Predicting nursing home admission in the U.S: a meta-analysis. *BMC Geriatr*, *7*, 13. doi:10.1186/1471-2318-7-13

Giannakouris, C. (2008). *Population and social conditions. Ageing characteristics the demographic perspectives of the European societies* (No. KS-SF-08-072-EN-N) (pp. 1–12). Luxemburg.

Glass, T. A., De Leon, C. F. M., Bassuk, S. S., & Berkman, L. F. (2006). Social engagement and depressive symptoms in late life - Longitudinal findings. *Journal of Aging and Health*, *18*, 604–628. doi:10.1177/0898264306291017

Gleick, J. (1996). *Chaos: making a new science.* London: Minerva.

Grammenos, S. (2005). *Implications of demographic ageing in the enlarged EU in the domains of quality of life, health promotion and health care* (pp. 1–199). Bruxelles: Center for European Social and Economic Policy.

Hannan, M. T., Felson, D. T., Dawson-Hughes, B., Tucker, K. L., Cupples, L. A., Wilson, P. W., & Kiel, D. P. (2000). Risk factors for longitudinal bone loss in elderly men and women: the Framingham Osteoporosis Study. *J Bone Miner Res*, *15*, 710–20. doi:10.1359/jbmr.2000.15.4.710

Haskell, W. L., Lee, I. M., Pate, R. R., Powell, K. E., Blair, S. N., Franklin, B. A., Macera, C., Heath, G. W., Thompson, P. D., Bauman, A. (2007). Physical activity and public health: updated recommendation for adults from the American College of Sports Medicine and the American Heart Association. *Circulation*, *116*, 1081–93. doi:10.1161/CIRCULATIONAHA.107.185649

Hawthorne, G. (2006). Measuring Social Isolation in Older Adults: Development and Initial Validation of the Friendship Scale. *Social Indicators Research*, *77*(3), 521–548. doi:10.1007/s11205-005-7746-y

Henchoz, K., Cavalli, S., & Girardin, M. (2008). Health perception and health status in advanced old age: A paradox of association. Journal of Aging Studies, 22(3), 282-290. doi:10.1016/j.jaging.2007.03.002

Hollenstein, T., Granic, I., Stoolmiller, M., & Snyder, J. (2004). Rigidity in parent-child interactions and the development of externalizing and internalizing behavior in early childhood. *J Abnorm Child Psychol*, *32*, 595–607.

Hopman, W. M., Harrison, M. B., Coo, H., Friedberg, E., Buchanan, M., & VanDenKerkhof, E. G. (2009). Associations between chronic disease, age and physical and mental health status. *Chronic Diseases in Canada*, *29*, 108–116.

Hopman, W. M., Towheed, T., Anastassiades, T., Tenenhouse, A., Poliquin, S., Berger, C., Joseph, L., Brown, J. P., Murray, T. M., Adachi, J. D., Hanley, D. A., Papadimitropoulos, E. (2000). Canadian normative data for the SF-36 health survey. *Canadian Medical Association Journal*, *163*, 265–271.

Idler, E. L., & Benyamini, Y. (1997). Self-rated health and mortality: a review of twenty-seven community studies. *J Health Soc Behav*, *38*, 21–37.

Inaba, Y., Obuchi, S., Arai, T., Satake, K., & Takahira, N. (2008). The long-term effects of progressive resistance training on health-related quality in older adults. *J Physiol Anthropol*, *27*, 57–61.

Janssen, I., Heymsfield, S. B., & Ross, R. (2002). Low relative skeletal muscle mass (sarcopenia) in older persons is associated with functional impairment and physical disability. *Journal of the American Geriatrics Society*, *50*, 889–896. doi:10.1046/j.1532-5415.2002.50216.x

Janssen, I., Heymsfield, S. B., Wang, Z. M., & Ross, R. (2000). Skeletal muscle mass and distribution in 468 men and women aged 18-88 yr. *J Appl Physiol*, *89*, 81–8.

Janssen, Ian, Baumgartner, R. N., Ross, R., Rosenberg, I. H., & Roubenoff, R. (2004). Skeletal Muscle Cutpoints Associated with Elevated Physical Disability Risk in Older Men and Women. *American Journal of Epidemiology*, *159*, 413–421. doi:10.1093/aje/kwh058

Janssens, J. P., Pache, J. C., & Nicod, L. P. (1999). Physiological changes in respiratory function associated with ageing. *Eur Respir J*, *13*, 197–205.

Jenkins, K. R., Pienta, A. M., & Horgas, A. L. (2002). Activity and health-related quality of life in continuing care retirement communities. *Research on Aging*, *24*, 124–149. doi:10.1177/0164027503024001008

Johnell, O., & Kanis, J. A. (2004). An estimate of the worldwide prevalence, mortality and disability associated with hip fracture. *Osteoporos Int*, *15*, 897–902. doi:10.1007/s00198-004-1627-0

Kaplan, R. M., Bush, J. W., & Berry, C. C. (1976). Health status: types of validity and the index of well-being. *Health Services Research*, *11*(4), 478–507.

Katz, S., Ford, A. B., Moskovitz, R. W., Jackson, B. A., & Jaffe, M. W. (1963). Studies of illness in the aged. The index of adl: a standardized measure of biological and psychosocial function. *JAMA: The Journal of the American Medical Association*, *185*, 914–919.

Kawachi, I., & Berkman, L. F. (2001). Social ties and mental health. *Journal of Urban Health-Bulletin of the New York Academy of Medicine*, *78*, 458–467. doi:10.1093/jurban/78.3.458

Kempen, G. I., Ormel, J., Brilman, E. I., & Relyveld, J. (1997). Adaptive responses among Dutch elderly: the impact of eight chronic medical conditions on health-related quality of life. *Am J Public Health*, *87*, 38–44.

Keysor, J. J. (2003). Does late-life physical activity or exercise prevent or minimize disablement? A critical review of the scientific evidence. *American Journal of Preventive Medicine*, *25*, 129–136. doi:10.1016/S0749-3797(03)00176-4

Kimura, K., Obuchi, S., Arai, T., Nagasawa, H., Shiba, Y., Watanabe, S., & Kojima, M. (2010). The influence of short-term strength training on health-related quality of life and executive cognitive function. *J Physiol Anthropol*, *29*, 95–101.

Kitzman, D. W. (2000). Diastolic dysfunction in the elderly. Genesis and diagnostic and therapeutic implications. *Cardiol Clin*, *18*, 597–617, x.

Kitzman, D. W., & Edwards, W. D. (1990). Age-related changes in the anatomy of the normal human heart. *J Gerontol*, *45*, M33–9.

Kramer, A. F., Colcombe, S. J., McAuley, E., Eriksen, K. I., Scalf, P., Jerome, G. J., Marquez, D. X., Elavsky, S., Webb, A. G. (2003). Enhancing brain and cognitive function of older adults through fitness training. *Journal of Molecular Neuroscience*, *20*, 213–221. doi:10.1385/Jmn:20:3:213

Kunnen, E. S. (2009). Qualitative and quantitative aspects of commitment development in psychology students. *J Adolesc*, *32*, 567–84. doi:10.1016/j.adolescence.2008.06.002

Kunnen, E. S. (2012). *A Dynamic Systems Approach of Adolescent Development*. Taylor & Francis.

Kunnen, E. S., & Bosma, H. A. (2000). Development of meaning making: A dynamic systems approach. *New Ideas in Psychology*, *18*, 57–82. doi:10.1016/S0732-118X(99)00037-9

Lam, C. L. K., & Lauder, I. J. (2000). The impact of chronic diseases on the health-related quality of life (HRQOL) of Chinese patients in primary care. *Family Practice*, *17*, 159–166. doi:10.1093/fampra/17.2.159

Latham, N. K., Bennett, D. A., Stretton, C. M., & Anderson, C. S. (2004). Systematic review of progressive resistance strength training in older adults. *J Gerontol A Biol Sci Med Sci*, *59*, 48–61.

Lee, C., & Russell, A. (2003). Effects of physical activity on emotional well-being among older Australian women: cross-sectional and longitudinal analyses. *J Psychosom Res*, *54*, 155–60.

Lee, L. Y., Lee, D. T., & Woo, J. (2009). Tai Chi and health-related quality of life in nursing home residents. *J Nurs Scholarsh*, *41*, 35–43. doi:10.1111/j.1547-5069.2009.01249.x

Leidy, N. K. (1994). Functional status and the forward progress of merry-go-rounds: toward a coherent analytical framework. *Nursing Research*, *43*(4), 196–202.

Lemon, B. W., Bengtson, V. L., & Peterson, J. A. (1972). An exploration of the activity theory of aging: activity types and life satisfaction among in-movers to a retirement community. *J Gerontol*, *27*, 511–23.

Lexell, J. (1995). Human Aging, Muscle Mass, and Fiber-Type Composition. *Journals of Gerontology Series a-Biological Sciences and Medical Sciences*, *50*, 11–16.

Lichtwarck-Aschoff, A., Kunnen, S. E., & van Geert, P. L. (2009). Here we go again: a dynamic systems perspective on emotional rigidity across parent-adolescent conflicts. *Dev Psychol*, *45*, 1364–75. doi:10.1037/a0016713

Lichtwarck-Aschoff, Anna, van Geert, P., Bosma, H., & Kunnen, S. (2008). Time and identity: A framework for research and theory formation. *Developmental Review*, *28*(3), 370–400. doi:10.1016/j.dr.2008.04.001

Lima, M. G., Barros, M. B., Cesar, C. L., Goldbaum, M., Carandina, L., & Ciconelli, R. M. (2009). Impact of chronic disease on quality of life among the elderly in the state of Sao Paulo, Brazil: a population-based study. *Rev Panam Salud Publica*, *25*, 314–21.

Lipscomb, J., Gotay, C. C., & Snyder, C. (2004). *Outcomes Assessment in Cancer: Measures, Methods and Applications*. Cambridge University Press.

Lubben, J. E. (1988). Assessing social networks among elderly populations. *Family & Community Health: The Journal of Health Promotion & Maintenance*, *11*(3), 42–52.

Luppa, M., Luck, T., Weyerer, S., Konig, H. H., Brahler, E., & Riedel-Heller, S. G. (2010). Prediction of institutionalization in the elderly. A systematic review. *Age Ageing*, *39*, 31–8. doi:10.1093/ageing/afp202

Manton, K. G. (1982). Changing concepts of morbidity and mortality in the elderly population. *Milbank Mem Fund Q Health Soc*, *60*, 183–244.

Manton, K. G., Gu, X., & Lamb, V. L. (2006). Change in chronic disability from 1982 to 2004/2005 as measured by long-term changes in function and health in the U.S. elderly population. *Proc Natl Acad Sci U S A*, *103*, 18374–9. doi:10.1073/pnas.0608483103

Marengoni, A., Winblad, B., Karp, A., & Fratiglioni, L. (2008). Prevalence of chronic diseases and multimorbidity among the elderly population in Sweden. *Am J Public Health*, *98*, 1198–200. doi:10.2105/AJPH.2007.121137

McAvay, G. J., Seeman, T. E., & Rodin, J. (1996). A longitudinal study of change in domain-specific self-efficacy among older adults. *Journals of Gerontology Series B-Psychological Sciences and Social Sciences*, *51*, P243–P253.

Mebane-Sims, I., & Association, A. (2009). 2009 Alzheimer's disease facts and figures. *Alzheimers & Dementia*, *5*, 234–270. doi:10.1016 /j.jalz.2009.03.001

Murdaugh, C. (1997). Health-related quality of life as an outcome in organizational research. *Medical Care*, *35*, Ns41–Ns48. doi:10.1097/00005650-199711001-00005

Netz, Y., Wu, M. J., Becker, B. J., & Tenenbaum, G. (2005). Physical activity and psychological well-being in advanced age: A meta-analysis of intervention studies. *Psychology and Aging*, *20*, 272–284. doi:10.1037/0882-7974.20.2.272

Pachana, N. A., Byrne, G. J., Siddle, H., Koloski, N., Harley, E., & Arnold, E. (2007). Development and validation of the Geriatric Anxiety Inventory. *International Psychogeriatrics*, *19*(01), 103–114. doi:10.1017 /S1041610206003504

Penedo, F. J., & Dahn, J. R. (2005). Exercise and well-being: a review of mental and physical health benefits associated with physical activity. *Curr Opin Psychiatry*, *18*, 189–93.

Rivner, M. H., Swift, T. R., & Malik, K. (2001). Influence of age and height on nerve conduction. *Muscle & Nerve*, *24*, 1134–1141. doi:10.1002/Mus.1124

Rogers, M. A., & Evans, W. J. (1993). Changes in skeletal muscle with aging: effects of exercise training. *Exerc Sport Sci Rev*, *21*, 65–102.

Roppolo, M. Mulasso, A., Magistro, D., Roggero, A., Andreoli, P., & Liubicich, M. E. (2012). Shintaido in the elderly: The new way for physical and psychological health. *Advances in Aging Research*, *01*(02), 22–30. doi:10.4236/aar.2012.12003

Rossi, A., Ganassini, A., Tantucci, C., & Grassi, V. (1996). Aging and the respiratory system. *Aging (Milan, Italy)*, *8*(3), 143–161.

Roubenoff, R., & Hughes, V. A. (2000). Sarcopenia Current Concepts. *The Journals of Gerontology Series A: Biological Sciences and Medical Sciences*, *55*(12), M716–M724. doi:10.1093/gerona/55.12.M716

Sabin, E. P. (1993). Social Relationships and Mortality among the Elderly. *Journal of Applied Gerontology*, *12*, 44–60. doi:10.1177/0733 46489301200105

Salat, D. H., Buckner, R. L., Snyder, A. Z., Greve, D. N., Desikan, R. S. R., Busa, E., Morris, J. C., Dale, A. M., Fischl, B. (2004). Thinning of the cerebral cortex in aging. *Cerebral Cortex*, *14*, 721–730. doi:10.1093/cercor/bhh032

Schroots, J. J. F. (2012). On the Dynamics of Active Aging. *Current Gerontology and Geriatrics Research*, *2012*, 1–10. doi:10.1155 /2012/818564

Sharma, G., & Goodwin, J. (2006). Effect of aging on respiratory system physiology and immunology. *Clinical Interventions in Aging*, *1*, 253–260. doi:10.2147/ciia.2006.1.3.253

Shephard, R. J. (1993). Exercise and aging: extending independence in older adults. *Geriatrics*, *48*, 61–4.

Sillanpaa, E., Hakkinen, K., Holviala, J., & Hakkinen, A. (2012). Combined strength and endurance training improves health-related quality of life in healthy middle-aged and older adults. *Int J Sports Med*, *33*, 981–6. doi:10.1055/s-0032-1311589

Small, S. A., Stern, Y., Tang, M., & Mayeux, R. (1999). Selective decline in memory function among healthy elderly. *Neurology*, *52*, 1392–1396.

Smith, L. B., & Thelen, E. (2003). Development as a dynamic system. *Trends in Cognitive Sciences*, *7*(8), 343–348. doi:10.1016/S1364-6613(03)00156-6

Sprangers, M. A., & Schwartz, C. E. (2008). Reflections on changeability versus stability of health-related quality of life: distinguishing between its environmental and genetic components. *Health Qual Life Outcomes*, *6*, 89. doi:10.1186/1477-7525-6-89

Steenbeek, H., & van Geert, P. (2008). An empirical validation of a dynamic systems model of interaction: do children of different sociometric statuses differ in their dyadic play? *Dev Sci*, *11*, 253–81. doi:10.1111/j.1467-7687.2007.00655.x

Tennant, R., Hiller, L., Fishwick, R., Platt, S., Joseph, S., Weich, S., Parkinson, J., Secker, J., Stewart-Brown, S. (2007). The Warwick-Edinburgh Mental Well-being Scale (WEMWBS): development and UK validation. *Health and Quality of Life Outcomes*, *5*(1), 63. doi:10.1186/1477-7525-5-63

Testa, M. A., & Simonson, D. C. (1996). Assessment of Quality-of-Life Outcomes. *New England Journal of Medicine*, *334*, 835–840. doi:10.1056/NEJM199603283341306

Thelen, E., & Smith, L. B. (1996). *A Dynamic Systems Approach to the Development of Cognition and Action*. Mit Press.

Thelen, E., & Ulrich, B. D. (1991). Hidden skills: a dynamic systems analysis of treadmill stepping during the first year. *Monogr Soc Res Child Dev*, *56*, 1–98; discussion 99–104.

Theofilou, P. (2011). Why is important to aseess health-Related Quality of Life? *J Palliative Care Med*, *1*, e104. doi:10.4172/2165-7386.1000e104

Thompson, W. W., Zack, M. M., Krahn, G. L., Andresen, E. M., & Barile, J. P. (2012). Health-related quality of life among older adults with and without functional limitations. *Am J Public Health*, *102*, 496–502. doi:10.2105/AJPH.2011.300500

Tomioka, K., Iwamoto, J., Saeki, K., & Okamoto, N. (2011). Reliability and Validity of the International Physical Activity Questionnaire (IPAQ) in Elderly Adults: The Fujiwara-kyo Study. *Journal of Epidemiology*, *21*(6), 459–465.

Tsai, S. Y., Chi, L. Y., Lee, C. H., & Chou, P. (2007). Health-related quality of life as a predictor of mortality among community-dwelling older persons. *Eur J Epidemiol*, *22*, 19–26. doi:10.1007/s10654-006-9092-z

Van der Maas, H. L., & Molenaar, P. C. (1992). Stagewise cognitive development: An application of catastrophe theory. *Psychological Review*, *99*(3), 395–417. doi:10.1037/0033-295X.99.3.395

Van Geert, P. (1994). *Dynamic systems of development: change between complexity and chaos*. Harvester Wheatsheaf.

Van Geert, P. (2008). Complex dynamic systems of development. In R. A. Meyers (Ed.), *Encyclopedia of complexity and system science* (Vol. 2, pp. 1872–1916). New York: Springer.

Van Geert, P., & van Dijk, M. (2002). Focus on variability: New tools to study intra-individual variability in developmental data. *Infant Behavior and Development*, *25*, 340–374. doi:10.1016/S0163-6383(02)00140-6

Wang, L., Larson, E. B., Bowen, J. D., & van Belle, G. (2006). Performance-based physical function and future dementia in older people. *Archives of Internal Medicine*, *166*, 1115–1120. doi:10.1001/archinte.166.10.1115

Ware, J. E., & Dewey, J. (2000). Health status and outcome assessment tools. *Int Electronic J Health Education*, *3*, 138–148.

Ware, J. E. J. (1987). Standards for validating health measures: Definition and content. *Journal of Chronic Diseases*, *40*(6), 473–480. doi:10.1016/0021-9681(87)90003-8

Weisstein, E. W. (2003). *CRC Concise Encyclopedia of Mathematics*. Chapman & Hall/CRC.

Wilson, I. B., & Cleary, P. D. (1995). Linking clinical variables with health-related quality of life: A conceptual model of patient outcomes. *JAMA*, *273*, 59–65.

Wolinsky, F. D., Unverzagt, F. W., Smith, D. M., Jones, R., Stoddard, A., & Tennstedt, S. L. (2006). The ACTIVE cognitive training trial and health-related quality of life: protection that lasts for 5 years. *J Gerontol A Biol Sci Med Sci*, *61*, 1324–9.

Wolinsky, F. D., Unverzagt, F. W., Smith, D. M., Jones, R., Wright, E., & Tennstedt, S. L. (2006). The effects of the ACTIVE cognitive training trial on clinically relevant declines in health-related quality of life. *J Gerontol B Psychol Sci Soc Sci*, *61*, S281–7.

Wyrwich, K. W., & Wolinsky, F. D. (2000). Identifying meaningful intra-individual change standards for health-related quality of life measures. *J Eval Clin Pract*, *6*, 39–49.

Yasunaga, A., Togo, F., Watanabe, E., Park, H., Shephard, R. J., & Aoyagi, Y. (2006). Yearlong physical activity and health-related quality of life in older Japanese adults: the Nakanojo Study. *J Aging Phys Act*, *14*, 288–301.

Yesavage, J. A., Brink, T. L., Rose, T. L., Lum, O., Huang, V., Adey, M., & Leirer, V. O. (1982). Development and validation of a geriatric depression screening scale: A preliminary report. *Journal of Psychiatric Research*, *17*(1), 37–49. doi:10.1016/0022-3956(82)90033-4

In: Psychological Health and Needs Research Developments
Editor: Raul Wolfe
ISBN: 978-1-63483-332-5

Chapter 8

STUDYING FAITH-BASED TREATMENT FOR SUBSTANCE ADDICTION IN HONG KONG: A THEORETICAL MODEL

Jerf W. K. Yeung*
Department of Applied Social Sciences,
City University of Hong Kong, Kowloon, Hong Kong

ABSTRACT

Substance addiction is described as a 'chronic relapsing disease', to which the Hong Kong government takes an 'enlightened prohibition' approach to stress on the provision of rehabilitative support to addicts instead of imposing stringent legal sanctions (Cheung, 2009).The treatment and rehabilitation of substance addicts is thus of utmost importance, in which use of faith-based approach to help addict patients keep abstinent is one of the main treatment interventions in Hong Kong. Faith-based addiction treatment is usually conducted and provided by local Christian therapeutic organisations in guidance of a Christian theory of substance addiction that recognises not only the psychological, social and physical determinants of addiction, but also the importance of the religious/spiritual dimension of abusing substance (Lyons et al., 2013). Despite the desirable treatment outcomes of faith-based treatment found in the West, little research has been performed with regard to its effectiveness and delivery mechanisms, especially in Hong Kong. This chapter will propose a theoretical framework to investigate the mechanisms by which faith-based addiction treatment delivers the desirable treatment outcomes and, in particular, the respective contributing factors in different levels of the treatment mechanisms. Pertinent research designs, measurement and statistical procedures are also addressed. The chapter will finally conclude with implications and contributions stemmed from the proposed study.

Keywords: Faith-Based treatment, religiosity/ spirituality, christian theory, treatment outcomes

* Corresponding author: Jerf W. K. Yeung, Department of Applied Social Sciences, City University of Hong Kong, Kowloon, Hong Kong; email: ssjerf@gmail.com.

1. Introduction

A recent report by the United Nations estimated that 243 million people aged 15 to 64 used an illicit drug at least once in 2012 globally, up 16.8% from 2006's estimated 206 million drug users (United Nations Office on Drugs and Crime, 2014). Both figures are double the rates anticipated in the 1980s (Bowser et al., 2014). In addition, it is estimated that there were 183,000 drug-related deaths in 2012 and a large number of newly inflected cases with life-threatening diseases, e.g., HIV, hepatitis B and C, caused by substance abuse reported every year (United Nations Office on Drugs and Crime, 2014). Such as, it is apparent that substance abuse has been a rampant social and public health problem since the early 21st century. In Hong Kong, the Central Registry of Drug Abuse reported 10,939 drug abusers registered in 2012, while the actual population of drug takers is considerably larger than the official statistics, due to the covert nature of substance-taking behaviour (Census and Statistics Department, 2013). In most developed societies, like Hong Kong, substance abuse continues to incur vast social, health and economic costs (Singer, 2008). Substance addiction is commonly described as a 'chronic relapsing disease' (Cheung, 2009), and the relapse rate can be as high as 56.8% to 81.8% (Donovan, et al., 2013; Nordfjaern, 2011). The estimated social cost incurred by substance abuse, exclusive of the costs in criminal justice system, health care, and workplace, was HKD 301.42 million in Hong Kong in 2010 (Cheung, 2012). Hence its treatment plays a key role in alleviating the suffering of patients with addiction and in relieving the burden of the wider society. Greater research effort is therefore needed to develop more effective treatment strategies and better delivery mechanisms.

In Hong Kong, both moral and medical approaches are used in coping with drug abuse. The moral point of view sees drug abuse as a violation of social norms and moralities that should be legally prohibited. The medical point of view sees drug abuse as a chronic illness and drug users as patients in need of treatment and care. The Hong Kong government tends to use less stringent legal sanctions against addicts. Providing treatment service is thus the main strategy to decrease drug abuse, and various addiction treatment programmes are therefore run by the government and local NGOs such as Christian therapeutic organisations (Cheung, 2012). Treatment approaches as such in Hong Kong are either secular-based or faith-based interventions, which represent two very different sets of assumptions and strategies for dealing with abusing behaviour.

Faith-based treatment is distinguished from secular intervention primarily in its root in the Christian theory of substance addiction. It presumes that substance abuse is a sin, showing the addict's movement away from God's will and their separation from Him (Lyons et al., 2013). A new, healthy, drug-free life that can only be accomplished by the addict is confessing her/ his sins, accepting Jesus Christ as their personal saviour and committing to the Christian faith in the process of sanctification by connecting with God, Christ and the Holy Spirit (Lyons et al., 2011). In contrast to the faith-based approach, secular treatment mainly adopts medical and psychosocial models to deal with addict patients' physical and social needs, with less regard to their spiritual status (Kelly et al., 2013; McCoy et al., 2004). Recent research conducted in the West on faith-based treatment, such as 12-step facilitated treatment programmes[1], has seen significant improvements in patients' recovery outcomes.

[1] By 12-step treatment programmes, it mainly refers to Alcoholics Anonymous (AA) and Narcotics Anonymous (NA). Although sometimes AA and NA are not organised by Christian organisations, the founders of the12-

These 12-step treatment programmes encourage the addicts to surrender their control of life to 'God', which is actually a 'transcendental Christian entity' (Sellman et al., 2007).Specifically, similar to the Christian theory of substance addiction, the 12-step treatment theorizes addictive behaviors as the result of one's inherent relationship with God being replaced by substance use, and abstinence can be achieved by "spiritual awakening" through confessing one's sins and re-building a close relationship with God. Hence, the 12-step treatment is largely built on the Christian approach in treating substance abuse (Neff &MacMaster, 2005).

Pertinent findings have shownthat patients in 12-step programmes have significantly lower rates of relapse and longer abstinence compared to those receiving secular treatment (Kelly et al., 2013; Robinson et al., 2007). These benefits are possibly a result of their treatment philosophy, which stresses the complete life transformation of addicts, by simultaneously triggering changes in spiritual, cognitive, psychological and social process factors conducive to abstinence (Kelly et al., 2009; Lyons et al., 2011). Although some research has regarded this transformation to be the result of a spiritual awakening, recovery is essentially reached through reforming and resocialising the addict's life, establishing healthy, prosocial routines and upholding total abstinence, rather than the 'controlled substance use' philosophy adopted by many secular interventions (McCoy et al., 2004). Some scholars consider the transformation process of recovery in faith-based treatment to be a behaviour change process involving changes in multiple religious, cognitive, psychological and social process pathways to achieve abstinence and prevent relapse (Greenfield et al., 2012). This agrees with the aforementioned hypothesis that the re-establishment of various healthy life aspects is favourable for abstinence. However, little research has investigated this behaviour change assumption, particular in non-Western societies such as Hong Kong. In this chapter, it will examine how participation in faith-based addiction treatment contributes to recovery through changes in multiple important factors in religious, cognitive, psychological and social processes and how these factors act and interact over time in a natural treatment environment.

THEORETICAL FRAMEWORK

Over the past two decades, many empirical studies have shown the salutary effects of religion on mental, psychological, behavioural and physical health (Rew& Wong, 2006;Yonker et al., 2012). Research has consistently reported negative associations between religious involvement and depression, anxiety, psychotic disorders, substance abuse and suicidal behaviour (Koenig, 2009) and positive relationships between religiosity and life satisfaction, meaning and purpose in life, self-esteem, prosocial behaviour and a healthy lifestyle (Rew& Wong,2006). However, most of these studies were based on general populations, such as adolescents, working adults and the elderly. Little is known about religion's effects on clinical populations, such as drug addicts, despite the faith-based nature of many addiction treatment programmes in Hong Kong and elsewhere. Christian organisations have long provided treatment for substance addicts in both the West and East (Chu et al., 2012). They first responded to the illicit drug epidemics among young people in

step treatment were members of the Christian-based Oxford Group. There are many similarities between Christian and 12-step theories of substance abuse (Lyons et al., 2013). As there is much empirical research on the effectiveness of 12-step treatment programmes (Donovan et al., 2013), this proposal will consider these to reflect faith-based treatment in general.

the 1960s and catered for their rehabilitative needs (White &Whiters, 2005). Currently, faith-based treatment is still the main service component of addiction rehabilitation in Hong Kong. Thirteen of the 17 residential treatment centres and programmes in Hong Kong are faith-based and organised by Christian therapeutic organizations, and the remaining is secular-based run by non-religious NGOs. The government is mainly responsible for providing substance abuse clinics and compulsory residential treatment services for sentenced persons. In this study, both religiosity and spirituality means the expression of a spiritual relationship with God through organised or private practices, and hence the term religiosity and spirituality will be used inter-changeably (Koenig, 2009; Yonker et al., 2012).

Prior relevant research in the U.S. has revealed that faith-based and spiritual-approach treatments have more desirable treatment outcomes than secular intervention programmes such as cognitive-behavioural therapy (CBT) and motivational enhancement therapy (MET) (Kelly et al., 2009), showing less relapse, longer abstinence and fewer addiction symptoms at relapse. Forman et al. (2001) reported that 84% of addiction treatment professionals (N = 317) supported an emphasis on religiosity/spirituality in treatment. Dermatis et al. (2004) stated that 84% of patients with addiction wanted their spiritual needs to be addressed in the treatment process. According to the Christian theory of substance addiction, addictive behaviour is regarded as a sinful substitute of God's will (Kaskutas et al., 2003; Lyons et al., 2013), and thus the restored religious belief may straightforwardly lead to abstinence. But in reality, the faith-based treatment is found to involve other pathways, regulating secular variables beneficial for recovery, such as changes in cognitive, (e.g., increase meaning and purpose in life), psychological (e.g., lessen depression and enhance self-efficacy) and social process (e.g., strengthen family support and pro-abstinent peer network) factors (Kelly et al., 2013; Krentzman et al., 2012; Lyons et al., 2011). To sum up, the behaviour change perspective assumes the importance of re-establishing various healthy, wholesome life aspects for abstinence. It is closely pertinent to the multiple pathways hypothesis, that faith-based treatment achieves recovery by simultaneously triggering multiple beneficial factors (Neff &MacMaster, 2005). The study proposed in this chapter attempts to construct a theoretical model that simultaneously investigates these multiple factors' contributions to treatment outcomes prospectively. In the following section, the associations between respective factor and treatment outcomes will be reviewed and a theoretical model to test the causal relationships is then made.

Growth in Religiosity and Treatment Outcomes

Faith-based treatment programmes lay stress on establishing close bonding with God and promote religious conversion (Chu et al., 2012). Change and growth in religiosity is therefore the central tenet of these treatment programmes. Recent studies have investigated the effects of religious growth and change on treatment outcomes. In a large longitudinal study of 655 treatment seekers, Kaskutas et al. (2003) found that individuals who experienced spiritual awakening during treatment were four times more likely to be totally abstinent three years after treatment than their counterparts without such experiences. Recently, Zemore (2007) investigated change in spirituality after AA participation and found that an increase in spirituality was significantly related to sobriety from heavy drinking at a 6-month follow-up.

In a more recent prospective study, Kelly et al. (2011) confirmed the significant mediational effects of religious and spiritual growth on better treatment outcomes across both inpatient and outpatient samples. Hence, we hypothesise that participation in faith-based treatment results in religious growth and change, which act as a pathway for recovery.

Meaning and Purpose in Life and Treatment Outcomes

As religion emphasises finding meaning and purpose in life, research has recently explored its role in treatment outcomes. People who perceive less purpose and meaning in life tend to have more pathological and maladaptive behaviour, such as substance use (Lyons et al., 2011).

Many studies affirm that a significant increase in purpose in life is related to less relapse after treatment. Carroll (1993) proposed that religiosity and spirituality might deter the impulse to abuse substances by conferring meaning and purpose to life, which fills the spiritual void that is a precursor of substance addiction. In a longitudinal study of spiritual-based treatment, Robinson et al. (2007) reported that significantly increased life meaning and purpose 6 months after treatment contributed to 12% fewer heavy drinking days. Cheng (2010) also found that enhanced life meaning and purpose was crucial for recovery from drug addiction in 12-step programs. In their recent prospective study with a latent class growth analysis, Cranford and colleagues (2014) found that purpose in life was a significant time-varying predictor of a decreased likelihood of heavy or heaviest-drinking memberships. Therefore, we propose that an increase in life meaning and purpose is a crucial cognitive factor leading to better recovery in faith-based treatment.

Depression and Abstinent Self-Efficacy and Treatment Outcomes

Changes in depressive symptoms and abstinent self-efficacy are thought to be crucial psychological factors contributing to better treatment outcomes. Religious involvement is negatively related to depressive symptoms and positively related to self-efficacy (Koenig, 2009).

Depression, characterised by a negative affect and hopelessness, is an important motivator and sustainer of substance abuse, as it impairs addicts' confidence to control the craving of re-using substance in tempting situations (Kelly et al., 2010; McKowen et al., 2013). Kelly and Hoeppner (2013) found that both depression and self-efficacy were crucial mediators predictive of percentage abstinent days and drinks per drinking day in 1726 treatment seekers for alcohol use disorder. Greenfield et al. (2012) found that an increase in self-efficacy during a 12-step treatment programme was positively predictive of abstinence from substance use 3 months after treatment across both depressed and non-depressed samples. We therefore predict that a decrease in depression and an increase in abstinent self-efficacy are important psychological pathways leading to recovery in faith-based treatments.

Supportive Family Relationships, a Pro-Abstinent Peer Network and Treatment Outcomes

Supportive interpersonal relationships that promote an abstinent culture, whether at the family or peer level, are indispensable for treatment success. It is believed that participation in faith-based treatment programmes will strengthen family support and pro-abstinent peer networks, as the restoration of constructive family relationships and the re-establishment of a drug-free social network are the main concerns of these programmes. Laudet et al. (2004) found that a supportive peer network in the first 12 months of treatment significantly mediatedthe effects of AA involvement on substance abuse among patients with co-morbid mental disorders. Recently, Litt et al. (2008) randomised alcoholic addicts to either a 12-step programme that emphasised an abstinent social network or two secular treatments. They found that the patients in the 12-step supportive network programme gained 20% more days of abstinence at the 2-year follow-up. Lavee and Altus (2001) reported that drug-free patients had closer, more supportive family relationships than their relapsed counterparts 6 months after detoxification in an in-home treatment programme. As healthy human relationships are particularly upheld by Christianity, we anticipate that strengthened family support and a pro-abstinent peer network will be a notable social process pathway leading to better treatment outcomes in faith-based treatment.

Summary

The main purpose of this study is going to evaluate the effectiveness of faith-based treatment among addict patients in terms of their post-treatment abstinence, addiction severity symptoms and quality of life after they completed their intervention (post-treatment), and 6- and 12-month after post-treatment (Donovan et al., 2013; Greenfield et al., 2012). Based on the behaviour change perspective, the study will investigate the interactions between the multiple factors involved in religious, cognitive, psychological and social process pathways in recovery simultaneously and longitudinally, in order to see how changes in these factors influence treatment outcomes. The following section will address the research methods, measurements and analytical procedures, and conclude with the potential contributions and implications of the current study.

Research Methods

This proposed study is a naturalistic treatment outcome evaluation with a 4-wave prospective design. It will investigate addict patients' changes in treatment outcomes and religious, cognitive, psychological and social process factors. It will explore how these factors influence the outcomes interactively and longitudinally in natural treatment settings by time-lagged mixed-effect and lagged-effect multiple-mediational modelling approaches. This type of study is more applicable than an experimental study, such as a randomised controlled trial, due to its prominent external validity and generalisability and the direct applicability of the findings in treating the target population (Singleton & Straits, 2010).

Sample and Procedures

Newly enrolled adult substance addict patients in the participating faith-based treatment programmes are the potential participants. Patients who have been in treatment for no more than 1 month will be considered newly enrolled and will be invited to participate in the study. The participants will also be invited to an interview immediately after being discharged from the faith-based treatment[2] and 6 and 12 months after treatment. A 2-year time span will be adequate to demonstrate the treatment effectiveness (Cheung, 2009; Robinson et al., 2007). In the implementation of the study, potential participants who have been enrolled in treatment for no more than 1 month will be approached by trained research assistants. Recruitment will be conducted over 3 months to recruit sufficient participants. Written consent will be obtained from the participants before the study. After the intake interview, the participants will be reminded to attend the future interviews at their discharge and 6 and 12 months after discharge. The prospective participants will be informed that they are not obligated to participate in the study. As it is well known for high attrition rates in following addict patients of drug abuse, the participants in this study will be compensated at a reasonable rate for their time and effort for decreasing attrition, which is common in addiction research (Cheung, 2009; Greenfield et al., 2012; Krentzman et al., 2012).

Measures

Percentage Drug-Free Weeks (PDFW). One of the comparatively objective approaches to measure post-treatment abstinence is to calculate the number of abstinent weeks over the period without residential treatment within the interval (i.e., from discharge to 6 months post-treatment and from 6 to 12 months post-treatment). A week is used as the measuring unit rather than a day because it is less affected by the problems of oblivion and being too short to reflect genuine abstinence (Cheung, 2009).

Severity of Addiction Symptoms (SAS). The 5-item Severity of Dependence Scale will be used to assess the participants' psychological dependence on substances. This measure has shown good reliability and validity (Tsai et al., 2012).

Quality of Life (QOL). The 26-item Brief WHO QOL Questionnaire will be used to measure the participants' perceived change in QOL. It has been used to measure improved life quality in addicted patients after treatment and has been shown to be a reliable measure (Feelemyer et al., 2014; Lin et al., 2011).

Religiosity/Spirituality. The 38-item Brief Multidimensional Measure of Religiousness/ Spirituality will be used to measure the participants' religiosity. It has been widely used in religious research in relation to health and risk behaviour (Kim et al., 2013). It has proven to be reliable and psychometrically sound (Masters et al., 2009).

Meaning and Purpose in Life. The 10-item Meaning in Life Questionnaire will be used to measure the participants' change in life meaning and purpose. Prior studies have shown very good reliability and validity (Kashdan& Kane, 2011).

Depressive Symptoms. The 20-item Centre for Epidemiologic Studies-Depressed Mood Scale will be used to measure the patients' depressive symptoms (Radloff, 1977). It has been

[2] Generally, the duration of faith-based residential treatment is around a-year period.

widely used in health and addiction studies and shown to be a very reliable measure (Yeung & Chan, 2014).

Abstinent Self-Efficacy. The 8-item Situational Confidence Questionnaire will be used to measure the participants' confidence and self-control to remain abstinent in tempting and difficult situations, which is crucial for predicting future relapse (Miller et al., 1989). The measure has good internal consistencyin addiction research (Wong et al., 2004).

Family Support. The 17-item Family Support Function Scale will be used to measure supportive family relationships. This scale has been used to predict current use/non-use among heroin addicts in China and has demonstrated good reliability (Lin et al., 2011).

Pro-Abstinent Peer Network. A 5-item pro-abstinent peer network measure will be adopted from Cheung (2009) to measure the drug-free culture in the participant's peer circle. The measure demonstrated excellent reliability across the three waves in Cheung's study.

Treatment Involvement. Recent addiction research has shown that active involvement rather than superficial participation in treatment contributes to recovery (Kelly et al., 2013, p. 21). Active treatment involvement has been shown to have strong effects in predicting abstinence and better psychological health (Kelly et al., 2013). Due to cultural considerations, an 8-item Treatment Involvement Scale is developed for this study by referring to relevant Western measures, such as the 12-Step Participation Expectancies Questionnaire and the AA Involvement Scale (Tonigan et al., 1996) and by consulting the supervisors of local faith-based treatment centres/ programmes (Table 1 for details).

Socio-Demographic and Control Variables. The participants' age, sex, education, marital and employment status, religious beliefs and number of treatments prior to the current one will be collected as covariates at intake. Prior research has indicated the importance of these variables in influencing treatment outcomes and recovery (Kelly&Hoeppner, 2013; Robinson et al., 2007).

All of the study variables will be measured at all four time points, except for PDFW, which will not be measured at discharge as a drug-free status is assumed then, and Treatment Involvement, which will only be measured at discharge to obtain the magnitude of a participant's active engagement in on-going therapeutic activities and tasks. The socio-demographic and control variables will only be measured at intake to collect the participants' background information and important baseline covariates, to rule out possible confounding effects.

Analytic Techniques

Instead of using single-level fixed-effect models with repeated measures, e.g., ANOVA and MANOVA, which are conventional procedures for treatment research, this study will adopt time-lagged mixed-effect and lagged-effect multiple-mediational modelling approaches. This method is better suited for analysing the ever-changing data in a clustered structure in a longitudinal fashion, since it could accommodate the clustered nature of longitudinal data, differentiate fixed and random effects, and examine the interactions between concomitant effects of multiple predictors in relation to treatment outcomes (Little, 2013; Skrondal & Rabe-Hesketh, 2014).

In time-lagged mixed-effect modelling, two-level hierarchical models will be built to test the effects of the time-varying and time-invariant predictors on the treatment outcomes of PDFW, SAS and QOL. The changing nature of repeated-measure variables within participants (Level 1) will be assumed to nest in the between-subject average levels of the study variables (Level 2) (Galwey, 2014; Wu, 2010). The time-varying variables are the three outcomes, religiosity/spirituality, meaning and purpose in life, depressive symptoms, abstinent self-efficacy, family support and a pro-abstinent peer network. The time-invariant variables are the socio-demographic and control variables measured at intake. To assure the temporal precedence of the relationships between the predictors and outcomes and to fortify causal inference, a time-lagged design will be used. For example, predictors at intake, discharge and 6-month follow-up after treatment will be used to predict the outcome of PDFW at 6- and 12-month follow-ups after treatment, while adjusting for the initial status of PDFW. The time effect will be coded as 0, 1, 2 and 3. Its quadratic temporal effect will be coded 0, 1, 4 and 9, as a curvilinear trend has been observed in many treatment studies (Wu, 2010). To standardise the interpretation of the predicting effects on the outcomes, centred group means and grand means will be applied to the time-varying and time-invariant variables, respectively. Figure 1 illustrates this mixed-effect hierarchical modelling analysis strategy.

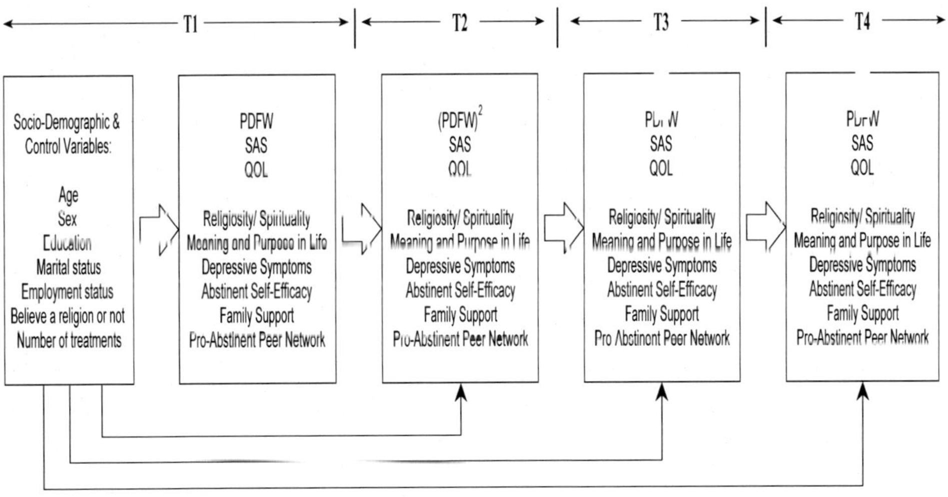

Note: T1, intake; T2, discharge; T3, 6 months post-treatment; T4, 12 months post-treatment.

[1] This modelling strategy will be used to investigate the effects of time-varying and time-invariant predictors on the treatment outcomes across the waves to ascertain random and fixed effects, respectively.

[2] The patient participants are assumed to be drug-free after treatment (T2), so the outcome of PDFW will not be incorporated in the analysis at T2. However SAS and QOL are assumed to change significantly after treatment, so are part of the analysis at T2.

Figure 1. Time-lagged mixed-effect modelling of the treatment outcomes PDFW, SAS and QOL[1].

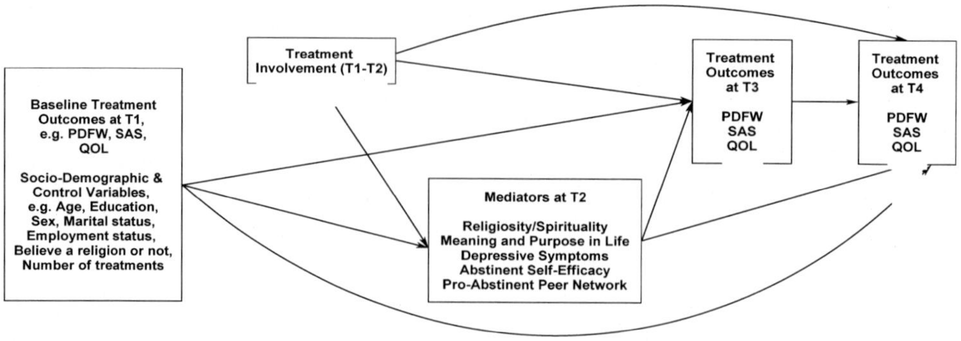

Note. T1, intake; T2, discharge; T3, 6 months post-treatment; T4, 12 months post-treatment.

[1] This modelling strategy will be used is to see how treatment involvement and changes in important mediators contribute to the treatment outcomes at T3 and T4 simultaneously and time-varyingly, while adjusting for baseline treatment outcomes and socio-demographic and control variables.

Figure 2. Lagged-effect multiple-mediational modelling of treatment involvement, changes in mediators and treatment outcomes PDFW, SAS and QOL[1].

Lagged-effect multiple-mediational modelling will be used to test whether the changes in religious, cognitive, psychological and social process mediators simultaneously and interactively predict the treatment outcomes of PDFW, SAS and QOL prospectively, while adjusting for the level of active engagement in treatment. Longitudinal structural equation modelling will be used to examine the effects of the participants' treatment involvement on their changes in the aforementioned mediators at discharge. Both treatment involvement and the mediators will be used to predict the treatment outcomes at 6 and 12 months post-treatment (Little, 2013). To prevent temporal confounding between treatment involvement, mediators and outcomes, a fully lagged mediational design will be used (Preacher & Hayes, 2008). The baseline levels of the mediators and outcomes and the time-invariant covariates, such as age, sex and education, will be adjusted. Figure 2 illustrates this lagged-effect multiple-mediational modelling strategy.

Conclusion and Implications

Substance addiction is a relapsing disorder of treatment complexity. It is characteristic of compulsive drug use and craving for re-use. If someone who is addicted, he or she is lack of control for drug use and may maintainabusing the substance irrespective of profoundly negative consequences (Laudet et al. 2004; Sellmanetal., 2007). Intense craving for the drugs once addicted makes abstinence and rehabilitation explicitly difficult (Cheung, 2012; White &Whiters, 2005). Lately, some scholars even claimed substance abuse as a "chronic debilitating disease," which is ascribed to, except the harmful effects it brings about,its compulsive, repetitive, relapsing and uncontrollable nature (Abadinsky, 2011; Walters, 2014). It is indubitable that the adverse consequences of substance abuse are far beyond the expected costs that we need to pay. The problems that are associated with abusing drugs, to name some such as permanent physical harm, loss of economic productivity, spread of transmitted diseases, criminal behaviours, family disruption, partner and child abuse, interpersonal violence, disorganization of public orders, public health issues, corruption of social morality and conventional values and so on., can contribute to long-lasting and irreversible calamities to the addict herself/ himself and human societies as a whole (Abadinsky, 2011; McKowen et al., 2013; Kelly et al., 2009; Walters, 2014). As mentioned in the beginning of this chapter, substance abuse is nowadays seen to be epidemic in most modern and industrialized societies. Accordingly, we need to strive for effective treatments through more research efforts in order to enhance our knowledge regarding the delivery mechanism and benefits for abstinence that these treatment programmes may bring, by which practitioners in the field of addiction treatment and rehabilitation can improve their treatment interventions for better catering the various needs of addict patients who want to do a new and drug-free life. As such, this chapter is with an attempt to construct a theoretical framework and introduce pertinent research methods and analytical approaches to investigate the effectiveness of those faith-based treatment programmes in Hong Kong, where relevant longitudinal evaluations are highly limited.

In sum, the study proposed in this chapter intends to investigate the mechanisms by which faith-based addiction treatment delivers its desirable outcomes and, in particular, how the multiple factors act and interact over time. This is a naturalistic treatment outcome study using a 4-wave prospective design, in which participants' information will be collected at treatment intake, discharge from treatment and 6 and 12 months post-treatment, covering 2 years. In methodology, we will use time-lagged mixed-effect and lagged-effect multiple-mediational modelling procedures to deal with the clustered nature of longitudinal data, to differentiate between fixed and random effects and to determine the interactions between the multiple predictors of the treatment outcomes. It is expected the proposed study can make valuable contributions in both the literature and the field of substance addiction treatment locally and internationally.

First, theoretically it may enhance our comprehension of the effectiveness of faith-based addiction treatment and its delivery mechanism, which could advance our knowledge of the rehabilitation of substance abuse. Second, practically its findings can inform policy making and resources allocation in relation to service betterment of substance abuse treatment and rehabilitation, which is owing to the prominent external validity and direct applicability inherent in the present naturalistic study. Third, internationally the current longitudinal investigation would act as a reference for academics in other regions, especially in Asian societies where pertinent studies are rarely conducted which may help to extend the scholarly work on faith-based treatment, and therefore may encourage large-scale cross-cultural studies in both the Asian and Western contexts. Fourth, locally the study results can help faith-based treatment practitioners to enhance their service delivery in the long run, as well as may inspire more indigenous research on addiction in the future, such as comparative examinations of faith-based vs secular-approach treatment, construction of more long-term longitudinal study with a more intricate framework and advanced methodologies to collect both quantitative and qualitative information. By the time to come, the advancement of our understanding of abusing behaviours and treatment recovery would be valuable assets for us to combat this lingering modern epidemic.

REFERENCES

Abadinsky, H. (2011). Drug use and abuse: A comprehensive introduction. Belmont, CA: Wadsworth/Cengage Learning.

Bowser, B. P., Word, C. O. & Seddon, T. (2014).*Understanding drug use and abuse: A global perspective*. New York: Palgrave Macmillan.

Carroll, S. (1993). Spirituality and purpose in life in alcoholism recovery. *Journal of Studies on Alcohol and Drugs*, *54*(3), 297.

Census and Statistics Department. (2013). *Drug abuse situation in Hong Kong in 2012*. Hong Kong: Census and Statistics Department.

Cheng, G. (2010). The Meaning of Suffering in Drug Addiction and Recovery from the Perspective of Existentialism, Buddhism and the 12-Step Program. *Journal of Psychoactive Drugs, 42*, 363-375.

Cheung, Y. W. (2009). *A brighter side: Protective and risk factors in the rehabilitation of chronic drug abusers in Hong Kong*. Hong Kong: The Chinese University Press.

Cheung, Y. W. (2012). *A Longitudinal Survey of Psychoactive Drug Abusers in Hong Kong*. Hong Kong: The Beat Drugs Fund.

Chu, D. C., Sung, H. E. & Hsiao, G. Y. (2012). Religious conversion and treatment outcome: An examination of clients in a faith-based residential substance treatment programme. *Journal of Drug Issues*, *42*(2), 197-209.

Cranford, J. A., Krentzman, A. R., Mowbray, O. & Robinson, E. A. (2014). Trajectories of alcohol use over time among adults with alcohol dependence. *Addictive Behaviours*, *39*(5), 1006-1011.

Dermatis, H., Guschwan, M. T., Galanter, M. & Bunt, G. (2004). Orientation toward spirituality and self-help approaches in the therapeutic community. *Journal of Addictive Diseases*, *23*(1), 39-54.

Donovan, D. M., Ingalsbe, M. H., Benbow, J. & Daley, D. C. (2013). 12-Step interventions and mutual support programmes for substance disorders: An overview. *Social Work in Public Health*, *28*, 313-332.

Feelemyer, J. P., Jarlais D. C., Arasteh, K., Phillips, B. W. & Hagan, H. (2014). Changes in quality of life (WHOQOL-BREF) and addiction severity index (ASI) among participants in opioid substitution treatment (OST) in low and middle income countries: an international systematic review. *Drug and Alcohol Dependence, 134,* 251-258.

Forman, R. F., Bovasso, G. & Woody, G. (2001).Staff beliefs about addiction treatment. *Journal of Substance Abuse Treatment*, *21*, 1-9.

Galwey, N. W. (2014). Introduction to mixed modelling: Beyond regression and analysis of variance. West Sussex: *Wiley*.

Greenfield, B. L., Venner, K. L., Kelly, J. F. & Bryan, A. D. (2012). The impact of depression on abstinence self-efficacy and substance use outcomes among emerging adults in residential treatment. *Psychology of Addictive Behaviours*, *26*, 246-254.

Kashdan, T. B. & Kane, J. Q. (2011).Post-traumatic distress and the presence of post-traumatic growth and meaning in life: Experiential avoidance as a moderator. *Personality and Individual Differences,* 50, 84–89

Kaskutas, L. A., Turk, N., Bond, J. & Weisner, C. (2003). The role of religion, spirituality and Alcoholics Anonymous in sustained sobriety. *Alcoholism Treatment Quarterly*, *21*, 1-15.

Kelly, J. F. & Hoeppner, B. B. (2013). Does Alcoholics Anonymous work differently for men and women? A moderated multiple-mediation analysis in a large clinical sample. *Drug and Alcohol Dependence*, *130,* 186-193.

Kelly, J. F., Magill, M. & Stout, R. L. (2009). How do people recover from alcohol dependence? A systematic review of the research on mechanisms of behaviour change in Alcoholics Anonymous. *Addiction Research and Theory*, *17*, 236-259.

Kelly, J. F., Stout, R. L., Magill, M., Tonigan, J. S. & Pagano, M. E. (2011). Spirituality in recovery: A lagged mediational analysis of Alcoholics Anonymous' principal theoretical mechanism of behaviour change. *Alcoholism: Clinical and Experimental Research*, *35*(3), 454-463.

Kelly, J. F., Stout, R., Magill, M., Tonigan, J. S. & Pagano, M. (2010) Mechanisms of behaviour change in Alcoholics Anonymous: does AA improve alcohol outcomes by reducing depression symptoms? *Addiction*, *105*, 626-636.

Kelly, J. F., Stout, R. L. & Slaymaker, V. (2013). Emerging adults' treatment outcomes in relation to 12-step mutual-help attendance and active involvement. *Drug and Alcohol Dependence*, *129*(1), 151-157.

Kim, S., Miles-Mason, E., Kim, C. Y. & Esquivel, G. B. (2013). Religiosity/spirituality and life satisfaction in Korean American adolescents. *Psychology of Religion and Spirituality*, *5*(1), 33.

Koenig, H. G. (2009). Research on religion, spirituality, and mental health: A review. *Canadian Journal of Psychiatry*, *54*, 283-291.

Krentzman, A. R., Brower, K. J., Cranford, J. A., Bradley, J. C. & Robinson, E. A. (2012). Gender and extroversion as moderators of the association between Alcoholics Anonymous and sobriety. *Journal of Studies on Alcohol and Drugs*, *73*(1), 44.

Laudet, A. B., Cleland, C. M., Magura, S., Vogel, H. S. & Knight, E. L. (2004). Social support mediates the effects of dual-focus mutual aid groups on abstinence from substance use. *American Journal of Community Psychology*, *34*(3-4), 175-185.

Lavee, Y. & Altus, D. (2001). Family relationships as a predictor of post-treatment drug abuse relapse: A follow-up study of drug addicts and their spouses. *Contemporary Family Therapy*, *23*(4), 513-530.

Lin, C., Wu, Z. & Detels, R. (2011) Family support, quality of life and concurrent substance use among methadone maintenance therapy clients in China. *Public Health*, *125*, 269-274.

Litt, M. D., Kadden, R. M., Kabela-Cormier, E. & Petry, N. M. (2008). Coping skills training and contingency management treatments for marijuana dependence: Exploring mechanisms of behaviour change. *Addiction*, *103*(4), 638-648.

Little, T. D. (2013). *Longitudinal structural equation modelling*. New York: Guilford Press.

Lyons, G. C., Deane, F. P., Caputi, P. & Kelly, P. J. (2011). Spirituality and the treatment of substance use disorders: An exploration of forgiveness, resentment and purpose in life. *Addiction Research & Theory*, *19*(5), 459-469.

Lyons, G. C., Deane, F. P. & Kelly, P. J. (2013). Faith-based substance abuse programmes. In P. M. Miller (Ed.), *Interventions for Addiction* (vol. 3, pp. 147-153). Boston: Elsevier Science.

Masters, K. S., Carey, K. B., Maisto, S. A., Caldwell, P. E., Wolfe, T. V., Hackney, H. L. & Himawan, L. (2009). Psychometric examination of the brief multidimensional measure ofreligiousness/spirituality among college students. *The International Journal for thePsychology of Religion, 19*(2), 106-120.

McCoy, M. L., Roberts, D. L., Hanrahan, P., Clay, R. & Luchins, D. J. (2004). Jail linkage assertive community treatment services for individuals with mental illnesses. *Psychiatric Rehabilitation Journal, 27,* 243-250

McKowen, J. W., Tompson, M. C., Brown, T. A. & Asarnow, J. R. (2013). Longitudinal associations between depression and problematic substance use in the youth partners in care study. *Journal of Clinical Child and Adolescent Psychology, 42*(5), 669-680.

Miller, P. J., Ross, S. M., Emmerson, R. Y. & Todt, E. H. (1989). Self-efficacy in alcoholics: Clinical validation of the Situational Confidence Questionnaire. *Addictive Behaviours, 14*(2), 217-224.

Neff, J. A. & MacMaster, S. A. (2005). Spiritual mechanisms underlying substance abuse behaviour change in faith-based substance abuse treatment. *Journal of Social Work Practice in the Addictions, 5*(3), 33-54.

Nordfjaern, T. (2011). Relapse Patterns among Patients with Substance Use Disorders. *Journal of Substance Use, 16*, 313-329.

Preacher, K. J. & Hayes, A. F. (2008). Asymptotic and resampling strategies for assessing and comparing indirect effects in multiple mediator models. *Behaviour Research Methods, 40*, 879-891.

Radloff, L. S. (1977). The CES-D scale: A self-report depression scale for research in the general population. *Applied Psychological Measurement*, 1(3), 385-401.

Rew, L. & Wong, Y. J. (2006). A systematic review of associations among religiosity/spirituality and adolescent health attitudes and behaviours. *Journal of Adolescent Health, 38*, 433-442.

Robinson, E. A. R., Cranford, J. A., Webb, J. R. & Brower, K. J. (2007). Six-month changes in spirituality, religiousness, and heavy drinking in a treatment-seeking sample. *Journal of Studies on Alcohol and Drugs, 68*, 282-290.

Sellman, J. D., Baker, M. P., Adamson, S. J. & Geering, L. G. (2007). Future of God in recovery from drug addiction. *Australian and New Zealand Journal of Psychiatry, 41*, 800-808.

Singer, M. (2008). *Drugging the poor: Legal and illegal drugs and social inequality*. Long Grove, IL: Waveland Press.

Singleton, R. A. & Straits, B. C. (2010). *Approaches to social research*. New York: Oxford University Press.

Skrondal, A. & Rabe-Hesketh, S. (2014). Multilevel and Related Modelsfor Longitudinal Data. In J.D. Leeuw, and E. Meijer (Eds.), Handbook of Multilevel Analysis (pp. 275-299). New York: Springer.

Tonigan, J. S., Connors, G. J. & Miller, W. R. (1996). Alcoholics Anonymous Involvement (AAI) scale: Reliability and norms. *Psychology of Addictive Behaviours, 10*, 75-80.

Tsai, J. H., Tang, T. C., Yeh, Y. C., Yang, Y. H., Yeung, T. H., Wang, S. Y., & Chen, C. C. (2012).The Chinese version of the Severity of Dependence Scale as a screening tool for benzodiazepine dependence in Taiwan. *The Kaohsiung Journal of Medical Sciences, 28*(4), 225-230.

United Nations Office on Drugs and Crime (2014). *World Drug Report 2014*. Vienna: United Nations.

Walters, G. D. (2014). Drugs, crime, and their relationships: Theory, research, practice, and policy. Burlington, MA: Jones & Bartlett Learning.

White, W. L. & Whiters, D. (2005). Faith-based recovery: Its historical roots. *Counsellor: The Magazine for Addiction Professionals*, 6, 58-62.

Wong, C. J., Anthony, S., Sigmon, S. C., Mongeon, J. A., Badger, G. J. & Higgins, S. T. (2004). Examining interrelationships between abstinence and coping self-efficacy in cocaine-dependent outpatients. *Experimental and Clinical Psychopharmacology*, *12*(3), 190-199.

Wu, L. (2010). *Mixed effects models for complex data*. Boca Raton: Chapman & Hall/CRC Press.

Yeung, J. W. K. & Chan, Y. C. (2014). Parents' Religious Involvement, Family Socialization and Development of Their Children in a Chinese Sample of Hong Kong. *Social Indicators Research, 117*(3), 987-1010.

Yonker, J. E., Schnabelrauch, C. A. & DeHaan, L. G. (2012). The relationship between spirituality and religiosity on psychological outcomes in adolescents and emerging adults: A meta-analytic review. *Journal of Adolescence*, *35*(2), 299-314.

Zemore, S. E. (2007). A role for spiritual change in the benefits of 12-step involvement.*Alcoholism: Clinical and Experimental Research*, *31*(s3), 76s-79s.

INDEX

#

A

B

C

D

E

F

G

H

I

J

K

L

M

N

O

P

Q

R

S

T

U

V

W

Y